M000029168

THE LANGUAGE AND LOGIC
OF THE BIBLE

THE LANGUAGE AND LOGIC
OF THE BIBLE
THE EARLIER MIDDLE AGES

G.R. EVANS

CAMBRIDGE
UNIVERSITY PRESS

Published by the Press Syndicate of the University of Cambridge
The Pitt Building, Trumpington Street, Cambridge CB2 1RP
40 West 20th Street, New York, NY 10011–4211, USA
10 Stamford Road, Oakleigh, Melbourne 3166, Australia

© Cambridge University Press 1984

First published 1984
First paperback edition 1991
Reprinted 1996

Library of Congress catalogue card number: 84–3175

British Library Cataloguing in Publication Data

Evans, G.R.
The language and logic of the Bible
1. Bible — Criticism, interpretation, etc.
— History — Early church, ca 30–600
2. Bible — Criticism, interpretation, etc. —
History — Middle Ages, 600–1500
1. Title
220.6'09'02 BS500

ISBN 0 521 26371 9 hardback
ISBN 0 521 42393 7 paperback

Transferred to digital printing 2000

WD

CONTENTS

Preface   *page* vii
Acknowledgements   ix
List of abbreviations   x
List of ancient and mediaeval sources   xi
Biographical notes   xvi

Introduction   1
  1 The Fathers on the Bible's language   1
  2 *Lectio, disputatio, predicatio*   8

Part I   The background

1 *The monastic way*   13
  1 Rupert of Deutz and 'holy reading'   13
  2 Anselm of Canterbury: a new look at the Bible's
     language   17

2 *Bible study in the schools*   27
  1 The academic way   27
  2 Introducing the Bible   30
  3 The use of the *artes*   31

3 *A standard commentary: the* Glossa Ordinaria   37

Part II   *Lectio*: surface and depths

4 *Words and things and numbers*   51
  1 Words and things   51
  2 Numbers   59

5 *The historical sense and history*   67

6   *Exegesis and the theory of signification*   72
    1   The theory of signification   72
    2   Imposition   76
    3   Dictionaries   80
    4   Grammar and practical criticism   85
    5   Joint meanings: consignification   87
    6   More meaning than appears: implicitness in words   89
    7   Implicit propositions   91
    8   No meaning on their own   92

7   *Transference of meaning*   101
    1   Similitudes and analogies   101
    2   Figures of speech   105
    3   The four senses   114

Part III   *Disputatio*

8   *Questions*   125

9   *Contradictory authorities*   133

10 *A new approach to resolving contradictions*   140

Conclusion   164
Notes   169
Select bibliography   193
Index   197

PREFACE

For a thousand years in the West, from the fall of the Roman Empire to the Reformation, almost every man of culture and scholarship was a Christian, and most were clerics. Under the Church's guidance, the Bible was regarded as incomparably the most important book. In principle, everything else was studied in connection with it, in the light of its teaching, or in the hope of throwing light on what was difficult to understand in the text of Scripture. No task could be more urgent. Upon it depended the completion of the redemption of mankind. Sin lingered in the world, and although God had sent his Son to save fallen men and original sin no longer presented an insuperable barrier, each of the future citizens of heaven had need of divine instruction if he was to grow more perfect in this life. In the Bible God had provided detailed teaching and help for the faithful.

Even when, in the later Middle Ages, natural science or logic or the higher studies of law or medicine attracted fine minds and strong interest in their own right, theological questions and problems of exegesis presented themselves. Henry of Langenstein found it helpful to arrange a series of studies on scientific problems (in physics, optics, zoology, and so on) in an order dictated by the six days of creation as they are described in Genesis. It must of course have been the case that a number of scholars were drawn to these subsidiary subjects for their own sake, and secretly had little use for their theological application. But the study of such matters continued to be justified by the need to understand the Bible better.

Between the eleventh and thirteenth centuries two developments took place which, while they did not alter the fundamental principles of mediaeval exegesis, greatly added to its sophistication and brought it, in one area at least, to a high point of development in critical method.

The study of grammar had become an essential preliminary to the study of the Bible in Latin once Latin ceased to be a vernacular language. It raised a number of difficulties for the reader of Scripture because the text often failed to conform to the rules of syntax, or to use words in the usual way. In an attempt to resolve these problems some scholars explored the underlying structures of language and epistemological questions, and began to bring together the teaching of Aristotle and Boethius on the first principles of logic and the laws of the grammarians. As they tried to explain obscurities in the Bible in this way they were struck again and again – as Augustine and Gregory had been – by the inadequacy of human language. They confronted, with greater technical skill and newly sharpened tools, the problem of the nature of theological language.

Out of this work came many of the questions which led to the framing of theology as a new academic discipline. Questions about points of doctrine which the text raised were treated more fully under the pressure of student demand, until a systematic theology began to emerge. Attention to the details of the text was accompanied by a larger view of the place of each passage in the scheme of Christian theology, not for the first time, but in an altogether more comprehensive way.

This study is concerned primarily with the new work on the language of the Bible, and on the nature of theological language in general, which was one of the highest achievements of the theologians of the earlier Middle Ages. At a philosophical level they had something to say about the problem which has recently come to seem impressive, and of lasting value, in the light of modern work on the philosophy of language.[1] Their efforts carried through into preaching and pastoral work only in a much diluted form, and a good deal of its significance was to be lost upon the scholars of the Reformation, who rejected what seemed to them a debased scholasticism. But that is another story and must await another volume.

ACKNOWLEDGEMENTS

I should like to thank especially Professor C.N.L. Brooke, Dr D.P. Henry and Dr B. Smalley for their kindness in reading this book at various stages in its writing, and making suggestions. It is dedicated to Beryl Smalley in gratitude for her teaching and friendship.

ABBREVIATIONS

AHDLMA	*Archives d'histoire doctrinale et littéraire du moyen âge*
Beiträge	Beiträge zur Geschichte der Philosophie und Theologie des Mittelalters
Cahiers	*Cahiers de l'Institut Grec et Latin du Moyen Age, Copenhague*
CCCM	Corpus Christianorum Continuatio Medievalis
CCSL	Corpus Christianorum Series Latina
CSEL	Corpus Scriptorum Ecclesiasticorum Latinorum
JTS	*Journal of Theological Studies*
LM	*Logica Modernorum*, ed. L.M. de Rijk (Assen, 1967)
MARS	*Mediaeval and Renaissance Studies*
MGH	Monumenta Germaniae Historica: Quellen zur Geistesgeschichte des Mittelalters
PL	Patrologia Latina, ed. J.P. Migne (Paris, 1841ff.)
RBén	*Revue Bénédictine*
RTAM	*Recherches de théologie ancienne et médiévale*
SC	Sources chrétiennes
SSL	Spicilegium Sacrum Lovaniense

ANCIENT AND MEDIAEVAL
SOURCES

Abbo of Fleury (*On Hyp. Syll.*), *De Syllogismis Categoricis et Hypotheticis*, ed. A. Van der Vyver, Bruges, 1966

Abelard (*Comm. in Rom.*), *Commentaria in Romanos*, ed. M. Buytaert, CCCM, 11, 1969

Dialectica, ed. L.M. de Rijk, Assen, 1956

(*Hist. Calam.*), *Historia Calamitatum*, ed. J. Monfrin, Paris, 1959, 3rd edn 1967

In Hexaemeron, PL, 178

(*Log. Ingr.*), *Logica Ingredientibus*, ed. B. Geyer, Beiträge, 1, Münster, 1919

(*Prob. Hel.*), *Problemata Heloissae*, PL, 178

(*Sent. Par.*), *Sententiae Parisienses*, ed. A. Landgraf, SSL, 14, 1934

(*Theol. Chr.*), *Theologia Christiana*, ed. M. Buytaert, CCCM, 12, 1969

Adam of Balsham, *Ars Disserendi*, ed. L. Minio-Paluello, Rome, 1956

Adam the Scot, *De Tripartito Tabernaculo*, PL, 198.609–793

Alan of Lille, *Elucidatio in Canticum Canticorum*, PL, 210.51–110

Regulae Theologicae, PL, 210.621–84

Albinus, *Rhetorica*, ed. C. Halm in *Rhetores Latini Minores*, Leipzig, 1863

Alcuin (*In Eccles.*), *In Ecclesiasten*, PL, 100.665–721

(*Q. in Gen.*), *Quaestiones in Genesim*, PL, 100.515–67

Anselm of Canterbury (S), *Anselmi Opera Omnia*, ed. F.S. Schmitt, Sekau, Rome, Edinburgh, 1938–68, 6 vols.

Anselm of Havelberg, *Dialogi*, PL, 188; Book I, ed. G. Salet, Paris, 1965

Aquinas, *Summa Contra Gentiles* and *De Veritate*, ed. P. Marc, Rome, 1961–7, 2 vols.

Summa Theologiae, ed. P. Caramello, Turin, 1962–3, 3 vols.

Aristotle, *Categoriae*, ed. L. Minio-Paluello, Oxford, 1949

(*De Interp.*), *De Interpretatione*, ed. H.P. Cook, London, 1962

Sophistici Elenchi, ed. W.D. Ross, Oxford, 1958

Augustine (*Conf.*), *Confessiones*, ed. W. Watts, London, 1961–8, 2 vols.

(*De Civ. Dei*), *De Civitate Dei*, CCSL, 47–8, 1955

(*De Cons. Ev.*), *De Consensu Evangelistarum*, ed. F. Weihrich, CSEL, 43, 1904

(DDC), *De Doctrina Christiana*, CCSL, 32, 1962

(*De Div. Q.*), *De Diversis Quaestionibus*, CCSL, 44^A, 1975

(*De Gen. ad Litt.*), *De Genesi ad Litteram* and *De Genesi ad Litteram Imperfectus Liber*, ed. J. Zycha, CSEL, 28, 1984

(*De Trin.*), *De Trinitate*, CCSL, 50, 1968

(*De Ut. Cred.*), *De Utilitate Credendi*, ed. J. Zycha, CSEL, 25, 1891

(*En. Ps.*), *Enarrationes in Psalmos*, CCSL, 38–40, 1956

Bede (*De Sch. et Tr.*), *De Schematibus et Tropis*, PL, 90.175–86; and ed. C. Halm in *Rhetores Latini Minores*, Leipzig, 1863

(*De Temp.*), *De Temporibus*, PL, 90.187–277

(*In Gen.*), *In Genesim*, ed. C.W. Jones, CCSL, 148^A, 1967

Bernard of Clairvaux, *De Spirituali Aedificio*, ed. J. Leclercq, Studia Anselmiana, 20, 1956

Boethius, *De Institutione Arithmetica*, ed. G. Friedlein, Leipzig, 1867

(*De Interp.*), *I Commentarii; II De Interpretatione*, ed. G. Meiser, Leipzig, 1877–80

De Syllogismis Categoricis, PL, 64.793–829

De Trinitate, in *Theological Tractates*, ed. H.F. Stewart and E.K. Rand, London, 1918; revised by S.J. Tester, London, 1973

Bruno of Chartreux, *In Psalmos*, PL, 152.637–1420

Cassian (*Collat.*), *Collationes*, ed. M. Petschenig, CSEL, 13, 1886

Cassiodorus (*In Ps.*), *In Psalmos*, CCSL, 97–8, 1968

(*Inst.*), *Institutiones*, ed. R.A.B. Mynors, Oxford, 1937

Cicero, *Orator*, ed. H.M. Hubbell, London, 1962

Topics, ed. H.M. Hubbell, London, 1953

Eriugena (*De Praed.*), *De Divina Praedestinatione Liber*, ed. G. Madec, CCCM, 50, 1978

Ernald of Bonneval, *In Psalmos*, PL, 189

Garlandus (*Dial.*), *Dialectica*, ed. L.M. de Rijk, Assen, 1959

Geoffrey of Auxerre, *Expositio in Canticum Canticorum*, ed. F. Gastaldelli, Rome, 1974

Gerhoch of Reichersberg, *In Isaiam* and *In Psalmos*, PL, 194.9–1000

Gilbert Crispin, *Disputatio,* ed. B. Blumenkranz, Antwerp, 1956; and in *Opera,* ed. G.R. Evans and A. Abulafia, London, forthcoming

Gilbert Foliot, *Letters,* ed. Z.N. Brooke, A. Morey and C.N.L. Brooke, Cambridge, 1967

Gilbert of Poitiers, *Commentaries on Boethius,* ed. N.M. Häring, Toronto, 1966

De Gloria et Honore Filii Hominis, PL, 194.1074–160

Giraldus Cambrensis, *Opera,* ed. J.S. Brewer, London, 1861

Speculum Duorum, ed. Y. Lefèvre, R.B.C. Huygens and M. Richter, tr. B. Dawson, Cardiff, 1974

Gregory the Great (*Hom in Ez.*), *Homilia in Hiezechielen,* ed. M. Adriaen, CCSL, 142, 1971

(*In Cant.*), *In Canticum Canticorum,* ed. P. Verbraken, CCSL, 144, 1963

(*In Job*), *Moralia in Job,* ed. M. Adriaen, CCSL, 143 and 143ᴬ, 1979

(*In Reg.*), *In Librum I Regum,* ed. P. Verbraken, CCSL, 144, 1963

Guibert of Nogent, *Liber Quo Ordine Sermo Fieri Debeat,* PL, 156

Haymo of Auxerre, *In Isaiam,* PL, 116

Hermannus Judaeus, *De Conversione Sua,* ed. G. Niemeyer, MGH, Weimar, 1963

Hincmar, *De Praedestinatione,* PL, 125.55–471

Hugh of Amiens, *Hexameron,* ed. F. Lecompte, AHDLMA, 25, 1959

Hugh of St Victor (*Adnot. in Pent.*), *Adnotationes in Pentateuch,* PL, 175.29–85

(*De Inst. Nov.*), *De Institutione Novitiorum,* PL, 176.925–49

(*De Sacr.*), *De Sacramentis,* PL, 176.173–616

(*De SS*), *De Scripturis et Scriptoribus Sacris,* PL, 175.9–29

(*Didasc.*), *Didascalicon,* PL, 176.741–839; and ed. C. Buttimer, Washington, DC, 1939

(*Hom. in Eccles.*), *Homilia in Ecclesiasten,* PL, 175.113–255

Opera Propaedeutica, ed. R. Baron, Notre Dame, Indiana, 1966

(*Q. in Gen.*), *Quaestiones in Genesim,* PL, 175

Isidore (*Etym.*), *Etymologiae,* ed. W.M. Lindsay, Oxford, 1911

(*Q. in Vet. Test.*), *Quaestiones in Vetus Testamentum,* PL, 83.201–7

Jerome, *Commentarioli in Psalmos,* ed. P. Antin, CCSL, 79, 1959

(*In Hiez.*), *In Hiezechielen,* CCSL, 75, 1964

(*In Isaiah*), *In Esaien*, CCSL, 73–73[A], 1963

(*In Matt.*), *In Matthiam*, ed. F. Bonnard, SC, 1977

(*Tract. in Ps.*), *Tractatus in Psalmos*, ed. G. Morin, CCSL, 78, 1958

Lanfranc (*In Rom.*), (Commentary) *In Romanos*, PL, 150.105–56

    Letters, ed. H. Clover and M.T. Gibson, Oxford Medieval Texts, Oxford, 1979

Magister Bandinus, *Sententiae*, PL, 192.965–1115

Odo of Soissons, *Quaestiones*, ed. J.B. Pitra, Rome, 1886

Ordericus Vitalis (*Hist. Eccl.*), *Historia Ecclesiastica*, ed. M. Chibnall, Oxford Medieval Texts, Oxford, 1969–80, 6 vols.

Origen, *Homilia in Genesim*, ed. L. Doutreleau, SC, 7, 1976

Peter of Celle, *Mosaici Tabernaculi Mystica et Moralis Expositio*, PL, 202.1047–81

Peter the Chanter, *Summa Abel* and *Summa de Sacramentis*, ed. A. Dugauquier, Analecta Medievalia Namurcensia, IV, VII, XVI, XXI, 1954–62

    Verbum Abbreviatum, PL, 205.23–553

Peter Helias, 'The Summa of Petrus Helias on Priscianus Minor: I, II', ed. J.E. Tolson, *Cahiers*, 27–8, 1978

Peter Lombard (*In Ps.*), *In Psalmos*, PL, 191.61–1296

    (*Q. in Ep. Paul.*), *Quaestiones in Epistolas Pauli*, PL, 191.1297–696 and PL, 192.9–517

    (*Sent.*), *Sententiae*, PL, 192.519–963

Peter of Poitiers, *Allegoriae Super Tabernaculum*, ed. P.S. Moore and G. Corbett, Notre Dame, Indiana, 1943

    (*Sent.*), *Sententiae*, ed. P.S. Moore and M. Dulong, Notre Dame, Indiana, 1943

Philip of Harveng, *Epistolae*, PL, 203.1–180

Priscian (*Inst. Gram.*), *Institutiones Grammaticae*, ed. H. Keil, Grammatici Latini, 2–3, Leipzig, 1855–9

Prudentius of Troyes, *De Praedestinatione*, PL, 115.1009–363

Pseudo-Dionysius, *De Divinis Nominibus*, Patrologia Graeca, 3

Rabanus Maurus (*Hom.*), *Homiliae in Evangelia et Epistolas*, PL, 110.135–465

    (*In Ez.*), *In Ezechielen*, PL, 110.495–1083

Ralph of Beauvais, *Glose Super Donatum*, ed. C.H. Kneepkens, Artistarium, 2, Nijmegen, 1982

Remigius of Auxerre (*In Gen.*), *In Genesim*, PL, 131.51–134

Richard of St Victor, *Adnotationes Mysticae in Psalmos*, PL, 196.265–400

(*Trin.*), *De Trinitate*, ed. J. Ribaillier, Paris, 1958

Robert of Melun, *Quaestiones de Divina Pagina*, ed. R.M. Martin, SSL, 13, 1932

    Quaestiones (Theologicae) de Epistolis Pauli, ed. R.M. Martin, SSL, 18, 1938

    Sententiae, ed. A. Landgraf, SSL, 13, 1943

Rupert of Deutz (*In Deut.*), *In Deuteronomium*, ed. H. Haacke, CCCM, 22, 1972

    (*In Ex.*), *In Exodum*, ed. H. Haacke, CCCM, 22, 1972

    (*In Gen.*), *In Genesim*, ed. H. Haacke, CCCM, 21, 1971

    (*In Hiez.*), *In Hiezechielen*, ed. H. Haacke, CCCM, 23, 1973

    (*Sup. Matt.*), *De Gloria et Honore Filii Hominis Super Matthaeum*, ed. H. Haacke, CCCM, 29, 1979

    (*Trin.*), *De Trinitate et Operibus Eius*, ed. H. Haacke, CCCM, 21–4, 1971–4

Simon of Tournai (*Disp.*), *Disputationes*, ed. J. Warichez, SSL, 12, 1932

Thierry of Chartres, *Commentaries on Boethius by Thierry of Chartres and his School*, ed. N.M. Häring, Toronto, 1971

Tyconius, *The Rules of Tyconius*, ed. F.C. Burkitt, Texts and Studies, Cambridge, 1895; repr. 1967

Walter of St Victor (*Four Labyrinths*), *Contra Quatuor Labyrinthos Franciae*, ed. P. Glorieux, AHDLMA, 19, 1952, 187–335

William of Conches, *De Philosophia Mundi*, PL, 172.41–100

William of St Thierry, *De Sacramento Altaris*, PL, 180.341–63

    Epistola ad Fratres Monte Dei, PL, 184.365–77

    In Errores Abaelardi, PL, 180.547–694

    Vita Prima, PL, 185.222–68

Zachary, *Super Unum et Quatuor*, PL, 186.11–620

BIOGRAPHICAL NOTES

ALAN OF LILLE (d. 1202), was called *doctor universalis* because of the range of his knowledge. He taught at Paris and Montpellier in the second half of the twelfth century.

ALCUIN (fl. late eighth century), served Charlemagne in the palace school at Aachen, teaching grammar, logic and the study of the Bible, and reformed the liturgy.

ANSELM OF CANTERBURY (1033–1109), prior of Bec from 1063; abbot of Bec from 1078; archbishop of Canterbury, 1093–1109; theologian and teacher of the elements of the *artes* as aids to the study of the Bible.

ANSELM OF HAVELBERG (mid-twelfth century), visited Constantinople where he engaged in discussions with Greek theologians on the Procession of the Holy Spirit; author of a book on the problem which begins with a survey of the unfolding of human history as a continuation of the biblical narrative.

ANSELM OF LAON (d. 1117), ran the cathedral school at Laon with his brother Ralph; was, in his day, famous as a lecturer on the Bible; a major influence in the forming of the *Glossa Ordinaria*.

AUGUSTINE OF HIPPO (354–430), an African convert to Christianity who did more than any other Latin Father to work out the implications of Christian doctrine into a system of thought, and whose homilies and lectures on the Bible became standard works in mediaeval exegesis.

BEDE (672–735), product of the northern English monasteries of Wearmouth and Jarrow, to which Benedict Biscop brought the books he had collected on the Continent. Bede wrote a good deal of seminal scriptural commentary, as well as handbooks on dating and other mathematical matters, and his *Ecclesiastical History*.

BERENGAR OF TOURS (fl. mid-eleventh century), proponent of the use of grammar and dialectic in scriptural exegesis.

xvi

BERNARD OF CLAIRVAUX (1090–1153), abbot of Clairvaux and adviser of popes. Author of a series of sermons on the Song of Songs which had an enormous influence, and made use, among other sources, of Origen.

BOETHIUS (c. 480–c. 524), translator of the logical works of Aristotle which cover the first stages of the syllabus; author of a series of short theological treatises which make use of logical principles.

ERIUGENA, JOHN SCOTUS (c. 810–c. 877), an Irishman who taught under the patronage of the Emperor Charles the Bald of the Franks. He knew Greek and translated the works of Pseudo-Dionysius among others. He was involved in the controversy over predestination which arose about the figure of Godescalc.

ERNALD, ABBOT OF BONNEVAL (mid-twelfth century), biographer of St Bernard of Clairvaux and author of writings on the Bible.

GILBERT CRISPIN (abbot of Westminster from 1085), a pupil of Anselm of Canterbury and author in his own right of several theological treatises, notably a disputation between a Jew and a Christian.

GILBERT OF POITIERS (1076–1154), a controversial bishop whose purported views on the doctrine of the Trinity, developed in his lectures on Boethius' theological tractates, were condemned at the synod of Reims in 1148; his scriptural commentaries on several books of the Bible survive.

GILBERT THE UNIVERSAL (mid-twelfth century), bishop of London, contributed important elements to the *Glossa Ordinaria*.

GODESCALC OF ORBAIS (ninth century), controversial writer on predestination.

GREGORY THE GREAT (540–604), the most important Western influence in encouraging exegetes to divide the meanings of Scripture into the literal, allegorical, tropological and anagogical; author of homilies on the Gospels, Ezekiel and other books of the Old Testament which became standard sources of comment.

HUGH OF ST VICTOR (c. 1096–1141), studied under William of Champeaux, master of Peter Abelard, and taught the elements of the liberal arts and scriptural commentary in the school at St Victor in Paris. His sensible, schoolmasterly approach reveals a consummate grasp of essentials and a capacity for putting things simply.

ISIDORE OF SEVILLE (570–636), bishop and encyclopaedist.

JEROME (fl. late fourth century), equipped himself with Hebrew and made the Vulgate translation of the Bible from Greek and Hebrew, at the Pope's request, to provide a standard Latin version. In time his translation supplanted the Old Latin versions which were current in the Western Empire and contained a number of errors.

LANFRANC (1010–89), lectured at Bec on the liberal arts and some books of the Bible, before he became archbishop of Canterbury.

MANEGOLD OF LAUTENBACH (c. 1045 to early twelfth century), contributed to the work which went to the forming of the *Glossa Ordinaria*.

ODO OF MORIMOND (mid-twelfth century), abbot of the Cistercian house of Morimond and author of a study of Scripture's numbers.

ORIGEN (c. 184/5–c. 254), one of the Alexandrian Fathers, whose theology was not always orthodox by later standards, but who exerted an enormous influence in favour of the use of higher, 'spiritual' interpretations of the Bible.

PETER ABELARD (1079–1142), made his name as a teacher of logic, and then took to theology, to the disgust of St Bernard of Clairvaux. His Commentary on Romans is his principal surviving work of exegesis. It contains an account of the reason for the Incarnation which makes Christ's primary purpose the setting of an example to man.

PETER THE CHANTER (d. 1197), author of a manual on the use of the Bible in preaching, and a number of advanced study-aids for students of the Sacred Page.

PETER COMESTOR (late twelfth century), commentator on Peter Lombard's *Sententiae* and master of theology at Paris.

PETER LOMBARD (c. 1100–60), compiled the *Sententiae* which became a standard theological textbook throughout the Middle Ages and put topics arising from the study of the Bible into order in a course of systematic theology, with the aid of extracts from the Fathers.

RABANUS MAURUS (d. 836), a pupil of Alcuin, produced an enormous corpus of exegesis and an encyclopaedia, bringing together the critical work of the Fathers.

RICHARD OF ST VICTOR (d. 1173), pupil of Hugh of St Victor, a scholar and a mystic, author of exegetical works, notably of a literal reconstruction of the Temple in Ezekiel's vision.

ROBERT OF MELUN (d. 1167), succeeded Peter Abelard as Master of Theology in Paris.

RUPERT OF DEUTZ (1070 – c. 1129 or later), abbot of Deutz near Cologne, and author of a large corpus of exegetical writings, especially the comprehensive *De Trinitate et Operibus Eius*.

THIERRY OF CHARTRES, taught at Chartres in the 1120s, where he commented on Boethius' theological tractates.

THOMAS OF CHOBHAM (fl. late twelfth and early thirteenth century), sub-dean of Salisbury, was author of a manual for preachers.

WALTER OF ST VICTOR (mid-twelfth century) wrote a diatribe attacking the theological errors of four scholars of his day, whom he felt to have departed from the methods developed by the Fathers.

WILLIAM OF CHAMPEAUX (c. 1070–1121), master of Hugh of St Victor and Peter Abelard.

WILLIAM OF CONCHES (c. 1080 – c. 1145), grammarian and Platonist.

WILLIAM OF ST THIERRY (c. 1085–1148), Benedictine abbot, later Cistercian monk at Signy; friend of Bernard of Clairvaux and accuser of Peter Abelard.

INTRODUCTION

1 The Fathers on the Bible's language

I

When God had created Adam and placed him in the Garden of Eden, he talked to him, telling him that he was free to eat the fruit of every tree in the Garden except one (Gen. 2:16–17). Adam understood him perfectly. Even immediately after the act of disobedience in which first Eve and then Adam ate the forbidden fruit both were able to hear 'the voice of the Lord God walking in the garden in the cool of the day' and to hear the sentence he passed upon them (Gen. 3:8–19). The changes which then took place as a result of Adam's sin are described in some detail in Genesis, but they amount to this: the harmony of Adam and Eve's relationship with the rest of the created world and with God himself was broken (Gen. 3:14–19).

The most important effect, in the eyes of a number of early Christian writers, was the breakdown of communication between man and God. As Gregory the Great put it in the sixth century, after man was expelled from the joys of paradise and began his exile in this present life in the world, he became blind in his spiritual understanding. When God spoke to him directly, telling him plainly to follow him or to love him, man was unable to take in what he had heard, because he was 'frozen in a stupor of faithlessness'.[1] It is upon this supposition, that man, through his own fault, is no longer able to understand what God says to him except dimly and imperfectly, that the whole of mediaeval exegesis is founded.

Augustine, writing three or four generations earlier, explains that God in his mercy continued to speak to man, but adapting his Word to man's damaged understanding. He met man on man's terms, speaking to him, no longer directly, but obliquely, in three ways: through the 'visual aids' of created things; by himself becoming man, so that man could hear what he said directly; and by inspiring the human authors of the books of the Bible to write down his Word in

1

a form intelligible to fallen man.[2] In these three ways, 'in his manner of speaking taking upon himself our ignorance', God ensures that man is able to arrive at a shadowy notion of that divine love which he cannot grasp when he is told about it plainly. In the words of Scripture, Gregory the Great notes, he even goes so far as sometimes to speak 'as if he shared our doubts', as in Luke 18:8: 'Nevertheless, when the Son of Man comes, shall he find faith on the earth?'[3] But this device, like everything in Scripture, is there to help us and instruct us.

The divine use of circumlocution and allegory, the divine way of putting himself in our place, is God's lifting mechanism, says Gregory; it raises the soul from its place at a great distance below God and brings it towards him.[4] It picks man up at the point his understanding can reach, so that as he recognises the 'outward words' he has something to hold on to while he is brought to know the meaning of their inward sense.[5] When the Book of Job has 'on a certain day' in the text, nothing is actually being said to have been done before God 'on a certain day'; God 'coming down to our level (*condescendendo*) uses our words, so that when he speaks in temporal terms about eternity, we who are accustomed to living in time' may be raised to the point where we can grasp eternal things.[6] Thus, if we laugh at certain passages in the Bible for their apparent banality, we are failing to see the great mercy of God in speaking to us in a way we can understand.[7] 'Humbling himself in speaking he exalts us in understanding.'[8]

These are ideas which would have been familiar to every Western reader of the Bible from the early Christian centuries to the Reformation and beyond. They are no longer a common heritage, and they require explanation if we are to understand the force they had for educated people for more than a thousand years. Their great attraction lay in the key they provided to everything which is obscure and apparently contradictory in the pages of the Bible. There would in any case have been a creaturely limitation on man's capacity to understand what God said to him, but the Fall had introduced a certain twistedness into human thinking. Indeed, Augustine saw such perversions and confusions as a characteristic effect of evil, and their straightening as a necessary work of the good. It became possible in this way to hold that the Bible is directly inspired word by word and that every word is true,[9] by transferring what might be called the 'blame' for the difficulties it presents from God to man, and making those difficulties not stumbling-blocks, but God's aids to a contorted human understanding. Each obscure passage or tortuous narrative, each ambiguity or contradiction, meets an obscurity or twist or confusion in human thinking and is thus more, not less, intelligible to man's clouded sinful mind.

Augustine placed an emphasis upon another aspect of the obscuring effect of sin upon the human mind to which he gave considerable currency in the centuries which followed. He himself had had the greatest difficulty as a young man in thinking in abstractions. He found that 'corporeal images', pictures of things which exist physically in the created world, consistently got in the way of his attempts to understand the incorporeal nature of God. 'My mind used to run on bodily forms',[10] he admits. This he put down to the dominance his body and its lusts had over his soul and the spiritual longings which were proper to it as God had originally designed it. His body controlled his mind, and so his mind could think only in 'bodily' terms.

At a stroke, this notion gave him a reason for God's use of stories about the created world and the comparisons the Bible makes between created things and the divine. It explains why God had to speak in such 'bodily' images in the allegories of Scripture if he was to make himself understood to fallen man (as Jesus deliberately did in telling his parables), and why it was necessary for him to act as a 'bodily image' himself when he became man. 'Our medicine Wisdom was by his assumption of humanity adapted to our wounds.'[1] 'Though he is everywhere present to the inner eye when it is sound and clear, he condescended to make himself manifest to the outward eye of those whose inward sight is weak and dim.'[12] 'Men, who in their eagerness to enjoy the creature instead of the Creator had grown into the likeness of this world . . . did not recognise him.'[13]

When we call the Bible the Word of God we are linking it with the act of redemption and looking at both in the same light, as God's ways of re-establishing his communication with man and bringing man back to the rationality and spirituality of vision with which he was created; restoring him, in other words, to understanding and the knowledge of God. Thus it is, emphasises Hugh of St Victor in the twelfth century, that there must be not only labour but rational effort in reading Scripture, for those who merely apply themselves with assiduousness are like men who cross a wood by a circuitous path; those who use their reason are like men who cross in a straight line and come quickly to the other side.[14] It is, then, of the essence of the interpretation of Scripture as God intends it to be read by faithful souls, that it should employ man's rational and spiritual capacities to the full, beginning from the 'bodily images' God provides in the text, and rising to an understanding of higher and spiritual truths. This is the pattern of exegesis in the West throughout the Carolingian centuries and beyond; the reader applies his mind and, increasingly, such technical aids as the study of the arts of grammar and logic and the other *artes* can provide to help his reasoning.

II

The principle that God had resorted to 'bodily images' and oblique means of declaring himself so that man's clouded understanding could grasp as much as possible of his meaning, made it natural to see passages which appeared obscure as expressing their meaning in a figurative way. To see a created thing as a representation of divine truth is to move beyond language into a region where things themselves are signs. Such 'things' (persons, places, events, animals, objects), must be accounted for as meticulously as the words of the text themselves. These figurative meanings are not thought of as additions or later interpretations, as being in any way imposed upon the text, but as so deeply embedded in it that they are acted out in the very events which the authors describe. Remigius of Auxerre, the Carolingian commentator, asks whether Abraham recognised those who appeared to him at Mamre as angels not men (Gen. 18:1). Did he know that he was being presented with a living figure or image, angels appearing to men? If he understood them to be more than they seemed, why did he prepare for them food such as only mortals need? Perhaps he first thought that they were men, and only later recognised their real identity beneath?[15] The human authors of Scripture, too, were sometimes aware that they were describing in figures and indirectly what could not be expressed plainly in human language. Augustine asks in what manner Moses (who was held to be the author of the Pentateuch) saw God on Sinai. The Lord spoke to Moses face to face, as a man speaks to his friend, but Moses was not able to see him in his glory, but only his 'back parts'; that is, he was not allowed to see the divine substance directly. Surely, says Augustine, Moses knew that he saw corporeally and he sought the true sight of God spiritually. That is to say, Moses understood the difference between the literal and the figurative.[16]

This is entirely in the spirit of Augustine's teaching about the need for God to make things easy for fallen man by speaking to him in terms of things in the world he knows. The Bible describes objects, creatures and historical events, so as to teach about the things of the spirit. It is an important part of this process that it does so in ways as various as fallen man in his needs as a sinner. 'Just as the divine Word exercises the wise with its mysteries', so it helps the simple with its superficial sense.[17]

If the Word was to speak to us in terms we could understand it was necessary for it to become many words, to multiply and diversify, to descend to the level of particular sounds for us (*descendit ad particulas sonorum nostrorum*); the one Word of God (*unus sermo Dei*) is expanded or diffused (*dilatus*).[18] There are, accordingly, several levels or different kinds of meaning, sometimes occurring all at once in a single passage, some of them literal, others conveying an image or comparison, a meaning beyond the obvious one. Under the influence of Origen, it became usual in the West to think in terms of four senses: the literal or 'historical' (the plain surface meaning of the words); and three 'figurative' senses – the allegorical or spiritual meaning, the moral to be drawn, or tropological meaning, and the anagogical or prophetic meaning.[19]

III

Augustine had difficulty, as a young man trained in the fine writing and literary appreciation of a late Roman rhetorical education, in finding the text of the Bible worthy of respect. It seemed to him crude and clumsy in expression. The Old Latin version his mother put into his hands was indeed full of archaisms and infelicities. The Christians who quoted from it in their talk in the market-place seemed to their listeners much as the Quakers must have seemed in the days when they preserved a similarly 'biblical' language in an antiquated version. But the Vulgate translation made by Jerome in Augustine's lifetime had its limitations, too. There were still obscure and difficult passages. Augustine reflected upon this in later years and came to the conclusion that it was to be explained by the fact that, because the Bible is God's own Word, it fills human words to bursting. The rules which govern grammar as we know it are often broken or modified by Scripture under the divine pressure to enlarge the frame of reference of ordinary human language. We may speak of Scripture's distinctive usages,[20] of the *locutio scripturarum*, or the *locutio divinae paginae*.[21] The Bible has 'modes' of speaking.[22] Its usage is different from common usage (*communis locutio*) and daily usage (*quotidiana loquendi consuetudo*).[23]

This awareness of extraordinary usage is present throughout the patristic and early mediaeval centuries. Writing on the first Book of

Kings, Gregory the Great asks, 'Why does the book begin with a reference to "one man" (*vir unus*). If this *unus* refers to the number one it seems superfluous, for what man is not "one"?' It is not to be believed that the holy Samuel, who wrote these words, began in a way contrary to the custom of other writers of Scripture. Yet he seems to have done so, if we compare the opening of the Book of Job, with its reference to Job as 'a man' of the land of Hus, and Luke 1:5, with its reference to 'a priest' of the line of Abidjah.[24] We do not have *vir unus* or *sacerdos unus* there. The reason, Gregory suggests, is that Samuel is not only a writer, but also a prophet. He knew not only of the story he tells, but of him 'whom the history spoke of; he knew whom it stood for'.[25] He therefore modifies ordinary usage for the sake of those who have a deeper understanding, and now the whole Church has adopted this new way of speaking, for 'Christ is one, God and Man'.[26] Therefore the *unitas* can fittingly be attributed to Christ.[27]

No attempt has been made in this example to explain the curious grammar of the phrase in terms of the rules of grammar itself. Yet the grammatical and rhetorical education of the late Roman world had made readers actively aware of the divergence from grammatical normality which is sometimes to be found in the Bible's usages. Cassiodorus wanted his pupils to learn not to be too quick to 'correct' the text when it differs from common usage (*ab usu communi*),[28] but to understand that the Bible's language has its own *puritas*, its own idioms which are perfectly proper to it.[29] Gregory himself, in a famous passage, exclaims that Scripture cannot be constrained by the rules of the grammarian Donatus.[30] The grammarian's approach to the Bible's grammar is of a piece with the application of reason to the understanding of the text, in its susceptibility to technical development when the study of the *artes* began to make such development possible. This was above all the achievement of the eleventh and twelfth centuries.[31]

IV

Gregory the Great thought it as absurd to ask who was the author of the Book of Job as if one were to hold a man's letter dictated to his secretary in one's hand and ask who had written it. God is the author of the Book of Job and his authentic voice is audible in every word of it.[32] But as the scholars of the West read them, those words were not in the original language in which God had inspired the human authors of Scripture to write, but in Latin. What was the status of the translation? Some interpreters held that the translators into Latin were not like the prophets. It was Jerome's opinion that God's inspiration worked upon the minds of the human authors of Scripture in such a way that he supplied the content of what they were to say, but left the choice of words and imagery to them, in their varied skills and educational conditions. This must be even more the case with the translators. If we confuse *vates*, a prophet, and *interpres*, an interpreter or translator, we shall have to say that Cicero, who translated some rhetorical works from Greek into Latin, was 'inspired by the Spirit of Rhetoric', or else we shall be inconsistent. If we insist that those who translated the Pentateuch were inspired by the Holy Spirit their errors will present us with a certain 'unfittingness' (*inconveniens*); if we concede that they spoke by a human not a divine spirit then there is no difficulty (*inconveniens nullum esse*).[33] Jerome was a Hebrew scholar and he knew Greek; he was, therefore, in a position to judge the accuracy of earlier attempts to render the Bible into Latin. He was himself the author of the Vulgate version, and was aware of the working of the translation process in his own mind, where it seems there was no conviction that he was being guided in detail by divine inspiration.

In practice, the majority of mediaeval scholars inclined to Gregory's view that the text remained the text even in translation. (He works from both old and new in the *Moralia in Job*, because he felt it his duty as Pope to give due weight to both versions.) Their attitude to the absolute literal truth of the Bible even in translation imposed upon them a set of strict rules in the reading of Scripture. Every word had to be accounted for, in its context. Specific explanations had to be found for every oddity of expression or grammatical superfluity; for each statement which, taken at its face value, presented some anomaly of Christian teaching had to be reconciled with orthodoxy. It was the interpreter's task, by prayer and thought, to penetrate to God's intention in framing the text as he had it before him in Latin, employing allegorical explanations where they seemed illuminating.

V

In this climate of interpretation, in which it is natural and proper to turn to a figurative interpretation where a difficulty presented itself in the literal sense, it was necessary to insist upon the importance of establishing the literal sense, lest it be ignored altogether. Its status was often felt to be modest. The Carolingian scholar Alcuin suggests that it may be wise to be 'content' with that sense, where deeper meanings are hard to ascertain.[34] He defends the literal sense. 'We shall deal with the literal sense, lest we seem to leave out the simple meaning altogether and despise the poverty of the historical sense while we pursue spiritual riches.'[35]

The possibilities of the literal sense began to become apparent in a fuller and more sophisticated way only with the development of refined technical skills in grammar and dialectic and the other liberal arts in the eleventh and twelfth centuries. Hugh of St Victor is able to regard the literal sense not as an inferior but as a fundamental one, a foundation not buried beneath the ground but a visible part of the beauty of the structure, upon which the others rest. He points out that those who disdain to learn the alphabet do not become masters of grammar; similarly, interpreters of the Bible must first master the 'primary signification' of each narrative.[36] The novel methods and principles which were developed in these centuries altered none of the fundamentals of the approach to exegesis of the earlier Middle Ages. Hugh of St Victor's truism that 'every Scripture, expounded according to its proper interpretation, both shines out more clearly and makes it easier for those who read it to find a way to understand it',[37] would have been acceptable in an earlier age, as would his warning that those who expound Scripture without reason and spiritual understanding succeed only in obscuring its beauty and truth,[38] but something new and important was happening to these ideas. It was partly a matter of emphasis, partly the result of the application of new skills.

2 *Lectio, Disputatio, Predicatio*

Towards the end of the twelfth century, Peter the Chanter, precentor of the cathedral of Notre Dame in Paris[39] compiled a manual for preachers. This *Verbum Abbreviatum*[40] begins with a discussion of the various approaches to Bible study with which Peter the Chanter and his contemporaries were familiar. They are three: *lectio, disputatio* and *predicatio*.[41] *Lectio* is the reading of the text with a commentary, either written in the margin and between the lines for convenient reference, or given by a master as he expounded the text to his pupils in a lecture. *Disputatio* is the discussion of the questions which arise in the exposition of difficult passages, and which prove to require fuller treatment than can be given in the course of the lecture. *Predicatio* is the highest form of exegesis, to which the others form a preliminary; it is a method of teaching by preaching. The preacher expounds the passage in a way which will show his listeners not only what it means, but how they are to apply its teaching to their own lives, bringing in other texts to illustrate and support what he says.

Thomas of Chobham, sub-dean of Salisbury, is the author of a *Summa de Arte Praedicatoria* written in the last years of the twelfth century or the first decades of the thirteenth, which has attracted attention because it is one of the earliest manuals to place preaching among the branches of rhetoric.[42] But it is remarkable, too, for the contribution it makes to the development of the view that preaching is the highest form of biblical exegesis.[43] It is possible that Thomas was Peter the Chanter's pupil;[44] but in any case Thomas knew of Peter's threefold division and mentions it in his *Summa*.[45]

Thomas gives a fuller account than Peter of the differences between preaching, disputation and commentary: 'Preaching is the announcing (*nunciatio*) of the divine Word for instruction in faith and behaviour (*divini verbi ad informacionem fidei et morum nunciatio*). For in preaching an announcement is made to others, which is not done in disputation. It is called an "announcement" because it involves the use of our own human arguments and explanations in which we use secular words not divine (*in quibus secularibus verbis utimur non divinis*).'

There is also a difference in subject-matter. Thomas points out that he has emphasised in his definition that preaching is 'for instruction in faith and behaviour', because it is the purpose of all preaching that it should instruct the listener in faith and in good behaviour. If it deals with anything else the order (*ordo*) of preaching is perverted, by which 'other things must be reserved for lecturing and disputing' (*qua alia locutioni et disputationi reservanda sunt*).[46] There is a clear distinction not only of modes of exegesis, but also of content and purpose.

The most important indication that Thomas was aware of the latest developments in exegesis and wanted to give preaching its proper place in relation to the other branches of Bible study lies in his account of the modes of signification which are found in Holy Scripture. Here he draws on contemporary work in grammar and dialectic as well as upon a tradition which goes back at least to Augustine in the Latin West. He has no doubt that the *artes* are to be regarded as theology's handmaids;[47] he compares them unfavourably with theology, but not with disapproval. 'The Sacred Page has its own

special topics', he notes, 'beside those of the dialecticians and rhetoricians, for the praise of God and the destruction of the vices.'[48]

That is not to say that he takes these technical principles very far.
Intelligibility ought to be the essence of preaching, he insists, citing
Cicero on the use of *cotidiana locutio*, everyday speech.[49] In this
fundamental requirement of the preacher's art lies perhaps the
reason why the detailed studies of the grammarians and dialecticians
on the theory of signification and on the theory of fallacy do not
appear to have carried over very far into the study of the Bible as it
was carried on in preaching to ordinary people. They form a sub-
stratum of technical exactitude on which the preacher may erect a
structure in which the scaffolding of theoretical analysis is not
apparent to the eye.

Peter's and Thomas's threefold division would not have come so
readily to mind in the earlier twelfth century. *Disputatio*, envisaged
as a distinct procedure and in connection with biblical study, was
something of a novelty; questions had proliferated in the schools of
the twelfth century to a point where it became necessary to set aside a
separate time to deal with them,[50] but commentary and preaching,
lectio and *predicatio*, had been established, and not always entirely
distinct, methods of Bible study since patristic times. When
Augustine and Gregory the Great expounded the text of Holy Scripture to their listeners, they included reflections on the Bible's
language and upon problems of a philosophical and doctrinal kind.
This study is concerned for the most part with *lectio*, as it is found in
the twelfth century because it was here that the most significant new
developments of the century took place in contemporary understanding of the nature of the Bible's language and its ways of conveying meaning. Technically speaking, *lectio* provided growing-points
for sophisticated work of lasting value. Some of this work spilled
over into *disputatio*, and we shall look briefly at the ways in which
it did so. *Predicatio*, in its twelfth and thirteenth century developments, is another subject and requires another volume.

Before we look at the direction of these new developments and
their technical implications (for some of them were of lasting philosophical importance), we must first try to get a picture of the work of
the scholars of the day in studying the Bible with their pupils.

PART I

THE BACKGROUND

1

THE MONASTIC WAY

1 Rupert of Deutz and 'holy reading'

A leisurely approach to the text, the cultivation of a quiet receptiveness which allows the Holy Spirit to speak in a man's heart as it will, patient reflection upon every detail of expression; these had long been the features of the 'holy reading' (*lectio divina*) of monastic life. At its best it led to a sharp and lively perception of the text and its meaning.

In the opening chapter of his *Proslogion*, written two decades before the end of the eleventh century, Anselm of Bec insists upon the importance of putting aside the distractions of business and creating a quiet place in the mind where there is peace to think about God.[1] Rupert of Deutz, abbot of the Benedictine house at Deutz near Cologne from about 1120, emphasises the same need. He complains to Cuno, abbot of Siegberg (where he had been a master),[2] that he has lately had no peace in which to think or write because of the cares of administration and the large volume of correspondence which has arisen in response to his published works. He compares himself to Zacchaeus, small of stature and weak, whom the crowds jostled and impeded, so that he could not force his way through to see Jesus (Luke 19:5).[3]

Writing on that most difficult prophet Ezekiel, Rupert points out that the Holy Spirit had previously spoken only in the ears of the prophets, but in Ezekiel's prophecy we find pictures painted, 'certain images, with which he may instruct more intimately the eyes of those who see'.[4] The pictures are not easy to understand. Jerome and Gregory have both commented on their difficulty.[5] Rupert wants his readers to find pleasure in them, and he knows that that will take time; they must, he argues, be patient in their reading and not reluctant to linger over the images until they have fully understood them.[6]

Rupert's enormous output is the work of an enthusiast for the richness and vividness of the Bible's imagery, the myriad pictures

13

counterchanging and reflecting one another in its pages. Rupert loved the details of the sacred text, tracing patterns and connections, passages in the Old Testament which have echoes in the New, prophecies fulfilled. Before he became abbot he wrote within a decade a book on the liturgy (*De Divinis Officiis*); two monographs on Divine Will and Divine Omnipotence; a commentary on St John's Gospel; another on Job, and others on the Apocalypse and the Song of Songs; his *De Victoria Verbi Dei* and his massive study, the *De Trinitate et Operibus Eius*. At Deutz he wrote the *De Gloria Filii Hominis* on St Matthew's Gospel, the *De Glorioso Rege David*; commentaries on Ecclesiastes and on the rule of St Benedict; and polemical works against the errors of Jews and heretics.

All these reveal not only Rupert's love of detail, but also his grand sense of the wholeness of the Bible and all Christian learning. The *De Trinitate* takes the whole of Scripture and unfolds from it the historical plan of creation, the work of the Father (up to the Fall of Adam), then the work of the Son (from the Fall of Adam to the Incarnation and the redemption of the world), then the work of the Holy Spirit (whose age lasts until the end of the world). He pauses to discuss the Psalms between his treatment of the third Book of Kings and his examination of the fourth. He leaves out several books of the Old Testament altogether and treats the four Gospels in a single short book. When he comes to the work of the Holy Spirit he draws freely from the whole Bible.

In this last section of the work, Rupert discusses the role of secular studies, the grammar, logic and rhetoric of the quadrivium, in the study of the Bible. This was by no means uncontroversial, as we shall see, but Rupert himself was not hostile to the use of the liberal arts. He could see a place for them.[7] He speaks, in the part of the *De Trinitate* which covers Exodus, of the proper use of human skills, when men employ them not for their own profit but as God intends, using the talents committed to them. 'Who can doubt that these and all such arts are the gifts of God?' he asks.[8] But the *artes* are like silly giggling girls. They have to be disciplined if they are to make good servants. All in all, Rupert found the *artes* inferior, as mere knowledge (*scientia*) is to wisdom (*sapientia*).[9] The Bible speaks with wisdom.

Rupert discovered that wisdom principally in the figurative meanings of Scripture, where he found an infinity of subtleties. He won over the Jew Hermannus to Christianity by convincing him that the Jewish scholars with their concentration on the literal meaning were restricting themselves to the mere husk of the grain, while the Christians enjoyed the sweet kernel of the spiritual meaning.[10] 'The spark of the letter is very small' and gives little light, says Rupert; although with its aid the diligent reader may bring light to the whole passage.[11] The letter gives instruction in holiness, but the mystical sense is a demonstration or prophecy of something far higher.[12] Everywhere in Rupert's exegesis we can feel his consciousness of this lively tension between the literal and the spiritual senses,[13] as he looks for the 'incorporeal and invisible' which is to come and which is foreshadowed by the 'corporeal and visible' deeds done in the past.[14] The literal sense is a veil[15] over the beauties which Grace reveals,[16] and which a man must search for in the mirror of his sense-impressions.[17] When Moses spoke with God in the mountain his face was transformed; it seemed to shine. The meaning of what he had been told could be read in his face, and so it was proper for him to veil it, for many of the children of Israel could not have endured the splendour if they had seen it uncovered. When he went in to speak with the Lord and removed the veil, it was as though he took away the 'letter' and exposed the 'spirit', the spiritual sense which represents most closely the original brightness of what God said to Moses (Exod. 34:29–35).[18]

Rupert had a strong visual sense, which was undoubtedly an important contributor to his pleasure in the images he discovered in the Bible and the large and small patterns they seemed to him to make. In comparing the genealogies of Christ given by Matthew and Luke respectively, he suggests that Matthew's is like a straight line, a sword drawn out of its sheath (Matt. 1:1–16), while Luke's is circular, like a round shield, beginning with Jesus the man and coming round to God, so that the end meets the beginning (for, in Christ, God and man are one) (Luke 3:23–38).[19] In a passage on Deuteronomy he speaks of scent as well as colour, of the way in which the reader is to feel delight as he is drawn along by sight and scent (*ut lectorem visu et odore trahendo delectet*).[20] Everywhere Rupert finds an aesthetic satisfaction in Scripture which is inseparable from spiritual understanding for him as for others. Anselm of Canterbury, too, speaks of the satisfaction he finds in the beauty of reasonableness and harmoniousness.[21]

Strikingly different though these two monastic scholars are, they share a joy in the pleasures of the senses heightened and made spiritual, and in pleasures more purely intellectual.[22] Rupert has a delighted sense of discovery when he finds that things come together, and especially in the discovery of 'keys'. When we look at the puzzling *similitudo* of the four animals and the wheel in Ezekiel, all difficulty disappears, he says, if we understand that the vision is 'beautifully and rightly' (*pulchre et recte*) a revelation of the coming of Christ. The wind coming from the north, for example, is the Devil who, cold without the love of God, blew on the human race as from the north and bowled it over with the wind of temptation. The great cloud is the blindness of the human race when men's minds were clouded with sin.[23] The image of Christ as a lion allows Rupert to explain a passage in Proverbs: 'Like the roaring of a lion is the anger of the king, and his laughter is like dew on the grass' (*sicut fremitus leonis ita et ira regis et sicut ros super herbam ita et hilaritas eius*) (Prov. 19:12). Why was Christ like a roaring lion in his crucifixion? Because he was about to bring the Devil what he deserved. Why was he laughing with joy? Because of his chosen ones, who had been waiting for him since the beginning of the world.[24] In these and similar ways Rupert points out his correspondences.

This pattern-making is not always effected without contrivance. Looking for a 'trinity' in that 'sublime peak of the whole Bible' (*omnium vertex sublimis*), the first verse of Genesis, Rupert finds one with some difficulty. 'In the beginning God created the heaven and the earth' refers to the homeland, respectively, of the holy angels and of men, the invisible and the visible *patria*. The 'third' is the inhabitants themselves, angels and men who are the adornment (*ornatus*) of these realms. But for a reference to these we must wait until the end of the six days' work of creation (Gen. 2:1).[25]

An interpretation of a word or phrase in one passage will sometimes provide a key to another. When he discusses God's 'calling' the darkness night and the light day in Genesis (1:5), Rupert notes (in Gregorian vein) that he did so 'not in Hebrew or Greek and certainly not in Latin' and that he had no tongue or lips to move as he 'spoke'. This *appellatio* is not merely a calling by name, but an 'establishing' (*stabilimentum*), in one case of the *firmamentum* of grace and happiness which is 'day', and in the other case of that unending damnation of darkness which is called 'night'. Once this is understood, 'many things in the Scriptures grow clear', Rupert comments; for example, Job's words, 'Perish the day in which I was born and the night in which it is said, "a man is conceived" ' (Job 3:6–7).[26]

We shall see more of such devices in interpretation. Rupert was exceptional in his range and in both the grandness and the minute brilliance of his evocation of the Bible's images, but he stands squarely within a tradition of patristic and monastic exegesis which underlies all the new work of twelfth century scholars with which we shall be concerned.

Rupert of Deutz and Anselm of Canterbury represent two extremes which show how broad a range monastic scholarship covered. The cool rationality of Anselm had profound spiritual depths, where faith and reason met with utter simplicity. The Bible held none of the mysteries for him which it possessed for Rupert, and which were for Rupert the very stuff of its teaching. In Anselm's view there was nothing a devout and right-minded man could not unravel, so as to arrive at a point where he could contemplate unimpeded the 'inaccessible light' in which God himself dwells.[27] The Bible did not seem to Anselm, as it did to Rupert, a vast puzzle to which keys must be sought if it was to be solved. Rupert's busy intellect worked over the text, building up his account of the truth from its details, and constructing a ladder up which the soul could climb step by step, so as to gain an ever better and fuller view of the glories spread before it on the sacred page in all their variety and detail. Rupert approaches the Bible in the expectation that it will reveal more and more complexities as he comes nearer; Anselm comes to it expecting it to become clearer and simpler as he does so.

2 Anselm of Canterbury: a new look at the Bible's language

In his youth, Anselm of Aosta (1033–1109) left an aristocratic home in northern Italy to travel in Burgundy and northwards into France as a student. His search for the best masters led him eventually to Bec, where a fellow-countryman of his was teaching. Lanfranc of Pavia had set out some years earlier on a similar journey and was now running a highly successful school there as prior under Herluin, Bec's founder-abbot. With Lanfranc as his master Anselm continued his studies in the liberal arts, especially logic, and took his monastic vows. He remained at Bec for thirty years, wholly content as a monk and a teacher, and when, after a few years, Lanfranc went to Caen Anselm was made prior in his place and, on the death of abbot Herluin fifteen years later, he became abbot. When Lanfranc died as archbishop of Canterbury in 1089, Anselm seemed his natural successor. From 1093, the rest of his life was spent uncomfortably in the archbishopric, in conflict first with William Rufus and then with Henry I, as Anselm struggled to reconcile his duty to the Church with his duty to the king. At heart Anselm remained a monk and a scholar and the habit of teaching never left him. As archbishop he would address the community of monks at Christ Church Canterbury, or any other audience which came his way in his travels in exile; what time he could spare from administration and politics was spent in writing and thinking and discussion.

For Anselm of Canterbury as for any of his monastic contemporaries, the Bible was the foundation of Christian learning, the ultimate authority on matters of faith, something which repaid beyond measure the careful, reflective reading proper to *lectio divina*. Something of the flavour of such reading at its best is to be seen in the intense concentration of the 'seeking' which goes on in the first chapter of the *Proslogion*. Anselm tells his reader to 'enter into the inner chamber' of his mind, shut out everything but God and whatever can help him in the search for God, and 'with the door locked' to seek God (Matt. 6:6). That done, his heart can say to God in the words of the Psalmist: 'I seek your face; your face, Lord, I seek' (Ps. 26:8). But where is God to be found, he asks? Anselm asks for help, exploring the clues in finds in Scripture, the reference to 'inaccessible light' in 1 Timothy, for example (1 Tim. 6:16). Where is this 'inaccessible light'? Who will take Anselm into it, so that he can see God who dwells there? What is he looking for, for he does not know what God looks like? He does not know his 'face' (Ps. 1:13). Anselm draws out everything he can from each text so as to 'excite'[28] his own mind and those of his readers to contemplation.

In an age when almost every scholar of note was busy with just such exegetical exercises, Anselm of Canterbury wrote no commentaries on the Bible. He made almost no use of the Fathers as authorities quoted to illuminate the meaning of scriptural texts.[29] He was not attracted by the allegorical explanations which had played a major part in exegesis since patristic times.[30] Nevertheless, he made a unique and original contribution to contemporary work on the study of the Bible. He is the author of three treatises which he says he intended for the use of students of Scripture: the *De Veritate*, the *De Libertate Arbitrii* and the *De Casu Diaboli*.[31] The problems with which they are concerned (the nature of truth, freedom of choice and the way in which it was possible for God's highest creation, the angelic beings, to fall into sin) are explored by means of technical principles of grammar and dialectic.[32] But Anselm's main purpose is to outline a method of approach to the study of the Bible, a method which he himself employed when he had to resolve a difficulty in the text of Scripture, but which is quite different from anything else in use in the eleventh and twelfth centuries.

The circumstances of composition of the 'three treatises pertaining to the study of Holy Scripture'[33] are described by Anselm himself. He wrote them not all at once but from time to time, perhaps working on them at intervals as he saw further into their possibilities. They are both the product of his teaching and designed to teach in their turn, so that his pupils and others who might be interested could have something to refer to in making their own study of the Bible.

Anselm's first book had been the *Monologion*,[34] written at the request of the monks of Bec. He had been in the habit of exploring various aspects of the 'Divine Being' with them in his talks,[35] and he himself describes the *Monologion* as a 'meditation'. Yet the *Monologion* already breathes the atmosphere of that teaching which made the monks of Bec seem to one chronicler like philosophers – even the simple (*rustici*) among them:[35] a gentle but insistent reasonableness with which he led others to think for themselves. The *Monologion* was, like almost everything Anselm wrote, intended to equip men's minds for their own reading and reflection, to encourage in them a certain approach to the faith. Anselm was left with a feeling of intellectual dissatisfaction because what he had said in the *Monologion* seemed to him to make up a chain of many arguments, and he wanted to find a single *argumentum* which would, by itself, be sufficient to show the truth of all that we believe about the 'Divine Being'.[37] The result was the *Proslogion*.

The *Monologion* had a further outcome. In the discussion the subject of 'truth' had arisen. One of Anselm's monks asked for a definition of truth, and the *De Veritate* was written with the purpose of finding one.[38] The other two treatises follow on in subject-matter. From the idea that truth may be defined in terms of 'rightness', freedom of choice rightly used can be shown to be a matter of uprightness in willing. It no doubt seemed natural enough to look (in the treatise on the Fall of Satan) at the way in which it was possible for angels to abandon uprightness in willing and make a wrong choice.

It is not immediately apparent how discussions such as this can be helpful in the study of the Bible. Anselm takes no text as his starting-point. Indeed, a complete list of quotations from the Bible in all three treatises is not a long one. In the *De Veritate* Anselm begins with an oblique reference to the teaching of John 14:6 that God is truth; he gives John 3:20–1 to illustrate the principle that there may be truth in actions (he who *does* evil hates the light; he who *does* the truth comes to the light); to show that 'doing' includes 'suffering' or having something done to one, he cites Matt. 5:10 (on suffering persecution for righteousness' sake) and 2 Cor. 5:10, which says that each man shall receive a reward 'in accordance with what he has *done*'. To illustrate the way in which Scripture describes the righteous as 'upright in heart', he gives two texts from the Psalms (Pss. 31:11 and 106:42).

In the *De Libertate Arbitrii* there are only two quotations, John 8:34: he who *does* sin is the servant of sin; and Ps. 77:39: 'A wind that goes out and does not return', used of free will which, when it abandons uprightness of will, becomes a slave to sin.

For the *De Casu Diaboli* we have a reference to 1 Cor. 4:7: 'What do you have that you have not received?' This provides a foundation for a discussion of Satan's lack of perseverance. Isa. 45:7 is brought in as an illustration of Scripture's sometimes apparently saying that God causes evil or not-being. John 8:44 appears again (Satan did not stand in the truth). There is Gen. 3:5 on Eve's willing to be like a god and Ps. 35:7 and Rom. 11:33 on the unsearchable ways of God, used to show that Satan could not have known what would happen to him if he sinned and would not have been prevented by fear of the terrible consequences we know to have followed.

This extreme economy in the use of texts is the first and most striking thing which distinguishes Anselm's approach to the study of the Bible from that of the commentator, and therefore from the work of the vast majority of his contemporaries, as word by word and phrase by phrase they make their way through the text. Anselm admits in a letter to Maurice, a former pupil of his now in Canterbury with Lanfranc, that he always found it wearisome to plod through a text with his pupils in this manner. Although he is referring to the elementary teaching of grammar traditionally based on the Latin poets[39] it is difficult to believe that he would have approached the glossing of the Scriptures with any substantially greater enthusiasm. In the three treatises on the study of Scripture he is helping his monks to see their way into the Bible's language, so that they will understand its workings. Individual scriptural texts enter the discussion only rarely, but when they do so they fall under a searchlight. Brilliantly illuminated, they yield up their implications so that the reader sees at once how to approach the investigation of other texts.

Anselm takes the word 'truth' and other terms, such as 'freedom' and 'will' which are used in the Bible and are also of philosophical and theological interest and importance. Citing them in scriptural contexts where appropriate, he asks how they are to be defined. It is clear from his mastery of the classical technique that he had learned in his study of dialectic how to arrive at a formally correct definition, continually refining it and making it more precise until it exactly fitted the thing defined, neither taking in more than the thing defined nor failing to include everything relevant to its definition.

But more than this, he was interested in the relationship of signification between the word for the thing and the thing itself. He discusses 'signification' in the second chapter of the *De Veritate*, in an effort to pinpoint what it is in which the truth of a statement (*enuntiatio*) consists. It seems to him self-evident that a statement is true when what it states is the case (*quando est quod enuntiat*), whether the statement is negative or affirmative.[40] Is the thing stated (*res enuntiata*) then the truth of the statement? No, because – and here Anselm characteristically rests his case upon what appears to him to be a self-evident truth – nothing is true except by participating in the truth (*nisi participando veritatem*). The thing stated (*res enuntiata*) is not 'in' the true statement. Therefore it is not itself the 'truth' of the statement. Rather it must be called the 'cause' of the statement's being true. This notion of a 'cause' of truth in statements is borrowed from Boethius' commentary on Aristotle's *Categories*. Anselm does not develop it; it merely provides him with a means of giving an account of what the *res* does for the statement. It makes it true, but it is not itself its truth. The truth must lie in the statement itself.[41]

If it is in the statement we may ask 'where' in the statement it lies. Is the truth of the statement the statement itself (*ipsa oratio*)? Is it its *significatio*? Is it one of the elements in its definition? It seems that it can be none of these, because then the statement would always be true, for these things would always be present.[42] Perhaps the truth of a statement is to be found by asking 'when' it is true rather than 'where' it is true. This proves a much more satisfactory line of enquiry. A statement may be said to be true when it fulfils certain conditions, that is, when it signifies that what is is or that what is not is not, when, in other words, it signifies 'as it ought' or 'rightly' or 'correctly'. The truth consists in this rightness.[43] Anselm is not far here from a distinction made with increasing confidence later in the century, between signification, of which a given *vox* may possess several, and the signification a certain *vox* has at a certain time and in a certain context, when it may be called a 'supposition'. We shall return to this distinction in due course.

Anselm goes on to distinguish two kinds of truth in a statement's 'doing what it ought'. It may be said to do what it ought when it signifies that which it has received the capability of signifying (*accepit significationem*). This happens whenever it signifies. 'It is day' is true in this sense, even if it happens to be the middle of the night.[44] Or it may be said to do what it ought when it signifies what it is designed to signify (*ad quod facta est*); this happens when it signifies: 'it is day' when it actually is day.[45] In some statements these two kinds of truth are inseparable, as in 'a man is an animal' or 'a man is not a stone', because such statements always signify in both ways.[46]

There is no general discussion here of the theory of signification, but elsewhere Anselm has a good deal to say on the matter. In the *De Grammatico*, the only treatise he wrote which is concerned exclusively with a grammatical and dialectical problem, he explores the ways in which a word or expression may be said to 'mean' the thing it stands for, the case of double meanings, where a word appears to mean one thing directly and another obliquely, the Augustinian notion of 'common usage', and a number of other problems of signification which his twelfth century successors were to tackle, like Anselm with the aid of Boethius, but not always with the same result. It is clear that he is approaching the analysis of the text in a manner and in a spirit quite different from that of the majority of his contemporaries, looking not for images and correspondences but for the exact relation at a literal level between the word or expression and what it designates.

This characteristic of Anselmian exegesis is evident in all his analysis. In the *Cur Deus Homo* the scriptural quotation is again used to carry the argument forward by providing material for analysis. In Book 1.9, Anselm considers an apparent paradox. It was necessary for Christ to die for man. God had been dishonoured by man's sin, and the debt to his honour must be discharged. No man could do what was necessary on his own; if an angel were given the task, man would owe allegiance to him, not God, in gratitude. Only God himself could carry out the task, and then only as man, since the debt was man's and the duty of discharging it rested with him. Thus the Son was, it seems, under a necessity to become man, although he was, as God, incapable of being under any necessity. The Bible says that he was 'made obedient even unto death' (Phil. 2:8). He himself says: 'I did not come to do my own will' (John 6:38) and: 'Not what I will, but as you will' (Matt. 26:39) as though he had his will overruled in some way by the Father. Anselm furnishes us with several such puzzling texts, and takes each in turn, scrutinising its implications, until he can show that there is no paradox at all.[47] The Son's will freely goes along with that which he must do, and so he is under no constraint. As in his studies of truth, freedom of choice, and so on, Anselm works by seeking and refining a definition, and by looking minutely at the signification of words in context.

Boso, the friend and former monk of Bec who is Anselm's partner in the dialogue, had listed a number of these texts in which Christ himself seems to be saying that he is acting not out of his own free will, but out of obedience to the Father: 'Father, not as I will but as you will', and others. Anselm puts it to him that he is not distinguishing clearly between that which Christ did because obedience required it and that which he allowed to happen to him even though obedience did not specifically require it, but because he was and remained in a 'state' of obedience.[48] That state of obedience Anselm equates with a steady adherence to justice and truth in deeds and words alike, an adherence he believes that God expects of every rational creature; every rational creature owes this to God. It is this perseverance in justice and truth that Christ maintained and in which his state of obedience consisted, and with which his will concurred. Since it was necessary (to maintain justice) that he should die for man's sake, he did so, not as a specific act of obedience to a will other than his own, but because within his condition of sustained obedience this was an act which he would automatically perform so as to keep to justice. God commanded that the death should take place, but this was to command a 'thing', in consequence of which Christ incurred death.[49]

This general explanation does not, however, quite cover all the points raised by Boso's texts. Anselm is interested in the further puzzling details of usage to be found in them. In each case a word or expression taken at its face value appears to present an anomaly when it is used of God. Anselm always looks for an answer in terms of the literal sense; he never resorts to the explanation that a word is being used figuratively. He tries to show by comparison with an idiom in ordinary human speech how the Bible's usage is to be understood in a way which presents no anomaly. How can Christ be said to have 'learned' obedience or 'become' obedient, when he is divine? Either 'he learned' is being used in place of 'he caused others to learn',[50] or else 'it is used to show that he learned in terms of experience what he already knew about in terms other than those of experience'.

To take another text: 'For this reason God has also exalted him'

(Phil. 2:9). There is something offensive at first reading about 'For this reason', because it suggests that had Christ not given himself up to death he would not have deserved his high place in heaven. Anselm cites as a parallel text: 'Therefore he lifted up his head' (Ps. 109:7). Two interpretations which would be natural on an ordinary reading of 'therefore' and 'for this reason' are unacceptable: either that Christ could not have been exalted except by dying; or that the exaltation was a reward for his obedience. Either of these would imply that he was less than God. There is, however, no objection to understanding the text to mean that the exaltation was a manifestation of Christ's glory to the world by God 'by means' of his death.

Is this an acceptable use of 'because'? Anselm is able to show from examples from common usage that it is. If I am planning to cross a river which may be crossed either on horseback or by boat and I decide to cross in a boat, I may be delayed because no boat is immediately available. When the boat comes, someone may say: 'The boat was ready, therefore he crossed over.' I have decided to do something by means of something else, and so my final action may appropriately be said to be 'because' of the earlier one.[51]

Another of Anselm's devices is to distinguish between the human and the divine response in Christ. When Jesus said: 'If it be possible let this cup pass from me', he was expressing a natural human desire for safety, for his human flesh shrank from the pain of dying. But since the Father was unwilling for the human race to be restored in any other way than by Christ's dying, he willed rather to let himself be killed than to see the human race lost. Here again a parallel suggests itself to Anselm in ordinary usage. If we say that someone 'does not will' to close a window through which a draught is blowing, and the draught blows out a lamp, then he can be said to have willed that the lamp should be blown out. Similarly, the Father willed the Son's death by not willing that the human race should be saved in any other way.[52]

Whatever force these arguments may seem to have now – and as we become familiar with their like in the generations after Anselm their sophistication becomes increasingly apparent – they have a subtlety beyond anything Anselm's immediate contemporaries can match. Anselm has put the question of method in the forefront and he teaches a system of exegesis in which the student learns to think about the way the Bible's language is functioning. Once he is familiar with its ways, he will be able to solve many problems for himself in his reading.

Anselm set a high standard. It did not prove easy for his pupils to follow him, nor for others to imitate him. Gilbert Crispin, one of the most able of his friends and pupils from Bec, whom Lanfranc took with him to Canterbury, later became abbot of Westminster. He was something of a theologian in his own right.[53] An Anselmian note creeps into his discussions from time to time. (In 'ordinary usage' (*usus loquendi*) he says in a favourite Augustinian phrase of Anselm's, we alter the verb, saying *erit* as long as we refer to the future, changing the verb to *est* in the present and *fuit* in the past.)[54] But his explanations are never as philosophically penetrating as Anselm's.

Gilbert's most famous work was the *Disputatio* between a Jew and a Christian, in which the two combatants put forward arguments supported by texts. He contrasts the *divinus sensus* and the *humanus sensus*, pointing out that if we read in the 'human sense' we shall find much that is contradictory (*multa sibi invicem adversantia et multa repugnantia videmus*).[55] But the divine sense has a 'higher' sound than the literal and sometimes that is the one we take, for it is not possible to read everything literally in a way which will be acceptable.[56] But whether the literal sense or the figurative one is appropriate, we can be confident that that is the due sense (*debitus sensus*). Thus we can obey all the commandments of the law, some literally and some 'in a figure' (*ad figuram*).[57]

Gilbert is cautious in his use of the simplest technical devices, so as to avoid there being any justice in the Jew's accusation: 'You do violence to Scripture, twisting it.'[58] Yet Gilbert stands exactly where Anselm does on the reliability of Scripture. He sums up his position in one sentence, quoting Ps. 61:12: it is impossible, he says, for any word of God to be nothing.[59] Where Anselm is confident that an explanation can always be found which will meet this requirement by presenting the exact words of Scripture literally, if we understand properly how those words have been used, Gilbert will sometimes turn to the figurative sense for a solution.

Anselm was able, then, to take his method further than even those he taught could do. Few of those who seriously pursued the study of the peculiarities of biblical language to which Augustine had pointed, employing their technical skills of grammar and dialectic, could approach him in the simplicity and profundity of his solutions. He combined the leisurely habits of *lectio divina* with the crisp technical exactitude of the student of the *artes* as few were able to do after him. Yet, although there is nothing quite like the 'three treatises' in the literature of the following century, Anselm was pioneering where others were to go in the attempt to interpret the literal sense seriously and fully and intelligently and to find in it matter worthy to set beside what might be learned from figurative interpretations.

2

BIBLE STUDY IN THE SCHOOLS

1 The academic way

Bec was exceptional under Lanfranc and Anselm, in Lanfranc's day in having external students, and under Anselm in the philosophical quality of the teaching. As a rule the monastic schools seem to have been modest in their aspirations and achievements on the intellectual side, however high the standard of spiritual striving they expected from their pupils. The primary need within the monastic life was for proficiency in reading and singing, so that the liturgical round could be sustained and each monk derive some benefit from his reading of the Bible and the Fathers over and above what he heard read to him each day in chapel or at mealtimes. It was a utilitarian education, in the mediaeval sense of *utilitas*: designed in the right proportions to be profitable to the whole man – body, mind and soul.

But there were schools of another sort, often ephemeral, consisting of a single wandering master and his pupils, or a small group of such masters. Anselm spent three years in Burgundy on his way from Italy to northern France in search of the best masters. He went to Normandy specifically 'to see, talk to and stay with' Lanfranc, says his biographer Eadmer. Anselm did not remain a wandering scholar for long, but he was for a time engaged in a search which attracted many able young men in the last decades of the eleventh and the early years of the twelfth centuries: for the best possible teaching, in the liberal arts and the study of the Bible. Peter Abelard (1079–1142) was one of the ablest. He studied under the best grammarians and dialecticians and Masters of the Sacred Page, and set himself up as a rival master, first in dialectic, then in theology.

It is difficult to see that there was anything that so many would-be students and academics could hope to gain by way of worldly advantage, for there was as yet no well-marked path from the schools to preferment; but it is clear that many thought a good education a desirable thing. Guibert of Nogent's mother, and Bernard of

Clairvaux's, too, went to some trouble to ensure that their sons had the best teaching they could procure for them in the late eleventh and early twelfth centuries.

If we may take 'academic' to refer to activities in which there is a driving intellectual curiosity, a love of learning for its own sake, then something of this sort was undoubtedly going on in the schools of northern France from the second half of the eleventh century. There is all the over-confidence and trivial curiosity which are the faults of the academic world, and the deep scholarship of fine minds given up to the pursuit of truth which are its virtues.

Providing fixed points and some continuity within the jostling throng of ambitious academics were the old cathedral schools, at Reims, Laon, Chartres, Paris, where there was almost always a school of sorts from at least Carolingian times (when Charlemagne laid on all cathedral chapters the duty of providing an adequate education for the clergy of the diocese).

A cathedral school had normally been of only moderate pretensions, with perhaps a single schoolmaster appointed by the chancellor, whose task was to give the clergy of the diocese such training as they needed in theology and canon law if they were to be administrators, probably often rather less. It was unusual for pupils to come from far afield, except where the master's reputation drew them, as seems to have happened for a time in the case of the brothers Ralph and Anselm at Laon at the end of the eleventh century and Bernard and his brother Thierry at Chartres. The cathedral schools had no continuous tradition of excellence such as an established institution is able to maintain; their standards were dependent upon those of the master available. Nevertheless, when the number of potential students began to increase at the end of the eleventh century, these schools had a certain attraction for those who wanted a good education but did not want to become monks.

One religious order made an attempt to embrace both the monastic ideal and the demands of the new academic life: the regular canons of St Victor in Paris.[1]

In earlier centuries the cathedral clergy had not been subject to a rule; many were non-resident and held private property. In the early years of the Gregorian Reform movement of the later eleventh century an attempt was made to reform the lives of such 'secular' clergy and bind them to poverty, chastity and obedience. The move was approved in 1059 and 1063 at Synods of the Latin Church. Not all cathedral clergy conformed: secular canons continued to live as they had always done. But those who put themselves under the Rule came to be known as 'regular' canons. The Rule eventually adopted was not that of St Benedict, which it would have been impractical for a member of the working clergy of a cathedral to follow perfectly, but a Rule based on the one Augustine of Hippo was believed to have devised for his own community in North Africa.

From the beginning of the twelfth century this *vita regularis et canonica* began to appeal to others who were not cathedral clergy. New orders of 'canons' were founded: the Premonstratensians, preachers who produced such scholars as Anselm of Havelberg and the Godescalc who drew up a list of points for St Bernard's use at the trial of Gilbert of Poitiers for heretical teaching on the Trinity in 1148. In the house of St Victor at Paris the Victorine canons endeavoured to be both monks and academics with a remarkable degree of success. There lay within the conception of their new order an implicit challenge to the growing contemporary assumption that monk and scholar had different purposes.

The order of canons of St Victor was founded by William of Champeaux, who had withdrawn in 1108 from the open, competitive world of the masters and pupils of Paris to the priory of St Victor – largely, it seems, because he could not endure the opposition of Peter Abelard, once his pupil and now his rival. He remained there only a few years after his retreat, before he was made bishop of Châlons in 1113, but his small chapel on the left bank of the Seine became the home of a community where the loyal pupils who had followed him there and whom he went on teaching in retirement remained and flourished. For thirty years at least the school seems to have remained open to pupils from outside the community, so that its students included both those who lived under a rule and those who did not.

St Victor was fortunate in the men it attracted and formed as scholars. Among them was Hugh, who came from Lorraine or the Low Countries about 1118 and taught in the school at St Victor from the mid-1120s until his death in 1141.

Hugh was a prolific author, with nearly forty treatises to his credit, every one of which is concerned directly or indirectly with the study of the Bible, some with its literal sense and others with mystical and figurative interpretations. We shall have little occasion to look at Hugh's work on the 'higher' senses, but they form a significant part of his œuvre, and he intended his pupils to see such exegesis as the higher ground to which they themselves should desire to move when they had mastered the literal interpretation.

Hugh taught the liberal arts, but as a preparation for the reading of the Bible only, and in the plainest and most straightforward manner. Among his earliest works are an 'Epitome' of philosophy, a little treatise on grammar and another on practical geometry, all of them modest and deliberately limited in scope. But his principal work of comprehensive instruction, which brings the liberal arts and the study of the Bible systematically together, is the *Didascalicon*. Here the arts are put in a nutshell, their main features listed in an encyclopaedia in the manner of Cassiodorus or Isidore, with nothing to tempt the reader to ask questions of an advanced or more technical kind. Hugh represents the arts always as the mere handmaids of theology.

Hugh's advice is to begin with those books of the Bible which strike him as being easiest for beginners: Genesis, Exodus, Joshua, Judges, Kings, Chronicles, and then the Gospels and the Acts of the Apostles.[2] At this elementary stage, he taught, the emphasis should be upon memorising persons, times and places; dull work but necessary and yielding unexpected rewards if carried out conscientiously.[3] Thus Hugh proceeds at a steady walking-pace, and his pupils accompany him, observing carefully what they find in the path, as on a nature ramble.

Hugh was methodical and sensible, but a number of practical and entertaining hints enliven his writings and show him to have been a gifted teacher. Yet these simple devices also mark the level of his instruction. He was simply trying to help those of his pupils without any particular academic gifts to grasp what they needed to understand if they were to make any progress in the study of Scripture. Where – as we shall see – Peter Abelard expects his students to interrupt him and ask questions, Hugh's students seem to have behaved more like the monks of Bec, regarding him respectfully as a master who could be trusted to give them sound teaching.

Here perhaps lies the difference between the monastic approach to Bible study and that of the schools which were springing up to meet a new demand. Hard and challenging questioning drives research forward.

2 Introducing the Bible

It had been usual for some generations for masters to begin the study of a new text with their pupils with an *accessus*: a short introduction which explained who the author was, what his purpose in writing and what was the subject-matter of his book, which all gave 'access' to the text.[4] This method of approach suggested itself equally naturally for books of the Bible. We find such helps for the student as: 'The *subject* of this book is Job . . . the *intention* is to give us an example.'[5] On Isaiah: 'At the beginning [the author] explains briefly the *name* of the author and his *origins* and the *subject-matter* of the work . . . when he says: "The vision of Isaiah . . . Son of Amos . . . in the days of Uzziah".'[6]

The device was used by masters whose discussions rise far above the level of simple pedagogy. In his commentary on the six days of creation in Genesis, Peter Abelard begins by 'placing' the text with an elaborate *accessus*. It is, he says, one of three *loci* in the Old Testament which everyone agrees to be especially difficult. (The others are the Song of Songs and the visions of the prophet Ezekiel, especially the first vision of the wheel and the last vision.)[7] The subject-matter (*materia*) of the first verses of Genesis is the creation and disposition of the natural world. The author's purpose (*intentio*) is to show by telling of these things how great an obedience man owes to the God who made him in his own image and placed him in paradise and gave him dominion over other creatures; and he also wants to lead the reader to worship.[8] The author (that is, the human author) is Moses. Gerhoch of Reichersberg expounds the Song of Isaiah so as to make clear its subject-matter (*materia*) and its meaning (*sensus*);[9] he further explains the *materia* of the Song of Ezekiel,[10] with the aid of Isaiah's reference to 'the writing of Ezekiel, King of Judah, when he had been ill and had recovered from his sickness'. 'In this brief preamble is implied the subject-matter of this song', he says. The *accessus* provided a structure within which the commentator could position the text before he began to examine it in detail.

3 The use of the *artes*

One of the questions commonly asked and answered in the *accessus* was: to what branch of philosophy does this work belong? Hugh of St Victor provided a comprehensive little handbook for answering this question in his 'Epitome Dindimi in Philosophiam'. The two speakers in the dialogue, Sosthenes and Dindimus, discuss the number of parts of philosophy. Dindimus says that there are four, corresponding to the fourfold nature of the human soul.[11] The four are *logica*, *ethica*, *theorica* and *mechanica*. Hugh goes on to divide each of the four into its branches: logic, or the art of language, is divided into grammar and argumentation (*ratio disserendi*);

argumentation may be further subdivided into probable, necessary or sophistical. Ethics has three principal parts: as it affects the individual (*solitaria*), his immediate circle (*privata*) and the public at large (*publica*). *Theorica*, too, has three branches: mathematics, physics and theology. *Mechanica* is something of a newcomer, he says, and scarcely deserves to be counted as philosophy;[12] it has seven parts, covering such subjects as navigation and agriculture. A number of schemes of this sort, with variations, are to be found in contemporary schoolbooks, as though, in an enlarging scholarly world, students felt a need to know how their studies fitted into an overall scheme.[13]

Within the brief compass of his 'Epitome', Hugh shows how the whole of philosophy may be seen as a way by which the student may gradually come to understand the highest truths of *theologia*, the topmost branch of *theoria*. Thus he brings philosophy firmly within the span of the proper studies of a Christian.

In his third century commentary on the Song of Songs, the Alexandrian Origen refers to a tradition which makes a connection between branches of philosophy and the writings of Solomon. In Proverbs it is as though a Father speaks to a beloved son, and that is like ethics; in Ecclesiastes it is as though the words were addressed to a grown man, and that is like physics; in the Song of Songs the reader is a fully-developed human soul, and the subject is *theologia*. This commonplace (as it became) lent a biblical basis to the study of the branches of philosophy. It was sometimes extended so as to cover further books of the Bible. We are told that physics may be found in Genesis as well as in Ecclesiastes; ethics in the Pauline Epistles and in the parables of Solomon and in Job. The Psalms, although they treat of ethics, are nevertheless principally concerned with *theorica*, the highest, theological study.[14]

The *locus classicus* for the proof of God's existence in the twelfth century was Rom. 1:18–19, with its insistence that even those pagans to whom the details of the Christian faith are not known have no excuse for not understanding something of God's nature from his revelation of himself in creation. Peter Lombard explains that the greatest philosophers perceived that God is not a body and that he is immutable. Some of them even understand dimly something of the Three Persons.[15] Philosophy at its best is, then, an unexceptionable introduction to Christian truth.

It was Hugh of St Victor's view, as it was Rupert of Deutz's, that the arts which make up philosophy are simply theology's handmaids.

Anselm of Canterbury saw no need even to comment on the matter, so obvious to him was it that clear reasoning could only help men to sound faith. But the use of the *artes* was by no means so uncontroversial for everyone. For many there was a tension between the *artes* as taught by ancient pagan thinkers and the Christian education which formed a preliminary to the study of the Bible.

Although Hugh of St Victor is quietly confident that there will be nothing but benefit in his students' mastering the *artes*, he never allows the technical principle to assert itself with a hard edge, as if it is of interest and importance in its own right. Like the dialecticians, Hugh taught his pupils to 'divide',[16] but he makes no reference to Boethius' monograph the *De Divisione*,[17] or to the technicalities of the subject as they were developed by the dialecticians of the day. He explains simply: 'The division is made by "distinguishing" when we separate those things which are confused', says Hugh. 'We divide by "investigating" when we open up those things which are hidden.'[18] This clearing of the ground so that he can see what he is doing is characteristic. It is a method used by his pupil Richard quite naturally and equally without pointing to the technical procedure involved. The fire which Jesus came to send upon the earth is one thing; the fire he came to put out is another.[19] There is one purity of mind and another purity of action.[20] 'It remains to learn what is the difference between the cedars of Lebanon and the bull-calves of Lebanon.'[21] We can appropriately understand by the 'Temple' not the present Church but the throng of the heavenly citizens.[22] The purposeful application of the elementary technicalities of the liberal arts in this way seems to have preserved Hugh and his pupils in some measure from a dilemma which had presented itself since early Christian times.

In the fifth century Cassiodorus faced the difficulty that there were no public teachers of the Divine Scriptures in his day, such as there were for the liberal arts.[23] He consciously tried to repair the gap in his *Institutiones*.[24] The methods of the existing masters offered the best starting-point not only because they had been tried and developed but also because they provided something familiar to all educated men. They were borrowed, albeit with caution and with modifications, for the use of the exegetes. With greater or lesser sophistication the liberal arts were used as a Bible study-aid in every century from the end of the Roman world, and rarely without controversy, because they were adapted for uses which they did not always closely fit.

Walter of St Victor, writing a diatribe against the misuse of the *artes* and other errors of the 'four labyrinths of France' puts the difficulty judiciously. 'We know that every art and wisdom (*sapientia*) is from the Lord God and also that Divine Scripture, Truth itself', uses syllogisms in the Gospel, 'proposing, assuming and concluding' in the formally recognised manner (*proponit, assumit et concludit*). But he is sure that it does so not contentiously (as it is suggested is the case with modern dialecticians) but with a 'truthfulness and weightiness of things and meanings' (*veritate et gravitate rerum et sententiarum*).[25]

The foundation study of the *artes* was always grammar. Rhetoric diminished in importance with the end of the Roman world because there was no longer the same need for speech-making either political or forensic. Dialectic did not capture wide interest until the eleventh century, but grammar never went out of fashion, and the Roman grammarians were read by Christians. (There was no difficulty in accepting the grammarian Donatus; he had been Jerome's master (*praeceptor meus*),[26] and might be regarded as an honorary Christian.) It was essential that the reader of the Bible should understand the Latin of the text and, as Latin ceased to be the vernacular, it had to be learned as a foreign language; therefore grammatical teaching was indispensable.

Both the Latin Vulgate and the Old Latin version contain much that is out of keeping with the normal rules of grammar, and it is therefore essential for the educated reader to have a view of the way in which such anomalies are to be regarded. We have noticed that Cassiodorus advises his readers not to 'edit' or force the text to fit the rules of grammar of ordinary human language (*humanarum formulas dictionum*).[27]

In his classic and much-quoted statement of the principle in the sixth century, Gregory the Great warns against trying to bind the inspiration of the Holy Spirit by the laws of Donatus (whose textbooks were the foundation of mediaeval grammatical studies where Priscian provided something more advanced): *indignus vehementer existimo ut verba caelestis oraculi restringam sub regulis Donati*.[28] Gregory's warning comes at the end of a letter to Leander, bishop of Seville, in which he explains his intentions in writing his *Moralia* on the Book of Job. The statement, in context, is part of Gregory's apology for the lack of felicity he fears his friend will notice in his own style. He has been ill, he says; he is a broken instrument who cannot play sweetly in tune. In any case, as Leander well knows, it is often the case that the art of rhetoric produces a luxuriant foliage and no fruit. It is for that reason that Gregory has not felt it important to write in a fine style. It is only thirdly that we come to the 'Rules of Donatus': no one, says Gregory, should read the Holy Scriptures in the expectation that they will obey the rules of human devising which govern our speaking and the writing of our human language.[29] Gregory makes a clear contrast between the human laws of the arts of language and the divine laws which will sometimes transcend them.[30]

Gregory's remark came to be well known because the *Moralia in Job* was widely read; numerous echoes of it are to be found in succeeding centuries: *nec per artem Donati;*[31] *sciens magis obedientiae Christi deberi quam Donato.*[32] It proved to be of importance in its implication that theological language has a grammar of its own, higher than humanly devised grammar, so that the Bible must always be read with an awareness that it may not obey the rules an ordinary text would be expected to follow.

The *Sententiae Parisienses* which are associated with the teaching of Peter Abelard include a discussion of the difficulty of talking about God in human language. The pagan philosophers, says the author, could not 'apply to God any word by which they can define or show what God was'. Neither by analysis (*per divisionem*) nor by words (*per aliquod vocabulum*) is it possible to 'learn anything properly' of God.[33] Hugh, bishop of Amiens, a monastic scholar and a former abbot of Reading, says that 'our words' cannot impose upon the Deity itself (*ponunt in ipsam deitatem*) any of the ordinary things they mean: 'action' or 'passion' or 'variety'. 'Therefore take careful note that words and any sayings which are taken to signify God' are not to be classified in terms of 'the parts of speech which the grammarians lay down'. They signify in a divine way (*ritu divino*), not in a grammatical manner (*non more grammatico*), nor in a dialectical way.[34] Thus it is that there is a serious obstacle in the way of the use of the arts of grammar and dialectic and rhetoric in the interpretation of Scripture.[35]

If human language must be regarded as necessarily limited in talking about the divine, and the three arts of language consequently suffered under a disability, the four mathematical arts of the quadrivium might seem likely to fare better. 'Number, weight and measure' are to be found in all created things according to Scripture,[36] and the symbolism of numbers played an important part in exegesis from early time.[37] The twelfth century contribution in this

area was chiefly arithmetical in character. Thierry of Chartres
analysed the properties of unity, duality and trinity with an arithmetical commentary in his treatise on the six days of creation, pointing out, for example, that $1 \times 1 \times 1 = 1$, just as the Three Persons
of the Trinity are so related to one another that they are one, while
the $1 + 1 + 1$ of things in the created world leads to a multiplicity.[38]

The speculations of Plato in the *Timaeus* provided a further
source of what we may call in modern usage 'scientific' thinking
about the creation of the world. Hugh of St Victor contrasts the
philosopher's account with that of Genesis in his commentary on
Genesis. Plato, he says, sees God merely as an *opifex*. He claims that
there are three first principles: matter, the archetypal forms of things
or ideas, and God himself who brought them together. The
Christians hold that there is only one first principle, God himself who
made both matter and form from nothing.[39] In a few lapidary sentences Hugh sets out the difference.

The quadrivium subjects and 'natural science' had a place, then,
but in comparison with the flourishing of the use of the arts of
language, their role remained small. Ironically, it was perhaps the
very difficulty which had been pointed out by the Fathers which
made the use of the *artes* so tempting. If language used of God broke
the rules of ordinary language, it might be illuminating to find out in
exactly what manner it did so, and, as the tools of grammar and logic
in particular grew sharper in the course of the eleventh and twelfth
centuries, there was a strong urge to try again, to see if with new
techniques the old barriers might be broken.[40] The practical usefulness of the *artes* over-rode all scruples and secular studies continued
to hold a place in commentary in every century. In the twelfth century their influence grew in a spectacular manner.

3

A STANDARD COMMENTARY: THE *GLOSSA ORDINARIA*

The running commentary had many merits as a vehicle of teaching on the Bible. In its written form it allowed the individual reader to turn to the margin or the space between the lines of the book he was reading and find a difficult word or grammatical construction explained, an extract from Gregory or Augustine to clarify a perplexing passage, ready selected for him and conveniently placed to hand. The student listening to his master's lectures was presented with an oral version of the commentary. He had an opportunity to ask questions and be further enlightened. (A number of twelfth century masters remark a little defensively even: 'At this point someone will ask', or: 'Perhaps here the question will be raised.')

The context of such teaching might be that of the schoolroom; Peter Abelard described how he went to hear the famous master Anselm at Laon and thought his lectures so poor and thin that he could do better himself, and the next day he lectured on Ezekiel (with the aid of a crib, or *Expositor*) to an admiring crowd. In this arena the teaching was businesslike and brisk.[1] Or in a monastic context or a house of canons like that in which Hugh taught at St Victor in the 1120s and 1130s, a commentary might be developed in a relaxed and companionable way in a series of talks to the brothers.[2]

The method was flexible and had all sorts of uses. A commentator might make his work a vehicle for special pleading. Gerhoch of Reichersberg (1093–1169), an ardent polemicist, turned his commentary on the Psalms into a diatribe against the present corruptions of the Church. He writes fiercely of the folly of the day in the choice of bishops. The faithful are being given into the charge of robbers not shepherds.[3] But running through this various and independent effort was steady work on the bread-and-butter task of compiling a complete gloss on the whole Bible.[4]

The *Glossa Ordinaria* is the product of protracted collaborative labour on the part of scholars who saw a need for a reliable commentary of manageable length. Standardisation can never have been complete. Some manuscripts carry a mixture of elements, some glosses which are the usual ones found in the *Glossa Ordinaria*, others which are not.[5] The *Glossa Ordinaria* could be neither definitive nor final when so much new work was constantly being done in the schools and by individual scholars.[6]

Since Carolingian times the text of the Vulgate had been copied with prefaces (which chiefly depend upon the Prologues composed by St Jerome) and explanations which differ a good deal in their length and in the sources from which they are taken. The whole apparatus – the 'crib' used by Peter Abelard – was known as an *Expositor*. Individual books had their commentaries from the Fathers already, in some cases several. The Psalms and the Pauline Epistles were especially rich; these were the books on which twelfth century Masters of the Sacred Page traditionally commented so as to establish a reputation.[7] The task of commenting upon the whole Bible involved different exercises for different books, sometimes reconciling or juxtaposing existing commentaries ('the expositors of this book are Bede and Augustine' says one commentary on St John's Gospel),[8] sometimes filling out earlier work as did Gilbert the Universal, bishop of London (1128–34).[9] The achievement of the eleventh and twelfth century scholars who put the *Glossa Ordinaria* together was to go over the existing commentaries, to select and prune, and to draw everything together into a relatively uniform whole, covering all necessary points briefly, clearly and authoritatively.

A few significant figures in pioneering this work have been identified. In her classic study Beryl Smalley lists Berengar of Tours,[10] and his friend Drogo at Paris; Lanfranc of Bec; Bruno the Carthusian (who seems to have taught at Reims before he withdrew from the world to become a monk and in due course to found the Carthusian order in the early 1080s); Manegold of Lautenbach;[11] Lambert of Utrecht;[12] and, above all, Anselm and his brother Ralph at Laon, with their pupils and collaborators, notably Gilbert the Universal. No doubt there were others whose names have been lost. It was rare for the author of a gloss on Scripture to attach his name to it, although it seems to have been common practice among the jurists, who were also making their glosses at this time, to identify them with their own *sigla*.[13]

The primary task, and one intimately related to that of the glossators, was to arrive at a correct text of Scripture itself.[14] As this work went on it brought about a heightened awareness of the problems of textual criticism, of establishing a preferred reading where there appeared to be a discrepancy, of the claims of rival translations, perhaps even a prompting towards the consultations with the Jews about the exact meaning of the Hebrew original which seem to have been a growing feature of mid-twelfth-century exegesis.[15] This labour of correcting the text was now to lead on into a 'speculative' approach which asked new questions about the nature of meaning and into the fresh work on the theory of signification with which we shall be concerned.

Lanfranc of Bec, like others before and after him, took the Psalms and the Pauline Epistles as a pair of books in which could be seen prophecy and its fulfilment.[16] His commentary on the Psalms survives in only two fragments quoted by Herbert of Bosham in his edition of the gloss of Peter Lombard.[17] The text of the commentary on the Pauline Epistles survives in a number of manuscripts.[18] The physical appearance of these manuscripts is striking because of their clarity of visual organisation.[19] British Library MS Royal 4.vii.C, for example, has the text copied so as to allow ample space for the gloss. The gloss itself is in a small clear hand in the margin, Augustinus and Lanfrancus and so on, indicated in capitals, with a system of symbols linking the glosses with their place in the text.

Of a piece with this concern to help the reader see at a glance what he needs to know about a passage is a brevity and economy in the commentary itself,[20] which contrasts with the expansiveness to which the Carolingians were prone.[21] The innovation was not, on the whole, in the selection of passages. The majority of Lanfranc's notes in the commentary on Paul are acknowledged as being drawn from 'Augustine' or 'Ambrose', and these in their turn seem to have come at second-hand from such ready-made collections as that of the Carolingian Florus of Lyons. Lanfranc certainly saw no need to seek out fresh texts by combing the Fathers afresh,[22] but he added notes of his own. We can see not only an interest in such straightforward dialectical devices as the syllogism, but also a concern with the deeper matters of grammar and dialectic which touch on the functioning of words as signs for things,[23] although Lanfranc was cautious and moderate in the use of dialectic in exegesis.[24] Over all there presides an air of practicality and common sense. Paul's authorship of Hebrews is disputed by some, Lanfranc comments. But in that case, he points out very reasonably, it can have no author at all, for there is no name in the title.[25] As to the argument that the style of Hebrews is different from that of other Epistles, Lanfranc employs a standard explanation: of course Paul is more eloquent in his own language, Hebrew, than in a foreign language like Greek in which he wrote the other letters.[26]

It is less easy to get a picture of the approach of Berengar of Tours or of Drogo. Berengar's fame depended more upon his part in the Eucharistic controversy (where Lanfranc was his opponent) than upon his scriptural commentaries.[27] Nevertheless, fragments attributed to him are to be found in several large collections of glosses, which also contain some of those attributed to Drogo and Lanfranc.[28] Berengar was, it seems, readier than Lanfranc to make use of the *artes*.[29] For Drogo, too, there is only a scrappy picture.[30] But he, like Berengar, is clearly at home with the technicalities of dialectic, not only with syllogisms, but also with the more difficult hypothetical syllogisms on which Boethius had written one monograph and at the end of the tenth century Abbo of Fleury had composed another.

> For if this had been so, justification would not
>   have been in Christ alone.
> But justification is in Christ alone.
> Therefore . . .[31]

Like Lanfranc,[32] Drogo shows a bent for law in his treatment of several of the texts in Romans which mention *lex*.[33] Slight though the evidence is, it seems that we can be confident that some technical aids from secular studies (and, again, especially from grammar and dialectic) were being employed to elucidate obscurities which the Fathers had not illuminated.

Bruno of Chartreux died in 1101, leaving an exposition of the Psalms and another of the Pauline Epistles.[34] Here, too, a fresh eye is apparent, and a clear mind. Bruno follows Cassiodorus in placing an emphasis upon the titles of the Psalms, trying to distinguish them from one another, and to make them individually memorable. 'The title of this psalm sends us (*mittit nos*) to the story of Abraham's two wives.'[35] 'Here the title of this third psalm expresses the purpose of the psalm.'[36]. He notices the duplication of the openings of the thirteenth and fifty-second Psalms, and of Pss. 39:18 and 69:6, and remarks that it is superfluous to repeat what he has already said, since both the literal sense (*littera*) and the deeper signification (*sententia*) are the same.[37] Manegold of Lautenbach shows a detailed interest in the workings of language in Scripture, and the 'grammarian's rule'.[38]

These masters teaching in France, then, seem to have brought a new crispness to commentary, to have made a businesslike selection from patristic opinion, and to have attempted a sensible application of the procedures of grammar and dialectic, with the exception perhaps of Lambert of Utrecht who seems to belong less closely with these language-conscious expositors. He prefers historical *exempla*,[39] the facts and events which instruct us directly as significant 'things'. It is difficult to do more than gain an impression of the quiet infiltration of technical aids drawn from the study of the *artes* into the work of these expositors. On the whole they seem to have used such assistance cautiously and with restraint, as part of their generally commonsensical approach to the Sacred Page. Their primary purpose was to provide the student with a complete account of the text, so that there should be nothing in it to puzzle him.

The central figure in the process of bringing this work together and developing it into what became known as the *Glossa Ordinaria* seems to have been the Anselm who, with his brother Ralph, ran the cathedral school at Laon until his death in 1117 (Ralph lived into the mid-1130s). We do not know where they themselves studied,[40] but Anselm lectured to many of the famous masters of the next generation: William of Champeaux, founder of the house of canons at St Victor at Paris and one of the masters of Peter Abelard; Peter Abelard himself, who spurned Anselm's lectures as the empty rattlings of an old man and gave his rival lectures on Ezekiel at the shortest of notice;[41] Gilbert of Poitiers, at the end of whose commentary on the Psalms is an uncharacteristically meek note to the effect that it was delivered before Anselm (who ordered it to be corrected at several points);[42] Hugh, abbot of Reading, later to be bishop of Amiens and archbishop of Rouen 1130–64 and author of several monographs.[43]

Anselm of Laon was a man of considerable capacities. In the later twelfth century Peter the Chanter laments: 'We ought still to grieve that Master Anselm was not permitted to complete the gloss on the Bible he began, for the canons whose dean he was, and many others, distracted him from his application to that task' by consulting him on administrative matters.[44] (It is a nice irony that as precentor of the cathedral of Notre Dame until his death in 1197, Peter the Chanter was to become personally well acquainted with such difficulties.)

The body of Anselm of Laon's work has proved difficult to isolate with certainty from the mass of texts which survive from his contemporaries and pupils and which are loosely identifiable as the work of his 'school'.[45] This is exactly what is to be expected, however, if Anselm was indeed the more or less central figure in so massive an

operation as the completion of a commentary on the whole Bible. He
and his helpers produced commentaries, and also 'sentences' which
survive more or less independently in the form of collections of
patristic opinions arranged under topic headings.

The most complete of these collections still extant is the *Liber
Pancrisis*. Its Prologue describes its purpose: 'The word *pancrisis*
means "all gold", for herein are contained the golden sentences or
questions of the Fathers, Augustine, Jerome, Ambrose, Gregory,
Isidore, Bede, and the modern masters, William, bishop of Châlons
(William of Champeaux), Ivo, bishop of Chartres, Anselm and his
brother Ralph.'[46] These 'sentences' were the first shoots of that
natural growth from the work of commentary to which we shall
come in a moment.[47]

As to Anselm's scriptural commentary itself: it seems that he more
or less completed compilation of the 'ordinary gloss' on the Psalms,[48]
the Pauline Epistles[49] and probably on Matthew, Luke and John,
though we must wait for Peter Comestor later in the century for a
complete set of lectures on the Gospels.[50] Anselm is patient[51] and
methodical rather than innovatory, although he was evidently, like
Hugh of St Victor, a teacher with a gift for helping his pupils to
understand. On Gen. 1:2 ('The Spirit of the Lord brooded over the
waters') we have the following explanation: 'By the word "waters"
is signified all matter in these two words.' When it says that: ' "the
Spirit of God brooded over the waters", it speaks through a human
analogy' (*per humanam similitudinem*); when someone has some
material from which to make something, his intention regarding that
material is turned over (*versatur*) in his mind while he is thinking
what he is going to do with it.[52] Such homely comparisons and the
exercise of common sense allow Anselm to bring out the signification
of the 'waters'.

Among the extracts from Anselm's commentary we find, on Gen.
2:2, a discussion of the signification of the 'rest' of the seventh day,
on which God rested from the work of creation. The 'rest', says
Anselm, is a figurative usage, standing for the 'true rest' in God
which is to last for eternity. Before, when men did not have 'the thing
figured' (*quia nondum figuratam rem habebant*), they hallowed the
seventh day, which was still *sub figura*. The Church, however, does
not lie 'under the figure of any thing' (*sub ullius rei figura*) but
already possesses 'that thing signified', rest in God, perfectly (in its
head, Christ) and in part (in its members, the faithful); and so it sets
aside the figure (*dismissa figura*) and celebrates the day of resurrec-

tion instead of the Sabbath or seventh day.[53] There are discussions of the signification of words, too, where he speaks of the 'force of the word excommunication' (*vis vocabuli*).[54]

The gloss on the Pentateuch and the Prophets was probably completed by Gilbert the Universal, a collaborator of Anselm's and perhaps his pupil.[55] Gilbert is mentioned among the clergy of Auxerre in 1110;[56] by the time he became bishop of London late in 1127 he was an old man, with a reputation for 'universal' learning because he was both a lawyer and a theologian.[57] He was sufficiently well known as a scholar for Peter Abelard to name him among the leading contemporary theologians of whose opinions he himself disapproves.[58] But although there are a number of early testimonies to his achievement as a scholar ('he was most learned in the arts and, unique in speculative theology, he stood alone'), there is no evidence as to what he wrote, except for Robert of Bridlington's remarks about his commentaries on the minor Prophets, and stray hints elsewhere which suggest that he was responsible for the Gloss on the Pentateuch, too.[59]

It is indicative of the nature of the *Glossa Ordinaria* that its compilers remain so elusive. Although it became so important that, by the mid-twelfth-century, commentary on the Bible often amounted to nothing more than commentary by the Gloss, it was never a finished work,[60] never a textbook like Peter Lombard's ordered collection of patristic sentences of the 1150s. Peter Lombard was an Italian who arrived in France from Italy in the mid-1130s, with a letter of recommendation from the bishop of Lucca, and quickly made his mark as a Master of Theology. His *Sententiae* remained for several centuries the standard work of reference for students of theology.

In the 1120s and 1130s, Hugh of St Victor preferred to write his own textbooks and to compose commentaries for himself so as to ensure that he met his pupils' needs as closely as possible.[61] Petrus Manducator expresses a later twelfth century view in his own commentaries on the Gospels. Sometimes, he complains, the *Glossa Ordinaria* is too brief 'and cannot be read without a supplement'.[62] Sometimes it is excessively wordy: 'You will find the whole genealogy expounded allegorically and tropologically.' Let 'the evil of the day be sufficient thereto and let us put in here no more than is proper', he suggests tartly.[63]

Peter Lombard's own efforts to expand and improve upon the work of Anselm of Laon show how live an organic growth the Gloss remained. He began his career as a teacher of theology in France by lecturing upon the Bible, expanding and improving two existing commentaries, on the Psalms and on the Pauline Epistles.[64] The first impression his writings give is one of largeness of scale. A late twelfth century manuscript of his commentary on the Psalms makes the point graphically. On each page of MS Bodl. 735 in the Bodleian Library, Oxford, a single sentence of Scripture at a time occupies a small rectangle to one side, and the commentary fills the rest of the page.

Peter feels a need to help the reader[65] keep his bearings in such a vast mass of material and he is careful to say at each stage what he intends to deal with next. In an *accessus* he tries to help the student to understand what kind of book the Pauline Epistles is; he explains the reason why the letters were written, the number and order of the Epistles, the subject-matter, the purpose and the mode of proceeding (*modus tractandi*). Besides these things, he tells us, we need to learn the specific intentions and subjects of the individual letters.[66]

The same thoroughness is apparent in Peter's commentary on the Psalms. Again he draws together the teaching which had become traditional. What kind of book is this? It is a book of prophecy. What does 'Psalter' mean? The term refers to a certain musical instrument which in Hebrew is called a *nablus*, in Greek a *Psalter*, from the Greek *psallein*, which means *tangere*, to touch. The Psalter is so-called because David used to sing the Psalms with this instrument before the Ark of the Lord and therefore it provides a title which is literally accurate; but the title is appropriate in a spiritual sense, too, since the instrument in question had ten strings and the Psalms teach the keeping of Ten Commandments. Just as the instrument makes its sound when it is touched by a hand from above, so the Psalms teach us to do good not for the sake of earthly but of heavenly things.[67] This book is a summary or consummation (*consummatio*) of the whole Bible; that is the reason why the Psalms have such an important place in the liturgy.

The Psalms are clear where other prophecies are obscure.[68] They are hymns. What is a hymn? It is a praising of God in song. What is a song? It is an exultation breaking into sound. These 'hymns' were written in metre in Hebrew, but that cannot be retained in translation.[69] So Peter goes on, into an explanation of prophecy and the way in which the Psalms can be said to be a book of prophecy (one book, not many, although there are a great many individual Psalms).[70]

A great deal of this material has been derived by Peter from the work of his predecessors, who in their turn took it from earlier authors.[71] His own contribution lies not so much in taking a fresh look, as in putting together traditional explanations. It is this large element of borrowing which made it seem credible for so long that the *Glossa Ordinaria* was the work of the Carolingian scholar Walafrid Strabo.[72]

Something of this process of growth can be traced. Few texts in Scripture so openly invite the use of aids from the arts of language as the first words of St John's Gospel: 'In the beginning was the Word', and the statement which follows, that: 'The Word was made Flesh' (John 1:1 and 14). *Verbum* was both a general term for 'word' and a specific term for those words which have the double function of signifying both some substance (in this case an action, such as 'going', 'doing', 'eating'); and the time at which the action takes place ('I go', 'I did', 'I shall eat'). This two-sided signification or *consignificatio* is discussed fully by Boethius in his commentary on Aristotle's *De Interpretatione*,[73] and we shall come back to it in due course.

When any verb is used of God a question arises about its power to refer to time in connection with the divine. The matter is taken up in a twelfth century gloss to the beginning of St John's Gospel. 'The verb "to be" has a double signification' (*duplex significatio*), he explains. Sometimes it declares motion in time, just as other verbs do. Sometimes it designates the substance of the thing of which it is predicated without any temporal motion, so that it is called a substantive. That is the case when it is said: 'In the beginning was the Word', as if the Son subsists in the Father. Then it is not used to refer to time. St John is affirming that the Son was indeed in the Father in the beginning; the Father was not before the Son. So the Son is a different Person from the Father, but of one substance with the Father.[74] This discussion, with some modifications, is to be found in the commentary on John by John Scotus Eriugena, perhaps the most able dialectician of the Carolingian period. He in turn borrows the term *proloquium* from Martianus Capella's book on logic in the *De Nuptiis Philologiae et Mercurii*[75] (where it means any proposition capable of being true or false) and applies it to the text: 'And the Word was made flesh'.[76] At many points he is able to introduce technical terms and principles from logic in this way, and our commentator is able to use his explanation of the use of the verb 'to be' in the past tense in 'In the beginning was the Word' as a technical explanation still up-to-date and helpful in the twelfth century.[77]

In many similar particulars the content of the Gloss in its more technical aspects can be seen to rest upon earlier work and to be only a modest advance upon it, if any advance at all. Important though the *Glossa Ordinaria* is, it is not in the Gloss that we shall find the most interesting and advanced developments in exegesis. That was not its purpose. It was simply a practical aid for students beginning on their study of the Bible.

The essence of the *Glossa Ordinaria* is the brevity and minuteness of its comments. Nothing can be developed at any length; no problem can be fully explored. A comment may touch on a major question such as that of the status of the Latin translation,[78] or upon a variant reading ('Some manuscripts have "*sapientissimus*" instead of "*prudentissimus*" '),[79] or upon a difficulty in equating the Latin with the Hebrew ('The meaning is different in Hebrew'),[80] all at much the same length.

This necessary economy greatly inhibits the exploration of the problem of the special difficulties posed by the language of Scripture in which twelfth century scholars were making such advances. We find a short note upon a passage where, for example, a plural is given instead of the singular,[81] or some other uncommon device is used.[82] 'But he said "I will call", not "I will be called", giving the active verb for the passive', remarks the Gloss; 'An unusual way of speaking (*genere locutionis inusitato*) in which perhaps he wanted to signify that he himself does this.'[83] When we read in Genesis that God 'saw' the corruption of the world, we should be aware, says the Gloss, that Scripture uses familiar words (*utitur Scriptura usitatis verbis*), 'fitting itself to our littleness', so that we may know the unknown through what is known. God does not 'see' as we do. If we read that he is angry we should realise that the anger of God is not a perturbation of mind,[84] Scripture is speaking to us in words we can understand. Many ways of speaking (*genera locutionis*) are to be noted in these words.[85] 'That is prophetic and priestly speech.'[86] The reversal of chronological order in a historical narrative may, too, be a 'way of speaking' (*genus locutionis*).[87] The *Glossa Ordinaria* contains many passing acknowledgements of such grammatical oddities and also of the peculiar behaviour of scriptural language, but there is no opportunity to explore the implications of their presence. Many such comments are simply borrowed from Augustine or some other patristic source.

In the Gloss to the story of the Tower of Babel in Genesis 11, Alcuin is quoted for his explanation of the way in which language was affected by what happened. In this division of tongues, he says,

God did nothing new, but he divided the modes of speaking (*dicendi modos*) and the *formas loquelarum* of different races. That is why we find the same syllables differently joined together in different languages, and often the same nouns and verbs, signifying different things.[88] The Gloss does not take the investigation any further.

The Glosses are often labelled to show whether they refer to the historical or to some other sense: *historice*;[89] *haec figurate et prophetice melius intelligitur*;[90] *moraliter*;[91] *mystice*;[92] *allegorice*,[93] but again, only as brief indications. There is no development of discussion of the various senses. Within the Glosses there is only the tersest of comment on the different senses. 'First the historical foundation must be laid', we are told.[94] If the historical sense builds up the kingdom of love, it is not necessary to expound allegorically.[95] 'Even according to the letter (*iuxta litteram*) this befits the beauty of the heavenly vision.'[96] The test of a sound interpretation is congruity. 'See it is fitting according to the order of history; and according to the allegorical interpretation, too, it is not inappropriate.'[97]

It is not, then, in this 'standard commentary' that we shall find the most important new work of twelfth century exegesis in understanding the nature of the Bible's language. The *Glossa Ordinaria* is above all a work of consolidation; distilling out the essence of the work of previous centuries it provides the student with a manageable and reliable textbook of Bible study, but a textbook for beginners, and requiring a competent master to develop its implications for the reader.

PART II

'LECTIO': SURFACE AND DEPTHS

4

WORDS AND THINGS
AND NUMBERS

1 Words and things

In his *Sententiae* of the 1150s Peter Lombard put together a collection of extracts from patristic and other authorities for convenient reference. He arranged them by topic, dealing first with the Trinity, then with creation and man's fall into sin, then with redemption and the virtues, and in a final book with the sacraments and the end of the world. He chose as the point of entry into his vast subject-matter Augustine's discussion of the way men learn about God: 'As the most learned Augustine says in his book *On Christian Learning*, all learning involves either things or signs.'[1] Peter explains that man learns about God primarily through the things which God provides to instruct him, and secondarily through the signs of various sorts which point to those 'things' and beyond them to God himself. He mentions in particular under the first heading the ways in which the Creator may be known through his creatures, and under the second the way in which he may be known through the words we use to talk about him.[2]

Peter Lombard's confidence that he is beginning from first principles here and will best carry his readers with him if he starts in this way, rests ultimately upon the general currency in his own time of Augustine's teaching on this point. But it is also a view which had done much to provide a thread of continuity of method in the study of the Bible since patristic times. The exegete's question is always: 'What does this mean?'; Augustine encourages him to look for an answer not only in the words of the text, but also in the things and events described.

Augustine's *De Doctrina Christiana* was written over a period of twenty years, the first three books (on the interpretation of the Bible) in 396; the last book (on preaching and teaching) in 426. The first three give aids for interpreting Scripture; the last provides instructions for conveying the interpretation to others.[3] Augustine begins by

51

asking himself what the process of learning and teaching involved. He concludes, as we saw, that it is always 'either about things or about signs'.[4] There is nothing else which can be taught or learned. This is, on the face of it, a startling claim, but Augustine includes under 'things' realities of every sort, from God himself to the smallest created thing, events and actions and objects alike, so that there is literally nothing outside the definition of 'things'; even signs themselves are things in a sense, 'for what is not a thing is no thing at all'.

Later in the *De Doctrina Christiana*, when he was trying to make a scheme of the ways in which 'things' act as signs in Scripture, Augustine drew upon the *Rules* of the Donatist Tyconius. The Donatists were a schismatic sect which had come into existence after the Diocletian persecution and which survived vigorously in North Africa. Their exclusiveness cut them off to some extent, and Tyconius framed his rules independently, with almost no resort to the work of other scholars.[5] The difficulty he attempted to meet was that of the signification of the many passages of the Old Testament which were generally held to prefigure or refer in some way to the events of the New Testament, but whose precise sense was not immediately apparent.[6] Tyconius saw these texts as 'a vast forest of prophecy',[7] through which it was necessary to cut a path with a few clear strokes.

He had in a simple form Augustine's much more developed notion of the special usages of Scripture's language. He speaks of the *modus* or 'mode' of speaking and of the *genus locutionis*.[8] But his first concern is with the strong repeated patterns of figures he perceives in Old and New Testament events. All prophecies, he says, fall into two classes: those which refer to Christ and the Church and those which refer to the Devil and his followers.[9] This bold division rests upon an infinitely subtle and complex network of detailed hints within the text of Scripture. The reader must be prepared to divide up the text very small. In Cant. 5:1 he reads 'I am black and comely'; here 'black' can be taken to refer to the bad in the Church and 'comely' to the good.[10] This combination of grand simplicity and infinite minuteness was most congenial to Augustine. He too looks for both bold patterns and fine detail in the 'things', the events and objects in Scripture, which seem to him to signify spiritual realities.

Strictly speaking, in Augustine's view, signs signify nothing but what they stand for outside themselves, but this, he concedes, can only be true of signs which are nothing but signs. Words are such signs, and so, as we shall see, are numbers. 'No one uses words except as signs of something else', says Augustine.[11] It is common experience that, in addition, some 'things' which are not merely signs may act as signs as well as being and therefore signifying themselves. Augustine begins, where Aristotle began,[12] by considering things in themselves and those signs, especially words, which stand for things. But he is also interested in 'natural signs' such as smoke, which tells us that there is a fire. All these types of sign belong to the great corpus of signs to be found in Scripture, where God teaches man in every way man can understand.[13] A piece of wood is normally nothing but a piece of wood, but the piece of wood which Moses threw into the bitter waters to make them sweet (Exod. 15:25) is a sign or symbol as well as a piece of wood. It was in making plain this significance of 'things' that the figurative interpretations of Scripture were believed to be illuminating.

The consensus of interest in the West had tended to lie in the investigation of the 'higher' or 'deeper' interpretations which make use of the power of 'things' to act figuratively, that is, as signs. That was where the kernel of the meaning was thought to lie. Gregory the Great, writing on the colourfulness of the language of the Song of Songs, remarks: 'He is a very stupid man whose attention is so captured by the colours in the picture that he does not know what is depicted. For we, if we embrace the words which are said outwardly and ignore the senses [within] are like those who do not know what is depicted, but grasp only the colours.'[14] This view is still to be found in the twelfth century, especially among scholars working within the monastic tradition, where 'holy reading' gave time for slow, reflective penetration into the depths. But the new taste for technical grammatical exactitude in the interpretation of the literal sense had its repercussions for the study of the figurative sense, too. They, too, raised questions of signification, as we shall see. 'Words' and 'things' are alike treated in terms of their meaning in this way.

Hugh of St Victor explains in the Prologue to his *De Sacramentis* that: 'In the Divine Word, not only words but also things have signification, which is not the usual way in other writings.'[15] The philosophers recognise only the signification of words, he says, pointing to Aristotle's account, but the signification effected by things is far better (*excellentior valde*), because a word has only the meaning given it by usage, whereas a thing has a meaning by nature.[16] Hugh was wrong in supposing that the 'philosophers' took so restrictive a view. The principle is found in Peter Abelard's discussion of signification in the context of dialectic: 'It is the property

not only of words but also of things to signify.'[17] But Hugh perceived
a principle which was especially important in its application to Scripture. He gives an example of the way in which this signifying by
things occurs in the Bible. In 1 Peter 5:8, we find the warning that 'the
Devil prowls like a roaring lion'. Here, if we say that the lion signifies
the Devil, we ought to understand not the word but the thing, says
Hugh. For if we are asked to believe that these two words, 'Devil' and
'lion', signify one and the same thing, the likeness fails. It is
incompetens. We must conclude that the word 'lion' signifies the
animal itself, and the animal the Devil, so that the point of comparison lies in the thing we call a 'lion' not in the word.[18]

A word may have more than one literal meaning. A bull, for
example, may be a papal edict or a male elephant. Neither meaning
is figurative. The word 'bull' in each case signifies a thing. If, however, we use the word 'lion' for, on the one hand, a great cat, and on
the other for Christ (as in 'the Lion of Judah') we are doing something different with it. Christ is not literally a lion, nor is there any
ordinary meaning of 'lion', unconnected with the beast, which can be
said to be in use here. The word 'lion' is being used metaphorically.
Christ is being *compared* with a lion. The comparison is instructive
because of the likeness of the *thing* compared, the lion itself, to
Christ, not because of any likeness or appropriateness in the *word*
lion.

A thing may be as multiple in its significations as a word, indeed
more so. Few words have more than two or three significations, but,
Hugh says, a thing can be as multiple in its significations of other
things as it has properties in common with them. 'Forasmuch as the
nature of everything is made up of different elements', says Gregory
the Great, 'in Holy Writ different things are allowably represented by
any one thing. For the lion has greatness of heart and also ferocity. By
its magnanimity, then, it represents the Lord, by its ferocity the
Devil.'[19] The bestiaries which are indebted to the *Physiologus*[20] are
impressive examples of this method of taking separate aspects or
qualities of a given thing in the natural world and making them stand
for different things in the supernatural world. To take the lion again:
we find the lion has three principal characteristics (*principales
naturae*). It covers its scent with its tail when it smells the hunter
coming, so that the hunter is confused. Just so did the Lord conceal
his divinity when Satan tempted him, so that Satan tried to tempt him
as though he were a mere man. The lion sleeps with its eyes open;
when Christ was crucified his divinity remained awake in the death

of his human body. The young of the lion are born dead; after three days the father comes and breathes in their faces and they revive. Just so did the Omnipotent Father resurrect Christ on the third day.[21]

Augustine laid the groundwork for this view of the signifying power of 'things' in his *De Doctrina Christiana*,[22] but the principle is to be found widely in his writings. In the *De Trinitate*, for example, we are told that where the Apostle says 'Which things are an allegory' (Gal. 4:24), some translators have rendered the passage: 'Which things signify one "thing" by another.'[23] Gregory the Great explains 'the method followed by Holy Scripture' in making 'things' significant, in a way entirely in keeping with both Tyconius' and Augustine's concern for detail. The position of the place may be referred to (Exod. 19:17: the people of Israel could not hear the words of God on the mountain but heard them on the plain, from which we understand that God was pointing to their subsequent weakness, for they were to live a lax life amidst the lowest things). The posture of the body may also be significant (Acts 7:55–6, Stephen saw Jesus standing, 'for standing is the posture of one in the act of giving aid'). The temperature of the air may be significant (John 10:22, Matt. 24:12: 'It was winter', from which we understand the frost of wickedness in men's hearts). The time may be significant (John 13:30; Luke 12:20: 'This night shall thy soul be required of thee.' That soul which is to be conveyed to darkness is appropriately said to be 'required in the night').[24]

A discussion of 'prophecy' which is commonly found carries through a similar line of thought. It involves an examination of the ways in which prophecy teaches not only through words but also through things. The Carolingian Haymo of Auxerre, for example, writes on the Psalms: 'Prophecy is divine inspiration which reveals the outcome of things (*rerum eventus*) through visions or through deeds (*facta*) or through the sayings (*dicta*) of certain men.'[25] The same list of visions, deeds and sayings, is found in the twelfth century in Peter Lombard's commentary on the Psalms,[26] supplemented by a fourth mode of prophecy (by deep and ineffable mystery as in the begetting of Christ; neither prophet nor evangelist would be able to speak of this unless the Holy Spirit had inspired him directly).[27]

It is in terms of 'things' signified, Hugh of St Victor explains, that Scripture deals with its subject-matter in its three ways: historically, allegorically (in which, for the purposes of discussion, he includes the anagogical sense), or tropologically. History is the narration of events or 'things done' (*rerum gesta narratio*), as it is contained in the primary or obvious signification of the words (*quae in prima significatione continetur*).[28] When the Bible uses allegory it tells us of something which has been done, not simply so that we may know of it, but in a way that refers beyond itself, so that we may understand that something else has been done or is to be done. When it speaks tropologically it means that something ought to be done.[29] The emphasis here is consistently upon what these 'things done' or 'things to be done' signify, that is, upon the meaningfulness of the things themselves, not the words.[30]

As Hugh's contemporaries saw it, the relation between particular words and the things they stood for was mutable. The lion, with all the other creatures, had been given its name by Adam at God's command (Gen. 2:19–20). The word for the thing was therefore of human choosing, and although thereafter that was its name, the name remained something 'imposed' upon the thing (*impositum*) and capable, in principle, of being changed. The episode of the Tower of Babel resulted in a confusion of tongues, and men of different races now have different words for 'lion'.[31] The 'thing', as Hugh of St Victor envisages it, is much more reliable because it stands by nature, not by imposition, for that which it signifies. It is God's language, his vehicle of communication and instruction through his created world.

It is this 'seeing into things' (rather than an understanding of the deep structure of language) which made the penetration of the allegorical, tropological and moral sense so important in the eyes of exegetes from at least the time of Origen. The idea that there are higher or deeper senses (*altior* covers both) stirs a profound excitement. Gregory the Great sees the historical sense as a surface (*superficies*) only, or as a plain with the higher senses stretching up like a mountain;[32] an image used by many other interpreters, so exactly did it convey their own feeling. The pursuit of these additional possibilities was so attractive that it was inclined to run away with the inexperienced reader. Hugh warns against hastiness in turning to the higher senses in exegesis for just this reason.[33]

The sense of the appropriateness and fittingness of the relation between the word and the thing was strong in the Bible's patristic and mediaeval readers. Cassiodorus applied the test of *convenientia* as readily as any twelfth century master.[34] Anselm of Canterbury and Gerhoch of Reichersberg speak of the beauty of the Sacred Page,[35] not only in its expression and use of language, but in the *res* or realities, the 'things' of which it speaks. As we penetrate the surface beauty of the language, we plunge into the reality of things beneath. Thus to leave the literal sense for the higher senses is to come closer to what the text really means. Its real meaning will always link the thing spoken of with a thing which it may fittingly be said to stand for. Donizone of Canossa in his versified *Enarratio in Genesim* of the early twelfth century suggests that the earth which produces vegetation in Gen. 1:11 can appropriately be said to signify the Church, and he goes on to show how closely the parallel matches, point by point.[36] Alternatively, the fittingness may consist in familiarity of association; the comparison may be a commonplace. But, in whatever way it is arrived at, a relationship of 'fitting together' is agreed to exist between the thing signifying and the thing signified, a relationship, that is, of 'signification'.

The principles are set out with elegance and economy at the beginning of the thirteenth century by Thomas of Chobham in his treatise on the art of preaching.[37] He says that there are two ways of understanding: according to the signification of the words (*secundum significationem vocum*) and according to the signification of things (*secundum significationem rerum*). He cites Aristotle's teaching in the *Perihermenias* that we understand through words and also sometimes by things, as when we see smoke and know that there is a fire.[38] The signification of words, says Thomas, is studied by natural scientists (*physici*) as well as by theologians, but only theology considers the significations of things. The signification of words is threefold: in *fabula*, *argumentum* and *historia*. 'Fable' contains neither truths nor verisimilitudes and it is to be rejected by theologians. 'Argument' – in its classical sense of the plot of a play – is a narration of things which might have happened, although they have in fact not happened. Theology does not reject this mode of signification, but makes use of it, for example, in parables. 'History' sets out things as they have actually happened. It has two modes of signification: by analogy and by metaphor. In analogy the words are used in their proper signification (*propria significatio*), as when Hannibal's wars with Rome are described. In metaphor there is an *impropria significatio* of words, as where *principium*, used properly to refer to the beginning of the world, is transferred (*transumitur*) so as to refer to the Son of God. This *impropria significatio* has various forms (with lovely names, Thomas notes, such as *tropus, metonomia, metaphora*). Each of them involves some *conversio* or *transumptio* or *transformatio* of the word or saying from its proper signification. The *artes* of grammar and dialectic deal with *propria significatio* and rhetoric with metaphors, for it teaches how words are shifted from their proper significations to improper ones through various rhetorical 'colours'.

He begins by looking at the three ways in which things may signify: tropologically, allegorically, anagogically, where one 'thing' is understood through another (*per unam rem alia intelligitur*). One thing is understood through another in a tropological way when it is made to convey a *moralis instructio* or when by *transumptio* 'night', for example, signifies sin and 'day' signifies virtue. One thing signifies another 'in another way', allegorically by changing the subject, as in: 'Come, my bride, my beloved' (cf. Song of Songs 7:11). Christ says this to the Church and thus the subject is changed there, for by (*per*) the bride of the flesh is understood the spiritual bride. The word *allegoria* is sometimes taken more generally to cover all three senses, but this is its strict sense, says Thomas. One thing signifies another in yet another way, when something concerning heavenly things is understood as concerning God and the angels and the saints in glory; this is the anagogical sense. *Anagoge* means *sursum ductio*, a leading above.

Thomas emphasises that allegory has nothing to do with the signification of words; it involves the signification of things (*sed fit secundum intellectum quam res significata facit*). He gives as an instance here: *Leo vincit de tribus Iuda*. The word 'lion' signifies (*secundum propriam significationem*) according to its proper signification, and the thing signified, that is the animal, signifies in its turn. 'It signifies fortitude to men', says Thomas, 'by which I understand Christ, and such signification of the "thing" is called allegory.' The essential element in allegory is divine inspiration. 'If I were to understand "a strong horse" by the lion, that would not be allegory, because God does not inspire such a signification nor does Holy Scripture teach it.'

All four kinds of signification, literal, allegorical, tropological, anagogical, 'may be understood in one word' of Scripture. The word 'Jerusalem', for example, signifies historically or literally the actual place, allegorically the Church Militant here on earth, anagogically the Church Triumphant in the world to come. In this way one word of the Sacred Page may have multiple significations, depending on the way it is interpreted, by the interpretation of a name, by quality, quantity, *habitus*, *gestum*, *factum*, *numerus*, *causa*, *modus*, *locus*, *tempus*. Rachel, for instance, was beautiful and through this *qualitas* she signifies the contemplative life. Leah, who was ugly, signified the life of vice.

This encouragement to analyse the properties of the 'thing' so as to extract from it the maximum signification further emphasises the fact that it is indeed the 'thing' which is doing the signifying in the higher senses, and not merely the word; and that the 'thing' and its various aspects or properties signify separately. 'Nothing moves the hearts of men more than the properties of animals and of other things of which they [the properties] may be predicated.'

2 Numbers

The mathematical arts of the trivium never attracted the same degree of interest in the Middle Ages as did the 'arts of language', especially grammar and dialectic. The academic study of the theory of arithmetic remained a specialist matter until at least the twelfth century, but a good deal of knowledge of the simpler principles of arithmetic entered early into two exercises which were commonplace necessities of monastic scholarship: the calculation of the dates of Feasts of the Church, and the working-out of the symbolism of the numbers mentioned in the Bible.

The lively tradition of number symbolism on which the latter rests found its way from Greek thought into the West through Augustine above all, but also through Martianus Capella and Macrobius, Calcidius' commentary on the *Timaeus*, Boethius and, among the Fathers, Jerome, Cassiodorus, Gregory the Great and Bede.[39] Examples are to be found everywhere in mediaeval exegesis, worked out according to principles which are sometimes stated and sometimes assumed to be familiar to the reader. In the middle of the twelfth century the Cistercian Odo of Morimond wrote a book on the theory of the subject in which he attempted – for the first time as he believed – to bring together the rules and principles on which it rests. His *Analectica Numerorum et Rerum in Theographyam*[40] is of importance for two reasons. Odo did indeed do pioneering work in reducing the art to order and he encouraged other authors such as his fellow Cistercians Geoffrey of Auxerre, Theobald of Langres and William of Auberive to follow him (William continues from three, where Odo leaves off, to twelve, and Geoffrey covers twelve to twenty; Theobald writes on the 'four modes of signification of numbers').[41] Odo's treatise, and to a lesser extent Theobald's, make a substantial contribution, too, to the contemporary discussions of signs and signification-theory in the context of exegesis.

Although Augustine insists that things as well as words can be significant,[42] his own training in the arts of language encourages him to place the theory of signification within the realm of the arts of language. It continued to be discussed in this context in the twelfth century. Odo's originality lies in his attempt to set the meanings of numbers beside the meanings of 'words' and 'things' by making a science of them. As he points out, he who does not learn the arts of grammar, logic and rhetoric (*artes loquendi, disserendi et dicendi*),[43] does not find it easy to understand the purpose of their underlying rules. Our understanding of the signification of 'things' is necessarily patchy (*sparsim*) and we find authors discussing individual examples rather than reducing them to order scientifically.[44] The same is true for the signification of numbers.[45] Previous authors have not collected examples and worked out *causae* and *species*.[46]

It is perhaps his determination to give this new science a proper standing which encourages Odo to talk about it in terms used in contemporary discussions of signification of 'words' and 'things'.[47] But there is really no need: number-symbolism had long been used in exegesis and exegesis remained the highest of scholarly activities in the twelfth century, in the monastic circles where Odo worked and in the schools alike. Nevertheless, a 'science' had a certain prestige over and above that of the subject-matter with which it might be concerned. Odo had a strong sense of the difficulty and importance of the task he had set himself: 'A heavy effort and a hard task fall upon us in conveying the significations of numbers, both because it is a new and untouched science and we institute it without the teaching of a master, and because the subtlety and nature of numbers presents many and complex questions.' He expresses the view of many scholars of his day, when he says that there is 'little benefit in knowing, if one knows the meaning and not the reason for it'.[48]

Accordingly, he works out the way of proceeding, the *agendi modus: enumeratio*, the listing of the significations which individual numbers and things have; *causa*, the reason why they have such meanings; *genus*, the mode of signifying in use in a particular instance.[49] This consciousness of the requirements of contemporary scientific method is present throughout. 'Let what is said be taken for the moment as a statement of opinion (*ad positionem sententie*); it will be discussed later (*ad discussionem*).'[50]

The central question with which Odo is concerned is exactly the same as the one discussed by a multitude of other authors from patristic times: why does God speak to man, not directly, but by making one thing stand for another? Odo says that 'the reason why things are represented by other things (*cur res presentantur a rebus*) is that visible things derive from invisible', created things from the Creator. It is possible for man to make the leap of understanding required because he can perceive a likeness (*similitudo; affinitas*) between the concrete and the abstract (*ex cognatione similitudinis surgit unius ad aliam*). Thus a pig signifies uncleanness and a dove simplicity, *ex affinitate morum ex similitudine naturarum*,[51] 'from the affinity of their behaviour and the likeness of their nature'. 'Thus most carefully (*cautissime*), the Divine Scripture speaks to us through the similitudes of things so that it may move us to faith.'[52]

This shifting from the literal to a figurative meaning is the *transumptio* to which Odo refers in his opening reflections in connection with numbers. It is not restricted to things of a concrete kind.[53] A *sacramentum*, Odo explains, is a 'spiritual representation' (*representatio spiritualis*) of one thing by another, while a *significatio* may be merely a 'representation'. All *sacramenta* are 'significations', but not all significations are 'mysteries'.[54] Odo defends his use of the word *sacramentum* to refer to the superior way in which numbers signify by insisting that numbers are higher than 'things' in their power of signifying (*pre rebus potior*).[55] This is partly because numbers never have an *acceptio vituperabilis* of themselves, although they may occasionally appear to be signifying something evil because of a juxtaposition, while 'things' are frequently bad in themselves.[56]

Numbers are superior to things in more important ways, however. Some meanings of numbers are older than the meanings of things and therefore *digniores*. It is true that '2' did not always signify a rational creature, or '4' the world, because these things did not always exist. 'Three', on the other hand, always signified the Trinity. There are no 'things' which were always significant, because no 'thing' has always existed. Adam did not signify the Passion of Christ and the opening of his side and the generation of the Church, until he slept and his rib was taken from him to make woman.[57] Numbers are an exemplar or pattern in the whole creation.[58] Number, Word and Wisdom are one, for all things were made *in numero* (Ecclus. 38:32) and all were made *in sapientia* (Ps. 103:24). These must be one with the Word, by whom all things were made, for there can be only one beginning of things (*principium rerum*). We read not *in principiis*, but *in principio*.[59] Odo is awestruck when he contemplates the mystery of numbers.[60] The superiority of numbers is still further apparent when we look at the relation between numbers and things. There are things which are signified and never signify anything but themselves, as the Father, Son and Holy Spirit may be signified by created things, but never signify anything other than themselves. Created things and the deeds of men and historical events both signify other things and are themselves signified by other things. Numbers, on the other hand, share the singleness of signification of the Trinity, but in reverse. They signify but are never signified.[61] The numbers are prior to the things they signify: *res a numeris processerunt*. When man was created with his twofold bodily and spiritual nature there was already a 'two'.[62]

Theobald of Langres chose to arrange his treatise in order of the 'modes of signification' possible to numbers. The expression *modus significandi* was to have a precise technical sense among the thirteenth century grammarians (the *modistae*), but it was used in the twelfth century in a wider and looser way.[63] Theobald indicates the existence of four broad categories of signification for numbers: they may signify by increasing (*generatio*) in themselves as they are (*secundum se*), by the way in which they are made up of component numbers (*secundum compositionem*), by their relation to one another (*secundum habitudinem*).[64]

Mathematically speaking nothing advanced is required, but a good deal of sophistication goes into the detailed work of discovering properties of numbers which will make it possible to detect or arrive at the numbers (of significance in themselves) whose meaning may be read into the passage in question. The exegete needs to be very thoroughly familiar with numbers and their relationships.[65] That familiarity shows itself in the choice of a vocabulary which reflects a sense that numbers are living and active beings. They are said to be 'born', 'created', 'generated', to 'progress', to have not only 'roots', but 'branches' and 'fruit'.[66] They have 'friends', 'relations', 'lovers'.[67] (The device recalls the attempts of some of the authors of treatises on the abacus to lend extra interest to mathematical calculation by using images such as that of fractions as crumbs on a tablecloth.)[68] As we watch the numbers breaking up and re-forming in new patterns the justness of some of these descriptions is striking. The integral factors of 30 make 42, which is 30 + 12; the sum of the parts of 42 is 54, which is 42 + 12; the sum of the parts of 54 is 66, which is 54 + 12; the sum of the parts of 78 is 90, which is 78 + 12. The 'fruit' of all these operations is 12.[69] Numbers are 'lovers' when the sum of the aliquot parts of both is the same – as is the case for 12 and 26, where 1 + 2 + 3 + 4 + 6 and 1 + 2 + 13 are both 16; and for 27 and 35, where $1 + 3 + 9$ and $1 + 5 + 7$ are both 13.[70] William of Auberive gives a description of numbers which have an 'affinity': where both generate the same third number by different methods. There is an affinity between 7 and 12, for $3 \times 4 = 12$ and $3 + 4 = 7$. Our authors outline progressions of numbers where there are regular gaps (*interscalaris*) or where the sequence does not begin with unity (*circumcisa*), multiplications and divisions, partitioning of numbers and proportions.

The underlying rules for interpreting the numbers to which any given figure in Scripture can be reduced are subtle, then, but not mathematically advanced. Their flexibility lies in this subtlety and in the authors' willingness to depart from the mathematical altogether and include other modes of resemblance. In discussing perfection in numbers, for example, we find not only the arithmetical definition of the perfect number as that which is equal to the sum of its parts, but also the idea that a number may be perfect because it 'creates' dimensions or is itself a dimension (the square and cubic numbers); if it has a beginning, a middle and an end (as 3 does); if it is engendered by another number which is perfect (the perfection of 3 is transmitted to 6 and 9); if it represents purity, as 7 does because it neither begets nor is begotten; if it is a 'limit' number – 10, 100, 1,000, 10,000; if it is a unity (monad); if it is indicated by the right hand in the system of calculation on the fingers; if it is even, and can therefore be divided into equal parts.[71] The rules are often conceptually striking in a simple way, but not always mathematical.

Whether the signs we are concerned with are words, things, or numbers, their relation to the things they signify is various. A word may have several meanings. So may a thing or a number. In Rev. 20:1–3 we read of Satan's being bound for 1,000 years. 'The number 1,000', says Gregory the Great, 'signifies not a quantity of time but the whole period (*universitas*) when the Church will reign.'[72] Just as a word may signify directly or obliquely (*per se*; *per aliud*)[73] or incompletely, as a preposition does when it stands alone,[74] or in such a way as to signify what is done and the time at which it is done simultaneously, as a verb does,[75] so a 'thing' or a 'number' may have various *modi significandi*, or ways of signifying.[76] Bede remarks on the 'many ways' in which the 'same mystery' of the Church of Christ is portrayed.[77] Noah left the Ark on the 27th day of the month, the cube of 3, which signifies the perfection of faith as it is sealed in baptism.[78] The building of the Ark was in hand for 100 years. The 100 years signifies the *universum tempus*, the whole period of this world's duration, in which the Holy Church is being built up. For there is no doubt that the number 100 signifies perfection, both because it is 10 × 10 and because it passes from the left hand to the right (in the system of counting on the fingers).[79] In a different way the 'length' of the Ark signifies patience because it stands up strongly to *adversa*; the width signifies the breadth of charity and the height the sublimity of hope which promises eternal reward in the heavens.[80] In another way again the thirty cubits of height may be seen to be meaningful in terms of the Decalogue and the perfection of the Trinity (10 × 3).[81] In a yet different way Noah's age (600) is significant because 6 is the number of days in which the world was made and 100 is what happens when *in computo digitali*, in finger counting, we pass from the left hand to the right; that is most appropriate (*maxime convenit*) to those who stand on the right at the Last Judgment and will hear: 'Come, blessed of my Father.'[82]

We can see much the same mingling of arithmetical principles and ideas about numbers in Hugh of St Victor's book on Noah's Ark. The 300 cubits of length are this present world, divided into three ages. The 50 cubits of breadth are all the faithful under their head, Christ (for 7 × 7 is 49 and 49 + 1 is 50). The 30 cubits of height are 30 books of the Bible, 22 Old Testament and 8 New Testament. The *tres mansiones* in the Ark are the three orders of the faithful. Those who are in the world legitimately are the largest number as theirs is the largest section. Those, fewer in number, who are in flight from the world, have the next biggest section. The fewest, in the smallest and highest *mansio*, are those who have forgotten the world altogether. Again, why is the Ark six·times as long as it is wide? These are the proportions of a man lying supine. 300 stands for the Trinity, or for the Cross, because Tau is 300 in Greek alphabetical numerals. The Ark takes the form of a *curta pyramis* as a sign that what is below God is less perfect than he.[83]

If numbers are signs they are themselves in turn represented by signs. A considerable variety of systems was in use in the twelfth century and exegetes were very conscious of the implications of the use of different sorts of 'signs-for-signs'. Although words, too, are signs which are written down by means of further signs,[84] there is not the same multiplicity in these as there is in the case of numbers. Apart from written devices there was the system of counting on the fingers and hands which Bede describes at length in his *De Temporibus*.[85] The parts of the body had significances in their own right, which they imparted to the numbers they were taken to represent. Theobald outlines the principles. A finger may signify a number by its place (*secundum ordinem loci*); the middle finger is the third finger, and so it signifies the third virtue, charity. It may signify by its length (*secundum quantitatem*); the middle finger is the longest finger; charity knows no limits (1 Cor. 13:8) and so it signifies charity. It may signify *secundum officium*: the index finger is so-called because it points (*ab indicando*); the little finger is called *auricularis* because it is used to clean out the ears. The fingers may signify by bending: the thumb and index finger can touch in a 'kiss' and so they stand for marriage. The right hand is more skilful than other parts of the body, and so it signifies heavenly life, where all is to be *decor et agilitas*.[86]

This practice of 'finger-counting' carried over into the concepts and vocabulary used by the abacists in their talk of 'digits' and 'articuli' for units and tens, hundreds, thousands respectively. Several authors of treatises on the abacus discuss the 'fingers' and the 'joints'.[87]

Words can be signs for numbers, in several ways: distributively, as *singuli, bini*; dispositively, as *primus, secundus*; respectively, as *unus, duo*; properly, as *unitas, binarius*; or we find *semel, bis*, or *monas, decem, viginti, triginta . . . centum, ducenti, trecenti* – the 'terminative' names for numbers.[88]

Letters may be signs for numbers, again in various ways. The Romans used C, D, I, L, V, X to signify numbers.[89] The Greeks had a set of alphabetical numerals.[90] Theobald gives a complete Roman alphabet with the numbers for which each letter may stand according to different systems of alphabetical numeration, and he gives an account of the reasons why these letters stand for these numbers. For example, U is the fifth vowel and stands for 5. L is the eighth consonant and stands for 50, because just as 8 exceeds 7 by 1, so 50 exceeds 7×7 by 1.[91] Letters may derive their numerical significance from their form – as in the example of the Greek letter Tau which as we saw stands for 300 – or from a mystery (*a mysterio*). (Pythagoras used Y to stand for a man because it has two arms, pointing one heavenward and one towards the earth.) Or a letter may derive its numerical significance *ab ordine*. Alpha is the first letter of the alphabet and so it stands for 1.[92] Letters may even be read together as a word. Forty-six is a number of significance because from the first day of Lent until Easter is forty-six days. A = 1; D = 4; A = 1; M = 40. 1 + 4 + 1 + 40 = 46. The number spells 'Adam'.[93]

Thus, in a multitude of ways, the signs for numbers confer signification upon the numbers themselves, or endorse their signification.

This building-up of significations into a complex harmony appears
in discussions of the ideas traditionally associated with, for example,
'unity' or 'perfection'. Unity signifies Deity not only because it is
simple and undivided, but also because it is the beginning of number
and all numbers proceed from it; because every number has unity as
one of its parts.[94] In discussing perfection – a favourite subject with
number-symbolists – it is possible to see a great many significant
ways in which a number may fail to be perfect, either by excess or by
falling short. In Rev. 17:1 we read that 'the Beast which was and is
not' is 8 (*ipsa octava est*). Eight is in excess of the sum of its parts
$(1 + 2 + 4 = 7)$ and those seven are the seven deaths, seven mortal
sins, says Theobald. He picks up such points with delight: 'Nor is it
without significance that . . . ' (*nec vacat quod*).[95] Perfect numbers
are rare, occurring in one case only under 10, between 10 and 100,
between 100 and 1,000, between 1,000 and 10,000, and their rarity
is itself significant, for perfection is by no means common or easily
attained.[96]

Theobald's *Epilogue* explains how the information he has
assembled is to be used. 'When you want to make a number holy', he
says (*quotiens igitur aliquem volueris numerum sacramentare*), you
should turn over the aforesaid ways of expounding in your mind, and
when you have done so frequently you may perhaps find what you
are looking for, lying hidden. There is, in other words, a search to be
conducted. The mystery will not be obvious. The properties of the
number will prove a good guide, but there are a great many other
types of signification to be considered.[97]

The interest and importance of these reflections, and of much the
other authors have to say, lies in the contribution they make to the
enlargement of contemporary thinking about the problem of signification. Signification is almost always discussed in the twelfth century
in terms of 'words' and 'things', words signifying things directly or
obliquely, completely or incompletely, properly or improperly, and
so on. Some consideration of the nature and function of signs other
than words has a place in these discussions, largely because
Augustine and Aristotle had pointed the way. In focussing attention
upon numbers as signs Odo was giving a new emphasis to such discussions and bringing the mathematical arts into line with the arts of
language in the service of the exegete.

5

THE HISTORICAL SENSE
AND HISTORY

In Carolingian times Alcuin had prefaced his *Quaestiones in Genesim* with the explanation that he had chosen to omit the more difficult questions and had concentrated for the most part on those to which brief answers could be given: the historical ones.[1] This view of the literal or historical sense as the simple sense might seem to make it of comparatively little account, merely a stepping-stone to those higher senses which were so much more rewarding; but Hugh of St Victor gives it a more important place.

Always an advocate of the laying of sound foundations, he insists that his pupils put the historical or literal sense first. He draws for them an elaborate picture of the 'house' of exposition. The foundation is laid in the earth. Its stones are not carefully cut or polished, but chosen for their solidity. Upon the foundation is raised the superstructure, where all is made level.

In the same way there are many words and phrases in the Bible, if we take it literally, which fit together like rough stones, leaving cracks and unevennesses. But the spiritual interpretation contains no contradictions. It rests upon the literal sense in such a way that it is like a series of stones cut to fit into the foundation stones below and to form a level surface above.[2] It follows that without its foundation the spiritual sense itself would not be 'level', that is, without anomalies and contradictions. The historical or literal sense remains the lowest, but it is the basis upon which all other interpretations must rest, for the varied stones of the spiritual sense would not fit together without it. Hugh's description is a particularly graphic one, but this 'architectural' image seemed to a number of mediaeval scholars to express exactly both the overall unity of the different senses and their relation to one another.[3]

Hugh points to the ocean of books the reader must master, the many winding paths in which he may lose his way without some line to guide him, and he tells him how to keep his bearings. When he begins to read and finds 'many things obscurely written, many

67

clearly, many ambiguously', he is to proceed methodically. 'Set upon its base whatever you find clear, if it fits; interpret what is ambiguous, so that it, too, fits. Put on one side what is truly obscure, if you can.'Hugh's advice to the beginner is to pass on when confronted with an obscure passage rather than to try out a novel interpretation without the learning to support it. The sure test is the 'architectural' one: if the interpretation fits together as a whole into the solid structure of the faith, then it cannot be false.[4] Hugh thus encourages his pupils to approach each passage as a whole, taking the literal and historical sense as the foundation and building upon it.

We shall see how those of his contemporaries who chose to employ grammatical and dialectical aids at a more highly technical level did so in the light of a new respect for the literal sense. But there was, too, some new thinking about the difference between the 'historical' or literal sense, and the idea of 'history' itself, which we must look at briefly first.

The literal sense had frequently been described as 'historical' throughout the earlier mediaeval centuries, because it is at this level that the text tells a story (*historia*). But in the first half of the twelfth century the use of the term was beginning to require its more exact definition. There existed already the germ of a distinction which Hugh himself recognised between *littera* and *historia*. In his treatise on the Scriptures and their human authors he distinguishes between 'history' which properly and specifically (*proprie*; *distincte*) has to do with the narrative of events (*res gestae*), and the larger sense of the term (*largius accipi*) to mean the primary relationship between the words of the text and the things they signify – what he describes as the thing signified 'in the first place' (*primo loco*).[5]

It was usual to identify Acts as a history book. 'The Acts of the Apostles, as the blessed Jerome says, seem to relate bare history and to set out the infancy of the new-born Church.'[6] Not all the text of Scripture by any means can be said to be historical narrative in this sense, although Hugh insists (against the view of some earlier scholars) that every part of it has a literal meaning. It is, nevertheless, evident that the 'things' signified by words are far more numerous and more various than historical events.

In the middle of the twelfth century Gerhoch of Reichersberg (following an older tradition) has *littera* and *historia* used in the same passage in two clearly different senses.Writing on Ps. 67 he says, 'See, in these words we have sought for the literal sense of the letter (*litterae litteralem sensum*) and we have found it, as far as we could, with God's help.'[7] It is also the case, he points out, 'that *historia praeterita*, past history, is commemorated in these words, so that at the same time future grace may be foretold' (*ut simul annuntietur gratia futura*).[8] He goes on to examine the use of tenses in connection with past history and future promise. 'Even the words hint at prophecies of future time, of a greater mystery to come, rather than forming a narrative of past history.' He comments that it is not unusual for prophets to introduce verbs in the past tense; 'they frequently foretell the future as though they were narrating the past'.[9] This marks history as being concerned not only with *res gestae*, but specifically with what took place in the past.

Hugh of St Victor had a great respect for history. He regarded it as an essential early discipline for his pupils.[10] If someone complains to him, 'I find many things in the histories which seem to be of little use; why should I bother with things like this?'[11] Hugh will answer that if these apparently meaningless bits and pieces are put together their meaning begins to become apparent. He advises: 'Learn everything; you will see afterwards that nothing is wasted.'[12]

Hugh's own historical work, the *De Tribus Maximis Circumstantiis Gestorum*, was written about 1130. He wanted to teach his pupils a method of mastering the large quantity of material which is the ordinary stuff of history, and reducing it to order. Accordingly, he prefaces the work with an explanation of the principles involved. Since historical narratives include persons, dates and places, these salient points may be taken out, tabulated and memorised. He explains how this is to be done and provides tables for his pupils to learn.[13]

Hugh employed the method himself in his own scriptural commentaries. In his first commentary, on the Pentateuch, written before 1125, the familiar historian's aids are there: Hugh discusses the *personae* by whom the sacrifices of Leviticus are made and the gifts given, the *tempora* at which the offerings are made, and the *loca* where they are made.[14] In Judges we have a reference in the commentary to the *tempora iudicium*, the times of judgment,[15] but most telling of all is a passage in the commentary on Genesis. In writing Genesis, Hugh explains, Moses is a writer of history (*historiographus*).[16] He sets out the history (*texens historiam*), from the beginning of the world up to the death of Jacob. Two things are accordingly to be looked for in reading Genesis, the *veritas rerum gestarum* or truth of the events, and the *forma verborum*; 'for just as we know the truth of "things" through the truth of words, so, conversely, when the truth of "things" is known, we may more easily know the truth of words. For through that historical narration we are carried on to the higher understanding of "things".'[17] It appears that the distinction between 'historical' strictly speaking and 'literal' lies close to the heart of the distinction between the significance of words and the significance of 'things' in Scripture.

This conception of history owes to the classical world a preoccupation with the general and eternal implications of the particularities of historical events, with what is to be learned from them as examples;[18] their temporal and incidental character almost disappears under the weight thus put upon them.

If we turn to the 'letter' properly speaking we move into the area of technically exact study of signification which was beginning to attract interest in Anselm of Canterbury's day and even more so during the first half of the twelfth century. Peter Abelard's commentary on Romans is on the whole notably free from figurative interpretation (although it is true that the Epistles did not lend themselves to spiritual interpretation at any time). He prefers to concentrate upon the letter. He asks the practical questions of the modern textual critic and sets about answering them in a strikingly modern way. Who had converted the Romans before Paul wrote to them? Eusebius (in his history of the Church), Jerome and Gregory of Tours agree in saying that Peter had done so. Haymo of Auxerre, on the other hand, thinks that the conversion was brought about not by Peter, nor by any of the other Apostles, but by certain Jewish believers who came to Rome from Jerusalem.[19] Abelard sets about reconciling these different opinions by reading the whole of the relevant chapter of Eusebius, so as to see what this 'authority' had really said. He discovers that Eusebius had said that Peter was the first of the Apostles to preach to the Romans, not that he was the first ever to do so. Therefore, he suggests, we may accept Haymo's account and say that when Peter came he made plain to the converts what had hitherto been obscure, and thus the difficulty will disappear.[20] This spirit of enterprise in research, this willingness to look at old questions afresh and to try to make some progress with them, is the motive force of much of the new work of the day on the literal sense and its difficulties.

More typical in Abelard perhaps than this independent recourse to the authorities is the close scrutiny of the way in which words are functioning in the text. This may involve nothing more advanced than the identification and discussion of the use of an ablative absolute.[21] But it often prompts the making of distinctions in the meaning of a word in its ordinary, proper usage which was to prove a fruitful line of investigation of the functioning of biblical language. Abelard discusses the two passages in John 15:15 where Jesus said to the Apostles: 'I do not call you servants but friends', and in Rom. 1:1 where Paul calls himself a 'servant'. There appears to be a contradiction here. Abelard gives the explanation – to be met elsewhere – that there are two kinds of servant, those who are subject from fear of punishment and those who are obedient out of love. When Jesus said that his disciples were not servants he was referring to the first type of servant. Paul is identifying himself as the second.[22] In both cases 'servant' is being used in what Hugh of St Victor has described as a 'primary' way; no figure or image is involved. In this instance it requires no very sophisticated command of contemporary signification theory to point to a difference between the two literal meanings of *servus*. Often such cases stretch the technical resources of contemporary scholars to their limit, providing grammarians and dialecticians with far more testing examples than they are likely to find in common usage or in the secular authors. The Bible proved to be a challenging field in which to make technical advance in understanding how signification-theory works.

6

EXEGESIS AND THE THEORY
OF SIGNIFICATION

1 The theory of signification

We have seen how the early mediaeval theory of signification rests upon two accounts: Augustine's talk of words and things and signs in his *De Doctrina Christiana* and Boethius' discussion in his commentaries on Aristotle's *De Interpretatione*.[1] Boethius approaches his subject, as Aristotle does, by distinguishing mere noise from those sounds we call words: a word is 'meaningful, signifying something by itself'; it is a *vox significativa per seipsam aliquid significans*.[2] A sound is a 'word' only if it means something.

Boethius goes on to explore the nature of the link between the word and that which it signifies.[3] He explains that every time we use language we are concerned with a chain: of things (*res*) which we want to talk about, 'understandings' (*intellectus*) with which we perceive and discern them in our minds, and the *voces* or words with which we signify that which we have grasped by understanding. If we want to record those words in written form, we shall also need letters (*litterae* or *notae*) with which to signify the words. Thus, the letters signify the words, the words signify what is understood, and the understanding grasps the things.[4]

In this chain of signifying, the letters and the words are arbitrarily chosen and 'imposed' upon the things. They may vary from language to language; but the *intellectus*, the *concept*, and the *res*, the thing signified, are natural and everywhere the same. Different races have different terms for the dog, but they all recognise the same animal, by a common *intellectus*.[5]

The chain may be broken in various ways, so that the signification process is interrupted. When Satan took possession of the serpent in the Garden of Eden, the serpent did not know what was being said through him 'and so the serpent spoke words which he did not understand', says Alcuin.[6] There was a gap between *intellectus* and *vox*.

There may also be an interrupted connection between understanding and words where the language is unknown to the listener. Something of this sort happened at the Tower of Babel. There, says Remigius of Auxerre, quoting Alcuin, the 'one tongue' which all men once spoke survived, and is now the Hebrew tongue, for it was fitting that the same language as the Devil used to seduce Adam should be the one in which the Saviour should speak to his people when he preached upon the earth; but many other languages came into existence. There is no need to postulate that God created any new language when he divided men's tongues. He merely reshuffled the *intellectus* and the *verba*, so that different words became attached to different 'understandings'. *Alma*, for instance, means 'secret' among the Hebrews and 'holy' among the Latins. *Sidera* are 'stars' to the Latins and 'iron' to the Greeks.[7]

When twelfth century masters began the study of a text with their pupils with a formal introduction or *accessus*, among other things, they explained to what 'part of philosophy' it belonged.[8] The classification of the sciences in a grand scheme was a favourite preoccupation, too.[9] This interest in the division of the sciences and in the definition of a 'science' was greatly increased from the end of the twelfth century, when the *Posterior Analytics* began to be more widely studied.[10] Aristotle insists that a true science must be reducible to principles which are either self-evident or which depend upon self-evident principles.[11] Throughout the later Middle Ages we find attempts to establish both the first principles and the status of 'politics' and other 'sciences' which were not among the standard liberal arts.

It had seemed to Gilbert of Poitiers that grammar was alone among the branches of study with which he was familiar in lacking such self-evident first principles. In his commentary on Boethius' *De Hebdomadibus*, he makes a list of the 'major premises' of logic, the *regulae* and *axiomata* and common *sententiae* of the other *artes*. But he points out that the rules of grammar are *positivae*, 'imposed' by man, and not to be counted among the *communis animi conceptiones*,[12] the principles grasped by every mind as soon as it understands them.

The *accessus* of the twelfth century sometimes gave way in commentaries of the thirteenth century to an enlarged discussion in which the 'placing' of the subject of the textbook to be studied among the sciences is of the first importance. This is the case with the commentary on 'Priscianus Maior' attributed to Robert Kilwardby, where grammar's claims to be a speculative or practical science – or indeed a science at all – are considered at length,[13] and where the problem of the nature of the connection between a word and what it signifies is taken a little further.

Our author proceeds, like Aquinas, by a set method of analysis, 'Kilwardby' – the attribution seems doubtful[14] – turns to Aristotle for assistance. Aristotle says that the subject of a science must be 'necessary'.[15] *Sermo*, language, is not 'necessary', if by 'necessary' we mean that vocabulary and syntax are universal and absolute, for it is clear that they are not so. Therefore it seems that grammar cannot be the subject of a science.[16] The problem is explored further in what follows.[17] *Sermo* is threefold: it is found in a written and a spoken form and also *in mente*. The objection that grammar is not a science proceeds from its variability in matters of spelling and pronunciation. When *sermo* is *in mente* its 'words' are universal; it is concerned not with the interpretation of the words the ears hear, but with the concepts abstracted from words in various languages and shared by all minds alike.[18] Such 'grammar' may certainly be a science. This account does not quite resolve the difficulty, however. 'Kilwardby' has not explained how grammar as taught by Priscian can be a science in this way,[19] for it is concerned with precisely the variable principles which he excludes from true science.

It is in his discussion of the theory of signification that 'Kilwardby' comes closer to solving the problem. He considers not only the relationship between the universal *intellectus*, the word in the mind, and the spoken word, but between the word in all its forms and the 'thing' it signifies. Here, albeit with a large debt to the dialecticians' work on signification (and covering some of their ground), the grammarian may concern himself with the stuff of textbooks of Priscian and Donatus as tradition obliges him to do, and at the same time consider universal and primary principles.

'Kilwardby' sets, and attempts to answer, a series of questions. Is it possible for a sound (*vox*) to be made to signify? If so, what form will this making-to-signify, or *institutio*, take? To institute a word for signifying is nothing else than to give it a signification which it did not have before. He suggests that perhaps to give it such a signification is to 'unite' a signification with it.[20]

It is the nature and mode of this 'union' with which we are concerned as grammarians interested in first principles. There are three things to consider: the basic material, which is an utterance; the signification; and their joining together. How is it possible for that which is inside the soul to be connected with what is in the air outside, the *significatio* or *species intelligibilis* with the *vox sensibilis*,[21] the sound we actually hear in spoken language? 'Kilwardby' is interested in the mechanics of this first operation in the process of effecting a union between the universal 'word' and the particular thing signified. He suggests that two distinct occurrences must take place. A sound is made which has no signification (*vocem non significativam proferre*). It is given a signification (*eam ad significandum instituere*).[22] Thus the audible *vox* is emitted and the signification is attached to it. A great many difficulties arise when we try to understand the mode of this 'attaching'. At what point does it take place: before the sound is emitted, simultaneously with its emission, or after it has been emitted? Can the speaker speak before he understands what he is saying,[23] that is before the signification of the noises he is making is known to him? Or does the 'institution' of the signification occur before the word is uttered?[24] Must we look for an intermediary, a connective of some sort?[25]

A further problem arises for our author out of the fundamental question of the connection between *voces* (spoken words) and *intellectus*, the 'words' which are ideas in the mind. As Aristotle says in the *De Interpretatione*,[26] *intellectus* and *res* are the same for everyone. Whereas the consistency of the former is easy to understand because human *intellectus* are reflections of the ideas in the mind of God – they are created things and 'natural';[27] in the case of *voces* 'nouns and verbs are not the same *apud omnes*', and therefore, it seems, 'they do not signify naturally'.[28] Indeed new words are 'derived' or given currency every day, nouns as well as verbs, and this *derivatio* is nothing more nor less than a 'new institution of a word to signify'.[29] The variability of attachment between a given sound and its possible significations in different languages is explored a little further. We are talking, says our author, not only of the Latin language, but of Greek, Hebrew and the vulgar tongues, where the same *res* may have different words imposed upon it by each language.[30] This possibility raises a series of further questions. Does a word always signify what it is made to signify by the 'institution' of its signification?[31] Can a signification change? Can a word be given any signification, like a lump of matter which can be adapted to any form?[32]

The technical term used by the dialecticians for this flexible attachment of words to the things they signify is 'imposition'. Words are chosen to fit certain *intellectus*, not because there is any natural or necessary relationship between them, but to suit the convenience of a given language,[33] or a given circumstance, as Garlandus put it in his *Dialectica* of the late eleventh or early twelfth century.[34]

2 Imposition

Abelard points out that words do not have the same meaning for everyone; to understand a word the listener must know its imposition *significandi officium apud omnes non tenetur, sed apud eos solummodo qui earum impositionem non ignorant.*[35] Priscian, too, has said that there may be many 'names' in a single word (*multa nomina incidere in unam vocem*). They are called 'many' or 'diverse' according to that very *significandi officium*, which gives them different 'understandings' (*intellectus*). They are one *vox*, for the *vox* is the actual form of the utterance or sound (*prolationis et soni forma*). For, as Thierry of Chartres says, it is their 'understandings' or significations which make sounds into words.[36]

There was a school of thought in the first half of the twelfth century which disputed this view of the chance and variable nature of imposition, at least in its beginnings. Thierry of Chartres believed that imposition is not a purely human activity, with all the unreliability and arbitrariness that would imply. 'For *vocabula* were united [with the things they signify] from eternity in the divine mind before they were "imposed" by men. The man "imposed" them on the things to which they were united in the divine mind. He "imposed" them, as it seems to us, at the prompting of the Holy Spirit.'[37] That is, he contends, what Victorinus means when he says that *nomina essentiant res*, names embody the being of things. 'That is nothing but the imposition of a name', he comments.[38] So the union of word and thing is ultimately an absolute one.

Nevertheless, language as we use it in our fallen condition has lost its perfect connectedness and Thierry is in a minority among his contemporaries in even attempting to maintain the primordial state of things in the context of human language.

More typical is the kind of debate in which we find Gerhoch of Reichersberg engaged as he quotes Gilbert of Poitiers in his *De Gloria et Honore Filii Hominis*. Gilbert had written in his gloss on Phil. 2:9: 'For this reason God exalted him and gave him the name which is above every name . . . It seems to some that this name was given to man, which is in no way in keeping with reason. This name is not one which can be given as we call someone by a name (*per solam appellationem*) but is itself God's very Being, the essence of

God (*hoc nomen esse deum*), and it belongs to the Son from eternity. It can only be said to have been given to man "by adoption".[39] Gilbert wanted to make a distinction between the ultimate and absolute union of word and thing in the Godhead and the flexible attachments of words to things in the created world. (Gerhoch said that Gilbert was a latter-day Nestorian, dividing Christ into two Sons, man and God, and he pursues the point with some subtlety.)

Whatever was to be said about the relation between word and thing in the Divine Mind, experience showed the human imposition of words upon things to be full of uncertainties, and by no means straightforward. The attempt to clarify matters led to the development of a new technical vocabulary. There may, for example, be an ambiguity in the use of the same word to speak of the particular instance or individual, and the class or category in general. I may want to speak of 'dogs' in a general way. The word 'dog' has been imposed upon the canine species, and so the word 'dog' may be said to signify that species. But if I wish to name, not dogs in general, but some particular dog, Abelard and some of his fellow-dialecticians would prefer me to speak not of *significatio* but of *nominatio* or *appellatio* when I speak of naming or calling the dog in question.[40]

Among the grammarians, too, William of Conches (c. 1080 – c. 1145) proposes a distinction between *significare* and *nominare*. The word *homo* 'signifies' the common quality of all men, their humanity. It 'nominates' or 'names' them individually. It would, however, seem absurd to make this distinction so sharp that there appears to be no conceptual or significative connection between the individual man and his kind. So William concedes that although *homo* properly (*proprie*) nominates the individual, nevertheless it also names the species obliquely (*ex adiuncto*). This habit of asking which is the 'proper' signification is widespread, but confusing, since *proprie* is in itself a term with many meanings in twelfth century dialectical usage.

Already in Anselm of Canterbury we find an exploration of the need for a fuller technical vocabulary and some pioneering thinking in this area. In his treatise *De Grammatico* he asks what the word *grammaticus* (literate) signifies. It may, he suggests, signify the man who is literate and mean 'a literate man', or it may signify the quality of literacy. There is no exactly comparable usage in English but there is perhaps a loose parallel when we shorten a phrase ('the Blue team') and speak of 'the Blues'. Both the team and its colours are being signified. Anselm says that in such a case 'literate' does not signify 'man' and literacy as a single whole, but literacy directly (*per se*) and man obliquely (*per aliud*). In Anselm's terminology this amounts to saying that the word *grammaticus* is *appellativum hominis*, 'appellative of man', but cannot properly be said to be 'significative' of man. He gives a definition of *appellativum* as 'that by which a thing is called in ordinary usage' (*usu loquendi*). Oblique signification, then, has to do with the *reference* of names, the way they are commonly and loosely applied to things, and direct signification has to do with their proper meaning.[41]

The eleventh century dialectician Garlandus's examples are all drawn from his reading of the logicians. He gives no scriptural illustrations. Nevertheless, within his lifetime the dialecticians' understanding of the multiplicity and complexity of signification in words and things was proving to be of the greatest assistance to interpreters of the Bible when they were confronted with apparently contradictory usages. Exegetes and dialecticians alike are to be found looking underneath the surface signification of a word or phrase to see whether something more might be 'understood'. Abelard, writing on dialectic, uses the term *subintelligere* to describe what happens when we read, for example, *Marcia Catonis* and understand that 'Cato's Marcia' is his wife. We mentally fill out what is said in order to complete the meaning.[42] *Subintelligere* is used in a singular way by Rupert of Deutz, writing on Scripture, in his *De Gloria et Honore Filii Hominis Super Matthaeum*.[43] *Subaudire* seems to have been a usage virtually interchangeable with *subintelligere* from an early date.[44] *Subinferre* is to be found, too.[45]

The underlying difficulty in all this is that the *vox* with which we are concerned is a *vox humana*. A dog may bark and make his meaning plain, but he does not speak in words. A meaningful sound (*vox significativa*) must have a mind behind it, and the will of a rational being to impose the signification. A *vox* without such an intellectual intention imposed upon it remains merely a noise,[46] but the mind which endows a *vox significativa* with signification is a fallible and changeable human mind.

The problem is compounded by the fact that the grammarian is not solely concerned with these audible *voces significativae* and their variability; indeed 'Kilwardby' believes that that is not primarily his concern at all. He deals with the written word (*De tali voce non est intentio apud grammaticum sed de litteratis solum*). The written word too, is a sign,[47] and it raises a fresh set of difficulties for

'Kilwardby' about the relation of signification which exists between word and thing. He says that the 'sign' ought to be 'proportionate' to the thing signified; *signum debet proportionari significato*.[48] This seems to 'Kilwardby' to raise special difficulties in the case of written signs. The thing signified, the *intellectus* or *passio* of the mind, is *simplex*. Among *signa vocalium*, the simplest is the letter, but the letter is an incomplete sign. It is a part of the syllable, and the syllable is a part of the complete *dictio*. Letters and syllables are merely the stuff (*materiale*) of which the *dictio* is made. A complete *dictio* is needed if the mind is to attach meaning to it. So the *dictio* emerges as the basic unit of signification and as having the simplicity required.[49]

Still further 'scientific' considerations are raised: if a word or saying is made to signify something and that something ceases to exist (*eo corrupto*), does the word lose its signification? No, because what is signified is ultimately in the mind, and there it is incorruptible.[50]

Can a word signify something which does not exist?[51] Here 'Kilwardby' raises one of the problems Augustine considers in the *De Magistro* and which had continued to exercise thinkers in Carolingian times and afterwards.[52] It would seem that it can, for Aristotle says that it is possible both to signify that what is not is, and to signify that what is is.[53] In a contradiction one premise signifies what is as it is, and the other signifies what is not as though it were.[54] On the other hand, the sign and the thing signified are *relative*. If one of a pair of relatives does not exist, the other disappears as well. A *vox existens* cannot be the sign of a *res* which does not exist.[55]

Whose task is it to institute *voces ad significandum*? It would seem that anyone can, for a *sermo* expresses the common will of any mind without distinction (*indifferenter*).[56] Indeed that is its task (*officium*). The *vox significativa* provides *mutae voluntatis indicia*, 'so that men can signify their wishes to one another, which cannot be done with exactness (*distincte*) by means of *voces* which are *naturaliter significativae*'.[57] But it might be argued on the contrary that it falls to him whose task it is to teach to give words their signification, for *sermo significativus* is the beginning of learning. This discussion leads 'Kilwardby' to ask whether creating significations is the work of a grammarian or a logician. The grammarian states what is signified by the word, and that is the prerequisite for all scientific studies, whether they are concerned with words or things. It is the grammarian who deals with nouns and verbs and the other parts of speech, under which all the *voces significativae* are contained. On the other hand, logicians may be said to have a claim, because, as we saw, the *institutio* must have a rational mind behind it, and reasoning is their province.

It cannot be said that these explorations penetrate very far into the problems of epistemology with which they are concerned. Their interest for our purposes lies in the way in which our author perceives the issues. He thinks about signification in connection with grammar in the philosophical terms to which the work of his twelfth century predecessors had pointed him. He asks what method is proper to the science of 'talk' (*scientia de sermone*). Is it to involve 'defining', 'dividing', 'collecting', as is the case in the other sciences which are concerned with 'things'.[58] He asks whether the 'science of signs' (*scientia de signis*) ought to be divided from the 'science of things', for in some cases a thing is just a *res* and has no signification and in other cases it is also a 'sign'.[59] This suggests to him a point of difference between logic and grammar. Logic is concerned with *sermo* as it is related 'to things' (*ad rem*). Grammar is concerned with *sermo* as it is related *ad modum significandi*.[60] We might add that exegesis is concerned with *sermo* as it is related both *ad rem* and *ad modum significandi* and thus brings the work of grammarians and dialecticians together.

3 Dictionaries

Towards the end of the twelfth century several of the leading Paris masters put together collections of *distinctiones*, or dictionaries of biblical terms. The first dictionaries to survive are the work of four masters who taught in Paris in the second half of the twelfth century: Peter the Chanter, Peter of Poitiers, Prepositinus of Cremona and Alan of Lille. Peter of Poitiers and Prepositinus confined themselves to the Psalms in making their collections. Peter the Chanter and Alan of Lille compiled more comprehensive dictionaries which drew upon the whole of Scripture.[61]

Each word was listed with a text to illustrate each of its meanings. Sometimes ten or fifteen literal and figurative senses were distinguished in this way. The term *distinctio* seems to have come into use to describe such collections in reference to this 'distinguishing'. Recent studies[62] have emphasised the usefulness of these collections to preachers, who could look up a word and find the theme of a sermon ready developed for them in miniature, together with quotations. There has also been a good deal of clearing of the ground so that we can see how the first collections were made, and how closely they were related to the development of 'finding-systems', symbols and other devices used to facilitate quick reference (see Fig. 1) in manuscripts of the late twelfth and early thirteenth century, when the *distinctiones* began to become popular as preachers' aids.

The entries in these dictionaries owe a debt to contemporary discussion of the theory of signification. Studies of individual words, designed to separate their meanings or significations had been a commonplace in exegesis for many centuries. In his *Moralia in Job*, Gregory the Great says that the word 'man' is used in three ways in the Bible: to refer to man's nature ('Let us make man after our own image and likeness', Gen. 1:26); in reference to man's frailty ('Are you not carnal and walk as men?' 1 Cor. 3:3); to refer to man's sinfulness ('Ye shall die like men', Ps. 82:6–7).[63] 'Brothers are so-called in Holy Scripture in three ways', Remigius of Auxerre explains: there are brothers like Jacob and Isaac who are brothers in nature; other 'brothers' who are kindred, such as Abraham and Lot; others who share only their race, as when all the Jews are called brothers.[64] Lanfranc comments on the usage of some secular authors who speak of leading philosophers as *principes* and suggests that that is the sense in which Paul uses the word in Rom. 2:4.[65] Hugh of St Victor analyses the *inanis* and *vacua* of Genesis, suggesting that *inanis* refers to a hollowness or concavity and *vacua* to the fact that in the 'hollow' there was neither air nor cloud.[66] The darkness which was

Fig. 1. Luke, with the *Glossa Ordinaria*.
Oxford Bodleian Library: MS Auct. D. inf. 27 (*olim* Fairfax 15), twelfth century, English, from St Mary, Bridlington; fo. 3, in the bottom margin in a later hand.

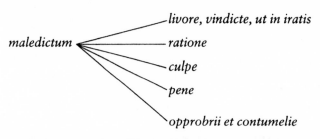

This note, distinguishing five kinds of 'cursed', is linked with the text by a symbol. The intention is to explain that Elizabeth was cursed in being shamed, not in any of the other ways, by a curse uttered in anger, by reason, by blame, by punishment (Luke 1:6).

upon the face of the abyss may be that very cloud, a mixture of the three elements of fire, air and water, the abyss the concavity or hollow; or alternatively the cloud, abyss and darkness may all be taken to refer to the absence of light.[67] Such potential 'dictionary entries' are commonplace, each commentator adding to them or modifying them or inventing them for himself as he saw fit.

There is no difficulty in finding examples of the method of *distinctio* or the listing of senses actually in use in the exegesis of the first half of the twelfth century. When Hugh of St Victor set about reconciling the two statements in St John's Gospel: 'The Father judges no one, but he has given all judgment to the Son' (John 5:22) and: 'I judge no man' (John 8:15), he did so by distinguishing the different senses of 'judgment' (*iudicium*). (He finds that there are four.) In this instance the first *iudicium* applies to the future judgment, which is to come at the end of the world, and the second to judgment in this present life. Gerhoch of Reichersberg interprets the 'reeds' of Ps. 67:31 as 'heretics' by analysing the meaning of 'reed'. The reed was used by the ancients as a pen, he says, and so it is appropriate to understand Holy Scripture by *arundo*; but these are *ferae arundines*, wild beasts or heretics who misunderstand and misinterpret Scripture. 'Reed' may also rightly (*recte*) be said to signify those who are unstable (*instabiles*), who, like reeds in the wind, are swayed this way and that by every wind of doctrine.[68]

Ernald or Arnold of Bonneval, mid-twelfth-century author of the second book of the *Vita Prima* of Bernard of Clairvaux, delivered a remarkable series of homilies on Psalm 132 in which he displays a command of a good deal of technical expertise in the liberal arts. The first homily deals with the verse: 'Behold, how good and how joyous it is for brothers to dwell together as one.' Methodically, Ernald takes the important words and distinguishes their meanings. 'I find the word "brothers" used in Scripture in four ways', he explains, in the same way as Remigius: according to nature, as in the case of Jacob and Esau who were brothers; according to kinship, like Abraham and Lot; according to race, or tribe, like the whole house of Jacob; according to faith, like all Christians.

'One' has many meanings. We speak of 'one' in the case of a collection, or collective class, as in 'one flock', which is composed of many beasts; there is 'one' *secundum similitudinem*, when many are alike in some respect as when many sing with one voice; we may say that those who are in harmony or reconciled are one; we call 'one body' that which is composed of different parts; we speak of 'one' when we mean that infinitesimally small quantity or 'atom' which cannot be divided; we call the 'soul' one *secundum simplicitatem*, for it is a simple substance although it has different powers. There follows a discussion of unity and simplicity (and the unique nature of the divine simplicity) in which Ernald displays some knowledge of the *quadrivium*.[69] Similarly, when he discusses *locus* he brings all his philosophical and mathematical knowledge to bear. A 'place' may be bodily or incorporeal, simple or composite. Composite 'places' are divided into solid and mathematical; incorporeal places may be *opinabiles, potentiales, naturales, personales, intellectibiles*. The *intellectibilis locus* may be *imperfectus* or *consummatus*. If it is *consummatus* it may be *superior* or *inferior*. 'And in all these I do not mention the dialectical *topos* or *locus*', concludes Ernald teasingly. He goes on to discuss the types of *locus* systematically and at length.[70]

Few of the commentators of the day took their explorations as far as Ernald, but his little treatise on the *locus* – for that is what it amounts to – emphasises the strong interest of his contemporaries in words and their meanings. 'Construe it this way',[71] recommends Abelard writing on the Hexameron. 'And the darkness was upon the face of the deep'; here *abyssum* is *profunditas*, the deep, he explains, and it refers to all that jumble (*congeries*) of elements which was not yet distinct as it was to be later. There follows a detailed analysis of Hebrew usages.[72]

The approach grew more systematic and thorough decade by decade during the twelfth century until in Peter of Poitiers's *Sententiae* the topics are arranged according to stated principles of *distinctio*. Chapter 2 is concerned with the *distinctio vocabulorum*, the distinction of the divine names, chapter 9 with the *diversae significationes* of *voluntas* in the discussion of divine and human will, chapter 11 with 'terms of a stated "kind" ', *posse de iustitia, posse de potentia, posse de misericordia*, and whether they are 'interchangeable in predication'. Other chapters deal with 'names which are as if abstractive', with 'these terms', 'this word', and a host of technicalities which would have been beyond the technical knowledge of Abelard, but which had become, within a few decades, the stock in trade of the theologian in his analysis of the language of the Bible.[73]

The differentiating or distinguishing of meanings is often directed to the pointing of a moral, much as it was by Gregory the Great. In his *Adnotationes Mysticae in Psalmos*, Richard of St Victor is anxious to allow the lessons of Scripture to show through: perhaps

Scripture wished to instruct us when it called some 'kings' or 'princes' and designated others 'races' and 'peoples'. If we seek to understand the difference between 'races' and 'peoples', we can easily distinguish them from one another. For one 'race' is distinguished from another by difference of custom or language, and often a 'race' contains many peoples. In one word therefore is implied a difference of behaviour and in the other is implied the greatness of their multitudes. Thus the reader is brought to a clear understanding of the precise point the text is making, and Richard is able to go on to draw out a moral.[74] A similar differentiation takes place with *videre*. *Videre* may be a seeing by faith or a seeing by contemplation or a seeing *per speciem* and we must read it with precision accordingly.[75]

But discussion of the signification of biblical terms often involves more explicit recourse than this to the developing technical language of the day. If we look up a word in a dictionary we expect to find one or more definitions of meanings the word possesses in its own right, independently of the context in which it is used, although the dictionary may also give some contexts for the sake of clarity. This dictionary definition tells us the *significatio* of the word, or its *significationes*. When a word (specifically and strictly a noun) is considered in the context of a sentence, that is, in use in a particular case, we should more properly speak, in mid- or late-twelfth-century usage, of its *suppositio*. Anselm of Canterbury does not use the word, but his distinction between *appellatio*, the specific naming of an individual, and *significatio*, the possible meaning or meanings of a word out of context, serves a similar purpose.

The first reference to *supposita locutio*, in a context where its technical import is clear, appears to be the one found in a gloss on Priscian in Oxford Bodleian Library MS Laud. Lat. 67, written in the last quarter of the twelfth century by a master who was continuing the work of William of Conches and Petrus Helias. The author of the gloss believed that each noun signifies a particular 'something' which 'stands under' (*sub-positum*) the verbal expression in a particular context. A word may be capable of signifying several things. These are its significations as they might be listed in a dictionary, but in a particular context it will normally have a particular meaning, which may be called its 'supposition'.[76]

Had the technical vocabulary existed when he wrote on the *principes* of Rom. 2:4, Lanfranc might have said that the word had a particular supposition. As it is, he simply speaks of the meaning in this context (*hic*): 'Here he calls "Princes" those outstanding philosophers by whom and through whom philosophy was discovered.'[77] The commentator of an interpretation of the Prophets which survives in an English Cistercian manuscript of about 1200 uses *supponere* familiarly, *secundum litteram supponenda est hec . . . ,*[78] but not perhaps with an exact technical import.

Supposuit is already to be found in Abelard, but not, it seems, in the precise technical sense it has in the later twelfth century.[79] Abelard discusses, for example, the clause *Dixit quodque Deus*, which is found with several variants: *Dixit vero Deus*; *Dixit autem Deus*; *Dixit etiam Deus*; *Dixitque Deus*. Abelard prefers *Dixitque Deus* because *quoque* carries a connotation of some addition or *augmentum*, 'and properly that *coniunctio* "also" ought not to be signifying some addition as being understood here'.[80]

The scholars of the twelfth century made *significatio* itself into a technical term with a new exactitude. It had long been in use in scriptural commentary in a general sense. 'What does this mean?'; 'What does that number signify?';[81] 'What is the significance of what Abraham said to his son?';[82] 'What is it that God meant when he said to Noah . . . ?'[83] The Carolingian scholar Rabanus Maurus explained to his pupils the way in which an event or action described in Holy Scripture may 'signify' something which the Christian ought to do in imitation.[84] This varied and relatively loose usage of *significatio* and *signo*[85] and related terms is to be found widespread in the earlier Middle Ages. Nor are *significare* and *significatio* by any means the only terms which had long been in use to describe what is to be learned from the words of the Bible. 'This can be understood in two ways':[86] 'This reading teaches or exhorts';[87] 'Through the names of the places in which the peoples once dwelt is expressed . . . '.[88] In the study of the liberal arts, on the other hand, the notion of 'signification' was technically relatively exact from an early date. The theory of meaning was one of the first areas of productive interplay between the study of grammar and the study of dialectic in the earlier Middle Ages.[89]

4 Grammar and practical criticism

'Kilwardby's' pretentious elevation of grammar to the status of a science in terms of signification-theory belongs to a later age, but it faithfully reflects the direction of earlier work. We can come close to the spirit of this earlier work in an earlier commentary, Ralph of

Beauvais's *Glose Super Donatum*, composed in the third quarter of the twelfth century.[90] Ralph depends substantially upon contemporary commentaries on Priscian's *Institutiones* and those of a still earlier generation, particularly William of Conches.[91] Ralph fills the gaps in Donatus from Priscian with their aid, and he generally prefers Priscian to Donatus where the two authorities are in conflict.[92] In these respects he places himself squarely amongst the grammarians of his day, and his examples are for the most part the traditional ones taken from the Roman grammarians and from Roman literature.

There is, however, one striking feature of his commentary which reminds us of the ultimate purpose of the contemporary study of grammar: to help the student of the Bible to read and understand the text of Scripture. Ralph uses several biblical examples to illustrate the points he makes in his commentary. It is evident that some of them have found their way in because they have been raised, often contentiously by pupils and fellow-grammarians. The argumentative tone is hinted at in such phrases as *sed opponitur*.

One such objection had been raised over the construction of 1 Cor. 13:13. 'Here it seems', says Ralph, examining *horum maior est caritas*, 'that "greater" governs (*regat*) this genitive: "of these".'[93] But 'greater' is not normally used with the genitive in this way. Some correct the text to read *hiis autem maior est caritas*; 'Charity is greater than these'. Others say that *numero* ought to be understood, and that 'of these' is governed by that. Ralph himself thinks that 'of these' is governed by the noun *caritas*, for whenever a genitive is used *in divisione* or with the force of division, it can be governed by any noun. This is the case here. The genitive is used *in vi divisionis*, for its force is to indicate the separation of *caritas* from the other virtues listed. Ralph is settling what was evidently a lively contemporary dispute.

Not all his examples are contentious. Many of them simply illustrate a principle. *In conveniendo populos in unum* from Ps. 101:23[94] serves to illustrate the way in which a gerundive may be formed from a *verbum absolutum*. The form *In . . . do* is construed with prepositions which take the ablative, as in *in convertendo* (Ps. 125:1).[95] The same text (*in convertendo Dominus captivitatem . . .*) serves to illustrate a difference between Latin and Greek usage where 'we are accustomed to say "Dominus", but *vitiose*,' that is, despite its strict grammatical inaccuracy.[96]

Priscian gives a list of prepositions taking the ablative which, he says, all have 'almost the same signification' (*fere eandem habere sig-*

nificationem). 'He says "almost" ', Ralph comments, 'because *ex* can be used where the others cannot, as when I say *ex illo tempore fui*. *De*, too, sometimes has its oddities, as when we read *de sub cuius pede*, where *de* stands in place of *de loco qui est* [*sub cuius pede*]. *De* is used similarly in the words of the psalm *de post fetantes* (Ps. 77:70).'[97] But even in these cases the text of Scripture often stretches the grammatical rule a little or tests it harder than ordinary usage can do. Ralph is showing us not only how the study of grammar benefited the student of Scripture, but also something not always so clearly recognised: how the study of the Bible was advancing the grammarian's thinking about language.

There appears to have been some contemporary debate over the use of the present participle. Some say that a participle ending in *-ens* can be used with a verb in any tense. William of Conches, however, says that it cannot be used with the future, but it may be objected, Ralph points out, that the Psalter says: *venientes autem venient* . . . William of Conches used to answer (*respondebat*) in Gregory the Great's words, that the Divine Page does not submit to the rules of grammar, or that in this instance *venientes* was a noun. But, Ralph accuses, he was not taking note of what follows in *portantes manipulos suos*, for if *portantes* was not a participle how would it govern the accusative? Ralph himself is of the opinion that conjugation with the future is permissible.[98] In this way, and not without the contentiousness which makes for advance, the work of the grammarians and dialecticians was coming together with the work of the exegetes in the course of the twelfth century.

4 Joint meanings: consignification

Sometimes a word has a secondary signification inseparable from its primary one.[99] This double signification is known as *consignificatio*: 'For to consignify is to signify secondarily' (*consignificare enim est secundario significare*) says the grammarian William of Conches.[100] *Equiferus* means 'a wild horse'. If it is a noun, it ought to be the case that no part of it signifies on its own, or it will not fit Boethius' definition of such a word as that which has no independently signifying parts: *cuius nulla pars est significata separata*.[101] But *ferus* does have a meaning when it is taken on its own. In its compound form we must think of it as ceasing to do so, and as having instead a joint meaning. Conversely, some words which look on the face of it as though they will have a secondary signification prove not to do so. If we divide up *domus* into *do-mus* or *magister* into *magis-ter* we have in each case two words joined together in the original word, but they bear no relation to the first word and consequently there is no 'con-signification'.[102]

All verbs have joint significations, because they signify not only 'to go' or 'to do' or 'to eat', or whatever their individual sense may be, but also the time of going or doing or eating, whether it is past, present or future. A verb has tenses.[103] Peter Abelard develops this principle further in his discussion of tenses. The *significatio* of the past tense is, he says, *infinita*, for once something is in the past it remains in the past. It is not so with the present and the future. What is present was future and will be past, and just as before it was present it was future, so once it ceases to be present it will be past, and the tense must change accordingly. There is much contemporary dis-cussion of the way tenses can be applied in speaking of God.

Thierry of Chartres insists that 'no verb adapted to speak of God (*ad loquendum de Deo translatum*) has this secondary signification of time'. When it is said, for example, that the Father begot the Son, 'begot' does not consignify past time but the completedness and per-fection of the begetting.[104] Alan of Lille, much later in the twelfth century, describes in his *Regulae Theologicae* the use of various parts of speech in talking about God. He agrees that tenses are quite inappropriate but he suggests that the present tense may be less unsuitable than the past.[105]

In relation to verbs in particular, the idea of consignification was not a new doctrine. It is to be found in Boethius on Aristotle.[106] But William sets out some additional types of consignification, in a way which shows how the notion was beginning to be enlarged in the first half of the twelfth century. He explains that a predicate may be said to 'consignify' its subject in the sense that the predicate implies its subject along with itself. Or we may speak of *consignificatio* in the case of parts of speech such as prepositions and conjunctions. These William notes from Priscian are called by the dialecticians *sincategoremata*, that is, *consignificantia*. 'A', for example, signifies nothing on its own, but in conjunction with something else it may have various significations. In *a domo*, 'from the house' it con-signifies a place, and in *a Socrate*, 'from Socrates', it consignifies a person.[107]

Garlandus has some further thoughts on *consignificatio*. He lists four types of regular propositions where the subject and the predi-cate are consignificant terms. In 'every man is an animal', 'every man' and 'animal' consignify; in 'a species is a genus' the thing signified by the subject consignifies with the predicate; in 'man is a genus' the thing signified by the predicate consignifies with the subject. In two further types of preposition the signifying term signifies what is signified and 'the genus is an animal'. In this way there can be said to be consignification when the subject term and the predicate term of a preposition refer to the same thing.[108]

It is clear from these explorations by dialecticians and grammarians alike that the principle that a word may signify more than one thing simultaneously was proving fruitful of further speculation in a way that was generating new technical categories. Although as yet these scholars largely confine themselves to secular illustrations, the helpfulness of the principle in exegesis is plain enough.

6 More meaning than appears: implicitness in words

As we decline a noun in Latin it runs through a series of changes of signification, taking on additional shades of meaning: 'to', 'for', 'by', 'with', 'from', 'at'. Sometimes a preposition is required before it, but not always. It is often the case that the noun contains the additional signification within it in the accusative, the genitive, the dative or the ablative. We might say that its consignification is implicit.[109]

Peter Abelard had said that: 'by the name of "Father" power is designated, by the name of "Son" wisdom, by the name of "Holy Spirit" goodwill towards creatures'.[110] He found himself challenged over the implication that these attributes of the Godhead may be regarded as proper to the individual Persons,[111] but not in his use of the expressions *nomine Patris, nomine Filii, nomine Spiritus*. In the 1140s Gilbert of Poitiers gave offence by a closely parallel usage when he suggested that God is not divinity (*divinitas*) but 'by divinity' (*divinitate*).[112]

The controversialist Gerhoch of Reichersberg contributed to this discussion in his *De Gloria et Honore Filii Hominis*, at once a work of apologetic and a work of polemic, in which he both defends himself against the accusations of those who have found stumbling-blocks (*offendicula*) in his writings, and attacks others for their errors.[113]

He himself makes full use of prepositions in discussing how Christ, in that he arose eternally from the height (*ex alto*) had no mother but only God the Father, and in that he rose from the earth of the Virgin's flesh, had no earthly father but only a mother. He fears it may be a stumbling-block to the simple to say that Christ was born in heaven *sine matre*, without a mother, on the earth *sine patre*, without a father, unless they understand that he had an adoptive father in Joseph. This is clear from the genealogies given in the Gospel which recognise him to be the son of David according to promise (*secundum promissionem*).[114]

Gerhoch goes on to consider the contemporary debate over the text: 'To him was given the name which is above every name.' Was this name given to the man Jesus? Can we believe that it is a proper name for humanity? Gerhoch distinguishes between the humanity 'which is the man' (*quae homo est*) and the humanity 'by which he is a man' (*qua homo est*). The humanity 'by which' Jesus is a man did not grow with him from infancy, it is not capable of growth; but 'the man who is a man by it' (*homo qui ea est homo*) grew up; but as God Jesus was *perfectus*, complete from the beginning. Therefore we may indeed say that 'man is in the glory of God' because *that* man is God and this man was never not God. From when (*ex quo*) he even began to be *homo perfectus* fully man, he was already perfect God *in seipso aeternaliter existens*.[115]

The point is consolidated by a reference to the rules of Boethius' so-called *De Hebdomadibus*, the most difficult of the 'theological tractates' of Boethius upon which several mid-twelfth-century masters chose to lecture, in which self-evident principles or *regulae* are used to resolve a philosophical problem as though they were geometrical axioms and the problem was mathematical.[116] The eighth rule, for example, states that: 'For every composite it is one thing to be and another [that] it is (*aliud ipsum est*).' This 'can be applied to man, for whom it is one thing to be "by" that which he is [that is, "by humanity"] and another to be himself, for the humanity by which he is a man is not the man himself'. Just as bodiliness (*corporeitas*), too, by which the body is, is not itself the body. There are many things in man which are not the man, such as memory, understanding, will, but nothing is found in God which is not God.[117]

Now 'humanity' is used equivocally by Christian writers (*in utraque significatione positum*) both for the humanity by which Christ is man and for the man that he is by that humanity: 'For where the assumption of humanity in God is predicated, "man" is signified by the noun of humanity' (*nomine humanitatis homo significatur*). Where the same man is said to be (*praedicatur*) equal with the Father according to his divinity, but less than the Father according to his humanity, by the name of humanity the human nature by which a man is a man and which is 'of a man' (*hominis est*) and itself is not man, is understood.[118] Gerhoch is anxious to make absolutely clear the difference between the particular man who is God and that humanity which all men have in common and which is not God, and he brings Hilary of Poitiers and other material to bear in support of his case.[119]

The discussion here has turned, not on the prepositions but on cases, on the difference of signification implicit within a difference of case, even where there is no sincategorematic preposition to point the way.

7 Implicit propositions

Alan of Lille perceives a difficulty in speaking of God which he states in Rule 10 of the *Regulae Theologicae*:[120] Every statement made about God is *copulata* and *conjuncta*, that is, it contains within it by implication far more than is explicitly stated. If I say that a man is good it does not follow that he is just and merciful. I must make separate statements to that effect (*divisim*). But if I say that God is good I am also saying that he is just and merciful and everything else that he is, because all the attributes of God are one with his very Being; they are not predicated of him in the usual way. As Alan puts it in Rule 12,[121] to be predicated of God is nothing else but to be in him, *praedicari nihil aliud sit quam inhaerere*. The point is further worked out in Rule 18.[122]

This sort of 'implicitness' is peculiar to statements made about God, but the general notion that something may be there within a proposition, even though it is not stated explicitly, was of some interest to Alan's contemporaries.[123] In a treatise which survives from the end of the twelfth century, the *Tractatus Implicitarum*, we find extended discussions of the difficulties raised by propositions which contain further propositions within them. Boethius gives an example of the implicit affirmation of a contrary. 'That which is good is not good' implies that 'that which is good is bad'.[124] The notion is taken up and developed in several treatises of the later twelfth century, for example the *Ars Meludina*:

Implicita dicitur propositio que preter principalem significationem . . . tamen implicit et continet vim alterius propositionis.[125]

If we say that *Socrates est aliquid qui currit*, we imply that 'something runs'. The *Tractus Anagnani* says that an implicit proposition contains the propositions into which it can be resolved.[126]

All these refer to sentences with relative clauses: Socrates is 'something which runs'. In 'the man who runs is discussing', 'who runs' is the *implicatio*. It is understood to restrict or narrow (that is, to make more precise) the range of reference of the term 'man'. This makes sense in terms of Priscian's teaching; the *nomen*, which together with its verb is equivalent to a participle (*currens*), has an adjectival function which restricts the reference of the term 'man' to the 'running' man.[127]

Were this the only sense in which the notion of implicitness in propositions could be taken it would be of limited help to our exegetes. But the treatise edited as the *Tractatus Implicitarum* includes clauses containing *solum, tantum, incipit, desinit, nunc primo, nunc ultimo*. There is a *general* idea of implicitness here,[128] which is of great assistance in elucidating the sometimes obscure text of Scripture.

8 No meaning on their own

The most renowned and influential of the masters who lectured on the work of the Roman grammarian Priscian, who was used as an advanced textbook for the study of grammar in the middle of the twelfth century, appears to have been Petrus Helias.[129] His lectures were more than a commentary. They summarise and assess the current opinions on each technical difficulty and provide a resolution. Petrus Helias's alertness to the topics of contemporary debate encourages him to concentrate upon precisely those points at issue between *grammatici* and *dialectici* which gave rise to disagreements about the fundamentals of the theory of language and its function. 'We grammarians say that every *dictio* is a part of speech', he reports, following Boethius, 'but according to the dialecticians there are only two parts of speech: that is the noun and the verb.'[130] This disagreement threw the other 'parts of speech' into a brief prominence because it made it necessary to determine their status. Thus grammarians and dialecticians alike were obliged to consider the powers of signification of prepositions, conjunctions and adverbs,[131] in a similar way to that already seen in the remarks of William of Conches on these *sincategoremata*.

In his *Dialectica* Peter Abelard asks whether prepositions and conjunctions have 'any meaning by themselves'. He believes that they must, or else they would be nothing more than collections of letters or syllables.[132] Nevertheless, it is not easy to see what exactly their *significatio* is.[133] If a listener hears 'and' or 'of', he waits for something to follow to complete the sense.[134] On their own, prepositions and conjunctions often have significations which are *confusae* and *ambiguae*. This is only as it should be. They are designed to be used in many different contexts.[135] Abelard does not find it easy to clarify the matter further. He is obliged to concede that there are many things we understand but are not able to put into words, which belong in some way to the deep structure of language.[136]

He does, however, set out clearly from the dialectician's point of view the differences between the grammarian's view of the matter and that of the dialectician. The grammarians say that in such expressions as *de homine*, the preposition points to the thing (man) and not to the word 'man'.[137] Abelard's own opinion is that this would make the use of cases superfluous. If the word *homo* points to the man, and *de* tells us that we thinking 'about' the man, there is no need for *homo* to take the form *homine*. On the contrary, *homine* already contains within it the sense of the *de* and the *de* must therefore be taken to refer to the word, not to the thing.[138] In this he is following the dialecticians, who hold with Boethius[139] that the noun and the verb are the only true parts of speech and that the others are merely supplementary (*orationis supplementa sunt*). The *de* in *de homine* is fulfilling no very important role in signifying in the strict logical sense (Abelard's *significatio per se*).[140]

But this is not to remove from these lesser parts of speech all possibility of signifying. They do, Abelard is sure, signify *per se*,[141] but only so as to determine certain properties of the things to whose words they are attached: *quod quasdam proprietates circa res eorum vocabulorum quibus apponuntur praepositiones, quodammodo determinent*. Thus, when I say *de homine* or *pro homine*, the prepositions *de* and *pro* designate certain properties which are 'in' a man. In the case of conjunctions, too, some property is 'determined', as when I say 'The man and the horse run', I show that they are *simul in cursu*, running as one.[142] Abelard's description of the limited and dependent power of signifying of these lesser parts of speech appears to have been in tune with what was held by the dialecticians of the twelfth century in general. The author of the *Ars Emmerana*, for instance, cites Boethius' dictum that prepositions and interjections are not parts of speech but *colligamenta*. They are connections between parts of speech, not categories; *consignificantia* not *significantia*.[143]

Petrus Helias tells us that many of his contemporaries reduced the number of these lowly parts of speech considerably; they take 'noun' so largely (*ita large accipiunt*) as to include in the class of nouns not only pronouns (adjectives are already classified as nouns by the Roman grammarians) but also adverbs. Into the class of verbs, taken similarly 'largely', fall the participles which form the eighth part of speech. It is on this view, he says, that the dialecticians teach that only nouns and verbs signify.

Setting aside the interjection, which falls in a class of its own, this leaves us with prepositions and conjunctions. Standing on their own (*per se probatae*), says Petrus Helias, they convey nothing to the understanding, but only when they are joined to others. This is why the dialecticians speak of them as 'connected' or 'joined up' parts of speech (*colligamenta partium*). Petrus Helias prefers to speak of *absolute* and *non absolute*; nouns and verbs make a complete *oratio* by themselves (*per se complent orationem*), prepositions and conjunctions do not. They merely co-predicate (*sincategoremata*) or co-signify (*consignificatio*).[144]

The adverb sits uncomfortably in the class of nouns. It is naturally associated with the verb (*poni cum verbo*), so as to show how the verb 'does' or 'suffers' (*modum agendi vel patiendi*). Following Priscian, Petrus Helias would like to group it loosely with prepositions and conjunctions among those words which are as a rule dependent upon their juxtaposition with others to render them significant, but capable in some cases of signifying on their own, and thus entitled to be counted among the parts of speech. The conjunction stands apart from prepositions in its turn because it is never compounded (*componitur*) with verbs (other than participles) as the preposition and the adverb often are.[145] As well as discussing them separately, Petrus Helias treats these three as a group.[146] For this last type of con-signification there is a parallel in a commentary on Priscian in Vienna MS VPL 2846:

In alius significat cum iungitur ablativo et aliud cum iungitur accusativo. Et coniunctio aliud [significat] cum est copulativa et aliud cum est disiunctiva.[147]

One thirteenth century writer makes a list of the *modi significandi* which are found in the parts of speech. Words, he says, contain things signified and consignified and modes of signifying, whereas things exist by 'modes of being' (*per modos essendi*), from which the 'modes of understanding' (*modi intelligendi*) in words proceed. He pursues the parallel between the 'modes' of existence of 'things' and the modes of signification of words as far as he can, dividing modes of signification into 'general', 'special', and of 'special' into 'essential' and 'accidental'. When these principles are applied to the parts of speech we find that the *modus significandi essentialis generalis* of the noun is to signify 'by the mode of substance' (*per modum substantie*). The mode of signification of the pronoun is to signify *per modum substantie*, but without *distincta qualitas*, whereas the noun signifies 'by the mode of substance' with a distinction of quality of this sort. The verb signifies *per modum motus*. The participle *per modum motus* but not *distans a substantia*, because it embraces both *actus* and *substantia*, without that separation from the substance which we find in verbs. The adverb 'determines' the verb absolutely, because it 'has no more respect to one verb than to another'. The conjunction signifies by saying how two *extrema* are joined. The preposition says what the *circumstantia* is. The interjection 'determines with respect to the verb' (*determinare respective verbum*).[148]

Without entering into those areas of doctrinal discussion in which from the earliest Christian centuries a preposition had lain at the centre of the doctrinal difficulty (Does the Holy Spirit proceed 'from' the Son as well as the Father? From the Father 'through' or 'by' the Son?) we can begin to see something of the application of all this in early scriptural commentaries. Alcuin discusses the problem of prepositions in his commentary on Heb. 1:2 (*novissime diebus istis locutus est nobis in Filio*). *In* is the exact equivalent of *per* in this passage, Alcuin argues, so that the meaning is that the Ancient of Days spoke to us *through* the Son. He cites 'many places' in Paul's Epistles where these two prepositions are used interchangeably (*indifferenter uti*),[149] but for a technically sophisticated treatment we must wait for the work of the twelfth century. In his *Regulae Theologicae* Alan of Lille asks how each part of speech in turn is to be regarded when it occurs in speaking of God, first nouns and verbs, and then adverbs and prepositions. Not all his illustrations are taken from the Bible but they show something of the spirit in which the Bible was likely to be read by men trained in the works of Priscian and Boethius. Alan himself, a product of the schools of northern France in the middle decades of the century, drew directly upon the work of Petrus Helias, and upon Gilbert of Poitiers and others among Abelard's contemporaries, too. His emphasis is exactly that of Thierry of Chartres in a remark on the form of words (*formula verborum*) by which Augustine seeks to explore the doctrine of the

Trinity; *in Patre unitas, in Filio unitas, in Spiritu Sancto unitatis equalitatisque conexio vel concordia.*[150] Augustine, says Thierry, wants somehow to insinuate (*insinuare*) what cannot be spoken.[151]

Adverbs, Alan explains, can be used with some degree of propriety (*proprie*) of God because they denote various circumstances or relations which are used in describing the substance of the Divine Being: *notant enim varias circumstantias, sive relationes, quae de Deo dicuntur secundum usiam.*[152] Every adverb of place (*adverbium locale*) said of God predicates the divine immensity: to say that God is *unique* or *alicubi* is not to place him but to say that he is beyond place.[153] Similarly, adverbs of time ('today', 'tomorrow', 'yesterday') predicate the divine eternity when they are used of God.[154] Adverbs denoting likeness (*quasi, sicut*) signify the substance of the Divine Being in different ways. Sometimes they refer to his true essence: 'We see his glory as of the only-begotten of the Father' (John 1:14), where *quasi* points to the true being of the Son who is indeed, not merely 'as if', the only-begotten of the Father. Sometimes there is an implied comparison or likeness: 'Just as the Father has life in himself, so he gives it to the Son to have life in himself' (John 5:26), where *sicut* points to the comparison. Sometimes there is an impropriety. Here Alan's memory fails him and he misquotes, conflating Dan. 7:9 and Ps. 77:65: *Antiquus dierum sedebit iudicans quasi crapulatus a vino.* Had this indeed been a scriptural text, there would certainly have been an implied impropriety in a *quasi* which compared the Ancient of Days with a drunkard. Lastly, Alan lists the *adiunctio* where, for example, the Father is said to be the *principium* of the Son, just as he is said to be the *principium* of the Holy Spirit; here, *sicut* behaves almost like a conjunction.[155]

'Similarly', says Alan, 'prepositions have *variae acceptiones* in theology.' The preposition *in*, for example, sometimes denotes identity of essence and plurality of persons (*Filium est in Patre*); sometimes a *quasi diversitas*, as when we say *Deitas est in Patre*, not meaning to imply that there is any difference between the Deity and the Father, for the Father is the Deity and the Deity is the Father. 'But it is as though a certain transition is denoted, when the preposition is placed there by apposition' *sed quasi quaedam transitio notatur, cum ibi praepositio per appositionem ponatur.* Sometimes *in* has an eternal predication, as in John 1:3–4. (Alan quotes: *Quod factum est, in ipso vita erat.*) That is, it is as if John said that in him, through eternal disposition of things, lived everything which was to be. Sometimes *in* refers to an efficient cause, as in 'in him were all things made'; *in* here is like *per*. Sometimes *in* has to do with a formal clause ('when he was in the form of God . . . ' Phil. 2:6). Sometimes, as when it is said that before the beginning of the world God was *in se* and *apud se*, *in* denotes identity.[156] Alan proposes similar variations for *secundum*.[157]

Alan worked out and made a list of some of the *variae acceptiones* of the *sincategoremata* in Scripture in his dictionary of the theological terms. He finds examples where *a* denotes (*notat*) place, time, eternity, the source of authority, origin or birth, procession from, separation, partition. *Apud* sometimes denotes place, sometimes person, sometimes the inherence of a property, sometimes identity, sometimes diversity.[158] *Contra* sometimes denotes contrariety, sometimes the presence of something, sometimes material, sometimes the inherence of a property in something, sometimes with or in a person (*coram*).[159] *Cum* can denote the plurality or diversity of things, the authority or dignity of the thing to which it is joined, contrariety, identity, abundance of a property, possession, being in the same place, being at the same time, a particular time, conformity of nature, the utility of something, authority.[160] *Praeter* can be used for near, to exclude or to include. Each has its scriptural text.[161]

It is clear that these are special usages, peculiar either to talking about God in such a way as to maintain doctrinal orthodoxy at whatever cost to normal grammatical usage, or to Scripture itself. Alan takes it for granted that the text as he quotes it is to be regarded as constituting an invariable standard. He does not discuss possible variant readings, or corruptions. He sees his task as being to explain it as it stands, in the terms of reference of the study of grammar, modified as it seems that scriptural exegesis demands.

Nowhere is the application of these discussions about the signification of prepositions and conjunctions and adverbs in scriptural and theological usages more fully worked out in the later twelfth century than in Peter the Chanter's *De Tropis Loquendi*, with which we shall be concerned in detail later (chapter 10). Peter the Chanter, precentor of the cathedral of Notre Dame in Paris (d. 1197) is best known for his preacher's manual, the *Verbum Abbreviatum*, and for his *Summa de Sacramentis* and *Summa Abel*.[162] Only the preface to the *De Tropis Loquendi* has been edited.[163]

Peter the Chanter was a grammarian and an exegete above all, although he had an up-to-date knowledge of the theory of fallacies. He draws upon Andrew of St Victor's commentary of between 1150 and 1163 on the literal sense of the Octateuch.[164] This interest in literal rather than figurative exposition encouraged him to avoid, in general, the solution of contradictions in Scripture by simply taking one or both of the contradictory texts in a figurative sense, in favour of a close scrutiny of their grammatical structure.[165]

In his preface Peter describes the dimness of that perception of the Divine which is possible to sinful man, and which makes it seem that Scripture contains contradictions. These 'contrarieties' are of several kinds. Sometimes Jesus spoke to unbelievers in what appeared to be a contradictory way, and then explained his words to his disciples later when he was alone with them (Matt. 21:25). Sometimes both *contraria* and *similia* are given in Scripture to encourage us to be on our guard; the contraries or contradictories so that they may be resolved or despatched to what seems *similia* so that they may be distinguished from one another, the truly *similia* so that their likeness may be demonstrated. For help in each of these cases we have Augustine, Gregory and Jerome.

There can be no question but that the *auctor* of the Scriptures was truthful, or that its writers did not in reality contradict one another. 'For truth is not contrary to truth' (*cum verum non sit contrarium vero*). Peter proposes to use dialectical methods – especially the detection of *sophismata* – as indeed he does in the latter part of the treatise.[166] But he is at bottom a grammarian as well as a dialectician, and he begins with grammatical attempts to reduce the *superficialis contrarietas* of words in a *unitas* of sense (*sensus*), so that in that way Scripture may be shown to agree with itself at every point. His list of those places where contradiction may be found puts great emphasis upon signification: *ex variis significatione dictionis; ex varia consignificatione*.

It is not without significance perhaps that Peter the Chanter mingles adverbs, prepositions and conjunctions in his discussion;[167] they have in common for him variability of signification, a variability which distinguishes them from even the most equivocal of nouns or verbs.[168] In the case of *sicut*, he is able to find the following senses,[169] all fine shades of *similitudo*:

1. *Diliges proximum tuum sicut te ipsum* (Matt. 19:19; cf. Mark 12:31; Luke 10:27). Here, *sicut* refers not to a similarity between the love I have for myself and that which I have for my neighbour, but to a single end or purpose (*finis*) in both. I must love my neighbour not 'like' I love myself, but 'just as' I love myself, that is in exactly the same way.

2. *Estote perfecti sicut et pater vester perfectus est* (Matt. 5:48).

Here there is again not a simple comparison between the way in which we are to be perfect and the way the Father is perfect. *Sicut* points to an imitation which is attempted from a great distance (*imitatio remota*).

3. *Sicut pater operatur et ego operor* (John 5:17; 10:15). Here, *sicut* denotes complete equality between Father and Son (*omnimoda equalitas*).

4. *Volo ut sunt unum in nobis sicut et nos unum sumus* (cf. John 17:11). There, the comparison is between human unity, which is a matter of mere union and *conformitas*, and the unity of the Godhead which is true *unitas*. In addition, Peter is able to list instances where *sicut* is used in place of *per* or *propter* or *et* (that is, *pro copulative conjunctione*), or to denote commensurability.

The preposition *secundum* receives similarly full treatment: it is used to denote *adiunctio* instead of *in*, to denote the divine power, or conformity, or the order in which something is to be understood, or the appearance of things, or proportion, or a reversed comparison (*similitudinis per contrarium*), or imitation. Peter the Chanter's examples here are often extraordinary scriptural usages, and he is forced to devise explanations well beyond the range of normal grammatical and dialectical explanations. *Praeter*, for example, is discussed by the dialecticians as being sometimes *localis* in its force, sometimes *exclusiva*, sometimes *additiva*.[170] Or it may come between the noun for a thing which does exist and the noun for a thing which does not, although this is a 'trivial usage' (*nugatorie*).[171] Peter the Chanter is able to add both common usage (*ambulans praeter mare*, walking by the sea, where *praeter* is used instead of *iuxta*), and a scriptural example, where *praeter* occurs instead of *super*: *Putatis quod ipsi debitores sint preter omnes habitantes in Ierusalem.*[172] He can furnish for every preposition, adverb and conjunction which he discusses something extraordinary of this kind by way of signification. *Ne*, for example, is a conjunction which can be used for *ut non* or for *ut* or for *si*.

Peter was not adding to the technical expertise of contemporary grammarians and dialecticians on the subject of signification. He was merely applying an existing system to the interpretation of Holy Scripture. The interest of his attempt lies in the extent to which he is obliged to modify, to create special cases for special usage. He deals, at a detailed level, with a problem drawn out by Alan of Lille in the opening remarks to his dictionary of theological terms. Alan notices that in Scripture all the rules of ordinary usage are turned upside down. Nouns behave like pronouns (where it is usual for pronouns to stand in place of nouns); adjectives behave like substantives. The construction of a sentence is not subject to the laws of Donatus.[173]

It appears that each master lecturing on the Bible was doing pioneering work for himself. (In Alan's dictionary the examples and the variants for each of the *sincategoremata* are different,[174] but that is where the growth receives its stimulus.) The problems posed for grammarians and dialecticians alike by the language of the Bible defy reduction to a few simple rules. They require a pioneering spirit in the reader who seeks to resolve them, and so we see hard thinking and experiment pushing forward the technical boundaries.

7

TRANSFERENCE OF MEANING

1 Similitudes and analogies

It was common doctrine that a likeness to help him understand (*similitudo*) is the best that can be made available to man when he seeks to know God. It is a device employed by God himself as author of Holy Scripture. 'The angels have the truth; you have a likeness', says Peter of Celle. The 'likeness' is the way to the truth. The mind may travel from what it understands easily and directly to what it can understand only by a 'sideways' or 'upwards' movement of comparison. If you believe you have a likeness and not yet truth, he promises 'you will come from the likeness to the truth'.[1]

The term *similitudo* came readily to mind because of the Genesis account of the creation of man in the 'image and likeness of God' (Gen. 1:26). In this connection the difference between *imago* and *similitudo* seemed to many commentators to require clarification. Sometime earlier, in the late eighth century, Alcuin had suggested a simple and patristic explanation in his *Quaestiones in Genesim*. The *imago* is eternal; the *similitudo* is not eternal, but a matter of *mos*, behaviour, for a man may 'behave like' God or he may not.[2] Hugh of St Victor takes a similar line. Man is the image of God in his very appearance: *imago est in lineamentis similibus*. The *similitudo* is a matter of 'participation in some divine property' (*in cuiuslibet eiusdem proprietatis participatione*). It can be lost to a man; it is variable, changeable, fleeting.[3]

The point is discussed in a more technical way, and with a slightly different emphasis, in a Carolingian gloss on the *Categoriae Decem*. The gloss comments on a passage derived from Aristotle's description in his *Categoriae* of the equivocal use of the word 'man' to describe both a picture of a man and a real man.[4] 'What likeness can there be said to be between God and man?' the commentator asks. A painted man and a real man are both called 'man'; they share a common name, but they do not share a common definition, *nomen aequale est, sed diffinitio aequalis non est.*[5] Similarly the soul has its image and likeness to God (the equivalent of having the same 'name') but it is not fully and really equivalent. The 'likeness' consists in that rationality and intellectuality of nature by which – as far as is possible to him – man knows himself and God.

The principle of *similitudo* is, then, built by God into the very creation. Man is designed to make the necessary movement from what he can directly and properly understand, to the higher things God wants him to understand. The *similitudo* or analogy does with 'things' what the word does when it is used in a 'transferred' sense so as to make the comparison which is implicit in every metaphor. (Augustine had already used the term *signa translata*, *De Doctrina Christiana*, I.ii.2.) 'Things' act as 'signs' by a process of borrowing or transfer which fits them for their new use.

Ernald, abbot of Bonneval, writes at length on *similitudo* in his second homily on Ps. 132:2. He brings out not only this grand purpose of the *similitudo* but also its humbler role in helping the understanding, and its function as a literary device where it is used merely as an ornament. He takes the text 'like an anointing oil on the head, which runs down into the beard': *sicut unguentum in capite, quod descendit in barbam.* Every *iota* or *apex* of this psalm is important, he says. *Sicut* is a *nota similitudinis*, an indication that a likeness is being drawn. He points out that the similitude is familiar to the theologian in its three typical uses: for decoration (*propter ornatum*); when an analogy is used so as to make something easier to understand (*commodum ad facilitatem intelligentiae*); or when it is employed out of necessity, because there is no other way of making something clear.[6]

It is the last of these which is important for the way it tests and stretches the very possibility of there being an analogy in the created world for such divine mysteries as the Incarnation, the Virgin Birth, the properties of the Trinity:

Necessitas quoque aliquoties cogit dari similitudinem in his dumtaxat quae etiam viros acris ingenii solent exercere,'et acutissimos sensus reddere impeditos.

Ernald says that the use of analogy out of necessity in this way is especially proper among theologians; other disciplines as well as theology make use of *similitudines* for their less essential purposes, to adorn what is said and to explain obscurities, but analogies are used in theology (and *a fortiori* in the Bible) because it would be impossible to convey (*insinuare*) these deep truths by open reasoning (*asperta ratione*).

In the *similitudo* with which he is concerned in interpreting, verses

1 and 2 of Psalm 132, Ernald finds all three present. In verse 1 we have 'How good and joyous it is for brothers to dwell together in unity.' Here there is beauty in the words (*urbane satis et eleganter*) where the Psalmist has introduced *bonum*, leaving 'like you' to be understood, and 'joyous', leaving 'like an unguent' to follow. Since the reference may be obscure to the simple – or even to those who are more intelligent – the Psalmist subjoins a *similitudo* so that his meaning may be more easily understood ('like an unguent upon the head running down into the beard'). But there is a third reason for the use of this analogy. A mystery is revealed here. The *unguentum in capite* is the divinity in Christ the man. Ernald investigates the beard. A beard is something which does not feel (*impassibilis*); it is above the whole body (*toti corpori praeeminens*); it is attached to the flesh (*carni adhaerens*); it grows from the flesh (*de carne incrementum accipiens*); but it is placed beneath the head. In this it resembles those high beings, the heavenly spirits, who are *impassibiles*, who stand in eminence (*privilegio praeexcellentes*) above the body of the whole Church in dignity, and who cling to the Word which was made flesh in an everlasting love.

The *similitudo* derives its 'necessity', then, from the fact that without it the deepest meaning of the biblical text remains unintelligible. In scriptural exegesis it does more than provide a picture to help the slow of understanding with a difficult passage; it helps the mind to penetrate into the things which lie beyond its normal scope. It forms the basis for all the figurative devices found in Scripture. It is the vehicle by which God signifies that which is beyond the powers of signifying of ordinary human language.

One type of figure would seem to fall into a class of its own. This is the *similitudo* which depends for its force not upon a putative likeness between the thing compared and the thing with which it is compared, between creature and Creator, but upon the perception of a similar relationship of parts. Gerhoch of Reichersberg uses the device in his *De Gloria et Honore Filii Hominis*. Just as (*sicut*) the Creator by an act of will (*voluntarie*) gave rise to us (*genuit*) by the Word of Truth, so that we might be the beginning of his creation; so (*ita*) by an act of will he begot (*genuit*) the New Man 'who was his Son and the Word', for 'the Word was made flesh and dwelt among us' (John 1:14).[7] The comparison here is between the patterns of events, the general shape or structure of the two things compared, as much as it is a comparison between the Old Man and the New Man.

'Structural' analogies such as this were used in patristic times to portray the relationship between the Persons of the Trinity. The sun emits light and heat without (it appeared to ancient man) being itself diminished. It would be hard to say where the light and the sun part company, or where the heat becomes light. Yet we recognise clearly that sun, light and heat are different.[8] This analogy was taken up and developed by Anselm of Canterbury. He made it encompass the Incarnation, by drawing a parallel with the way in which the sun's rays strike a prism or lens through which they can be directed on to a piece of wood so as to kindle it. The wood burns and is consumed. The lens is unaffected. Just so was the divinity of Christ made human through the Virgin Mary. She remained a virgin. The human flesh of Christ was able to die.[9] Anselm also adapted an image of Augustine's, describing the Trinity in terms of a river which comes from a spring. In Anselm's version the river Nile flows from its source into a lake or pool. The water which flows throughout the whole watercourse is the divine essence, and although it is clear to us that spring, river and pool are different, we cannot tell exactly where one ends and the next begins.[10]

These analogies could be controversial if they were pressed so far that they broke down. Anselm found the Greeks difficult to persuade that the Holy Spirit proceeds from the Father and the Son just as the pool comes from both the spring and the river. They pointed out that, if his analogy was to be taken to be exact, he was saying that the Holy Spirit proceeds from the Father through the Son, for the pool comes from the spring through the river.[11] With misgivings of his own, Peter Abelard discusses Anselm's Nile image in his *Theologia Christiana*. There has, he says, recently been a new use of Augustine's *similitudo* by Anselm, but it seems to imply a temporal succession of some sort in the procession of the Holy Spirit.[12] Abelard tries to expose the deep structure of the analogy, to see how far it may be of help in illuminating the 'structure' of the Trinity. He concludes that it is only from the Father that the Spirit can 'properly' (*proprie*) be said to proceed by this analogy, for the pool comes not 'from' but 'through' the river.[13]

Abelard's own principal contribution was the analogy of the wax seal. Here problems of signification-theory arise as well as difficulties over exact parallels in the structure. In a wax image the image is related to the wax as *materiatum* to *materia*, that is, as the thing made of matter is related to the matter from which it is made. Yet we speak of the image as if it were the wax when we refer to 'the wax image', so that it may be said that 'the image is wax' (*quod imago cerea sit ipsa*). Thus through predication (*per praedicationem*) we associate the image and the wax.[14] The analogy allows us to say that the wax and the image made by the seal are both identical and different, if we pay attention to the use of the words (*nomina*) for 'wax' and 'wax image'. They must be taken to be said not relatively (*relative*), but *absolute*, each word signifying in its own right, even though they are conjoined by predication so that they refer to the same substance of the wax. Thus when the wax is yellow and the image is accurate it is one and the same thing to say that the yellow (thing) is accurate or the accurate is yellow. But we cannot use interchangeably those terms (*nomina*) which refer to the generation or constitution of the wax image from the wax, and which are used relatively as *materia* and *materiatum*. We cannot say that the wax comes from the image though we can say that the image comes from the wax. If we now apply these principles to divine generation it is easy to see how they support the orthodox doctrine of the Trinity. Divine Wisdom, the Son, is from Divine Power, the Father, as the wax image is from the wax; the derivation runs only one way; the Power and the Wisdom are nevertheless the same, in something of the way that the wax and the image are the same.[15]

Several points of technical interest emerge. Abelard suggests that if we take the relation of the word and what it signifies in one way (*absolute*), a statement may be read in one sense, whereas if we take it another way (*relative*), the relation between word and thing signified yields another meaning. In this way irreconcilables may be present in a single statement and both be true. 'It is therefore not surprising if from this sort of discretion of the Persons these names [of Father and Son] are separated from one another by predication, although they also signify relations which join them (*copulent*)'.[16]

Such devices for reconciling contradictions were to be taken up and developed by later twelfth century scholars. As we shall see, pp. 161–2, Peter the Chanter includes the *materia/materiatum* principle in his own list, as well as the *continens* and *continentum* principle already noted by Bede, and other such pairs.[17] For him, as for Abelard, it proves to be impossible to discuss these analogies without the discussion of the language in which they are expressed obtruding its own technical difficulties; analogies, like the larger class of *similitudines*, remain a branch of signification-theory.

2 Figures of speech

Similitudes and analogies are a prime type, but only *one* type of figurative language. In his commentary on Genesis, Hugh of St Victor asks why Satan is called a serpent there. Satan put on the form of a serpent as if it were a garment (*eum quasi tunicam induerat*), but in mockery (*derisorie*). The usage is such as would be employed if a thief dressed up as a monk so that he could steal undetected among the monks of a house, and when he was caught in the act was derisorily called a 'monk' by those who had apprehended him.[18] In calling the Devil a serpent, the Bible ascribes to him the attributes of a serpent. This is a *historia metaphorica*, a metaphorical story. Similarly, the statement 'You will be like gods, knowing good and evil' is a mockery (*irrisio*); it is readily identifiable as a figure of speech, a *sarcasmos figura*.[19] Rupert of Deutz refers in a similar way to an 'ironical usage'.[20]

'When words taken literally give an absurd meaning', says Augustine, 'we ought forthwith to enquire whether they may not be used in this or that figurative sense which we are unacquainted with . . . in this way many obscure passages have had light thrown upon them.'[21] 'I would have learned men know that the authors of our Scripture use all those forms of expression which grammarians call by the Greek name "tropes", and use them more freely than people who are unacquainted with the Scriptures, and have learned these figures of speech from other writings, can imagine or believe.'[22] Augustine's immediate purpose in making these assertions was to convince his educated readers that the authors of the books of the Bible wrote not with the crudity and rusticity which he himself had thought he found in their pages when he was a young man, but with skill and polish, using all the figures of speech in the rhetorician's armoury. This identification by name and in detail of the use of *schemata* and *tropi* in Scripture persisted beyond the period when every educated man was something of a rhetorician. Cassiodorus gave classic expression to the Augustinian position in the Preface to his commentary on the Psalms. The holy profundity of the divine Scriptures has common expressions (*communes sermones*) so that everyone may receive it, but its meaning is hidden (*arcanum*) so that it must be sought for. It hides its mysteries in many ways, making use of definitions and syllogisms and figures.[23] These are beautiful, but not as in an ordinary use of such decorative stylistic devices, where the figures add an outward loveliness; for here the Divine Word itself confers beauty upon the figures.

Isidore lists *schemata* and *tropi* in his encyclopaedia among the aspects of grammar, along with barbarisms and solecisms. *Schemata* he identifies as 'figures' (*figurae*), 'which occur in words or sentences through various forms of words, for the sake of decorating what is said'. The trope is a 'way of speaking' (*modus locutionum*); it involves a transference, literally a 'bending' or 'turning' from 'proper signification' to some similitude which is not 'proper' (*ad non propriam similitudinem*).[24] These he applies to the study of Holy Scripture. In his *Quaestiones in Vetus Testamentum*, for example, he refers to the figurative usages of Scripture, those things 'which are figuratively said and done in it'.[25] He is aware of the subtlety of their application, how 'not everything which is written in the Law and the Prophets is shrouded in the enigmas of mystery'. Some parts are straightforward in their meaning. In a musical instrument not all the parts sound, but only the strings. The strings must be anchored to the fixed parts of the instrument, just as the figures of Scripture are 'anchored' by the parts with literal meanings.[26] Gregory the Great continues the tradition, in passages such as that where he describes Scripture as a mountain from which the Lord comes down into our hearts to bestow understanding. The mountain is shrouded in mystery: *condensus . . . per sententias*; *umbrosus . . . per allegorias.* If a man approaches the holy mountain like a beast, abandoned to irrational urges and therefore unable to interpret it correctly, he will be pelted with hideous incomprehensibilities (*atrocissimae sententiae*) like stones.[27] The mountain gives up its secrets only to the faithful, for whom the meaning of the figure is plain.

The first attempt after Augustine to set out the Bible's figures systematically was Bede's, in his *De Schematibus et Tropis*. The Greek word *schema*, he notes, means *figura* in Latin.[28] He repeats Isidore's distinction: the figure has a decorative function; the trope or *tropica locutio* involves a transference of meaning in which a word or expression is shifted from its proper meaning (*propria significatio*) to a likeness or comparison (*non propria similitudo*).[29]

The list of figures identified by some of the later Roman and Carolingian authors of rhetorical manuals is enormous. Bede selects from the 'many kinds of schemes and tropes' one, the metaphor, which is 'the most widespread of all', and then lists a number of others[30] commonly found in Scripture. These he illustrates in detail from the Bible. *Prolepsis* or *preoccupatio* involves a reversal of natural order, as in Ps. 86:1–2: *Fundamenta eius in montibus sanctis, diligit Dominus portas Sion.* Here the Psalmist first speaks of 'his foundations' and only afterwards tells us whose they are.[31] In *zeugma* oe *coniunctio* a long series of words or phrases depend on a single word or phrase or clause, as in Eph. 4:31: 'Let all bitterness and wrath and anger and clamour and evil speaking be put away from you, with all malice.'[32] These, as Bede says, are devices used solely for adornment, but he goes on to consider the tropes, which actually alter the signification of words and expressions.

The metaphor may involve a transference from one animate being to another, as in Ps. 2.1, *Quare fremuerunt gentes*, where 'the people' roar like a lion; or a transference which makes an animate thing out of an inanimate, as in Zech. 11:1, *Aperi, Libane, portas tuas*, where 'Lebanon' is asked to open its gates. When in Amos 1:2 we read of the withering of the top of Carmel we have a transference from inanimate to animate. In Ezek. 11:19 there is a transference from inanimate to animate in the reference to taking away a heart of stone. Metaphors are also, says Bede, used of God in many ways, in references to birds, wild beasts, parts of the human body (Isa. 40:12: 'Who has measured the waters in the hollow of his hand'), human emotions (Ps. 2:5: 'And he spoke to them in his anger'), inanimate objects, and so on.[33]

Katachresis is an abuse (*abusio*) of a noun or verb, making it signify what it fails to signify in its proper *appellatio* (*quae propria appellatione deficit*). It differs from a metaphor in that it constitutes an expansion or extension of the word to mean more than it strictly ought: we call a man who kills his brother a parricide; a pond with no fish in it is still called a 'fish-pond'. If Scripture had not imposed such words on things (*si Scriptura praefatis rebus non imposuit*) they would not, properly, signify them. A *metalepsis* is a saying which gradually moves towards its meaning, insinuating it, as in Ps. 103:26. 'That leviathan whom thou hast formed to play therein', is, says Bede, the Devil, but he is to be understood to have been made by God as a good angel.[34] *Metonymy* is a form of *transnominatio*, by which a signification is transferred to one close to it. Thus the container stands for what is contained, or the contained for the container, as in Gen. 24:20, with its reference to pouring out the water-jars; it is not the jars but their contents which are poured out. Similarly, the discoverer may be given for what is discovered or the cause for the effect and vice versa.[35]

Antonomasia involves the use of a word or expression instead of a name. In 1 Kings 17:4, Goliath is described as a man of six and a half cubits high, and we understand that he was a giant from the description of the size of his body.[36] In the *epitheton* the name is left out altogether as in Ecclus. 45:1, 'Beloved before God and men', which can refer only to Moses. *Epitheton* and *antonomasia* are similar, but in the first the name is absent and in the second something else serves in place of the name.[37]

Synechdoche is a signification which refers to the whole by a part.[38] *Onomatopoeia* is a name which represents a sound, such as the *tinniens* of 1 Cor. 13:1, which itself sounds like the clashing of the cymbal it describes.[39] *Periphrasis* or *circumlocutio* involves an oblique or circuitous way of speaking of the subject in hand.[40] *Hyperbaton* disturbs the order of the words for effect, in various ways.[41] *Hyperbole* is exaggeration.[42]

Allegory is defined here as a 'trope which signifies something other than what is said', as in John 4:35, 'Lift up your eyes and look on the fields, for they are already white for harvest', which means the people are ready to believe. It has the following seven types in Bede's list:[43] irony is a trope which says the opposite of what is meant, as does *antiphrasis*, but irony conveys its meaning by the tone of voice, whereas in *antiphrasis* there is some actual contrary stated in the words;[44] *enigma* is an obscure saying, containing a hidden comparison;[45] *charientismus* is a trope by which something mild is said as though severely; *paroemia* is a proverb adapted to fit the context;[46] *sarcasmos* is mockery prompted by hatred not humour;[47] *asteismus* is a multiple trope (*tropus multiplex*), its principal characteristic is that it makes a simple statement with polished urbanity.

All these allegorical tropes sometimes involve actions and sometimes words. Abraham had two daughters, one by a slave and one by a freedwoman, which are the two Testaments. This is an allegory not of words but of facts. In Isa. 11:1, 'There shall come forth a rod out of the stem of Jesse', the allegory is in words. Sometimes the allegory is in both words and actions. In Gen. 37:28 the actual pieces of silver for which Joseph is sold are an allegory. In Zech. 11:13 the allegory in the reference to thirty pieces of silver lies in the words.[48]

Although the principles which underlie these devices were useful to them at every point, the classical technical terms for the *schemata* and *tropi* were comparatively little used by mediaeval exegetes, with certain exceptions: notably *metaphora*, which Bede himself singles out for special mention as the most important of the *tropes*. Alcuin, writing in Eccles. 1:7, says that in this talk of the river returning to the sea we can perceive a metaphor for those who return to the earth from which they were taken, that is, mankind (*possumus . . . per metaphoram homines intelligere*).[49] It is not inappropriate, says Haymo of Auxerre, to understand metaphorically by the head (which has a kind of royal dominion over the members of the body) and the heart (where learning and wisdom reside) the princes who rule the people and the learned.[50] Elsewhere he notes that the prophet 'keeps to the metaphor' (*servat metaphoram*).[51] Hugh of St Victor speaks of *hyperbolica locutio*.[52]

In the case of *schemata* it is not difficult to understand why the habit of identifying each type should lapse in a period less concerned with the rhetorical aspects of grammar. Their purpose, as Bede describes it, is to adorn what would otherwise be less elegantly said.[53] They are merely decorative. The trope modifies ordinary usage more dramatically. It involves a shift of signification away from what is usual (*propria*), so as to make a comparison (*ad non propriam similitudinem*) and thus it lies at the heart of the work of the interpreters of the eleventh and twelfth centuries in their concern with the technicalities of signification in Holy Scripture.

Here a new technical terminology began to develop from the established vocabulary of ancient rhetoric. The most important of these for our purposes is the term *translatio*, a term already found in the rhetorical textbooks of the late Roman world. In Iulius Victor, for example, we find the explanation that words are often used in a 'transferred' sense because no word exists for the thing to be referred to, and a word has to be adapted. Words, he says, are also used in this way to enliven the writing, that is, for the sake of ornament.[54] The explanation became something of a commonplace.[55] The principal rule is that 'transference' ought to take into account the appropriateness of the real meaning to its metaphorical usage: we may say that the sea is in a fever and be readily understood,[56] but it would be less than illuminating to say that a cabbage is in a fever. As Robert of Melun puts it: 'The mystical signification is assigned by all the doctors of Holy Scripture to things and not to words.'[57] The *res* is the fixed point of reference. The meaning of the word may shift from 'thing' to 'thing'.

The technical term *translatio* is sometimes used by the ninth century controversialist Godescalc of Orbais and his contemporaries,[58] especially in connection with the need to adapt or borrow words, shifting their meanings where human language is inadequate. This is always the primary use of *translatio* in exegesis. Even though there is talk of the beauty of scriptural language it is not generally thought to be principally for the sake of adornment that such transference of usage goes on, but because human language is not adequate to talk about the Divine.

The thinking behind the use of the term is perhaps most clearly set out by John Scotus Eriugena in the treatise *De Divina Praedestinatione Liber* which he wrote about 850–1 against Godescalc. Eriugena was one of a number of Irishmen working on the Continent in the ninth century. Despite his position as head of the cathedral school in Paris, in many respects he was something of an isolated thinker, with interests beyond those of his contemporaries, in aspects of the Neoplatonic thought which were for the most part in abeyance among would-be philosophers. But, in his grasp of technicalities of argument and in his theory of language, his interests were very much those of his contemporaries.

He addresses himself to the question in terms not dissimilar from those of Aquinas four centuries later.[59] He asks whether words which signify the limitations inseparable from created things can be used literally of God, or only by way of comparison. He considers, in other words, the problem of analogy. Can we say something about God as he is, or must we always talk in terms of what he is 'like' amongst the things we are capable of understanding? The words 'foreknow' and 'predestine' imply time. To foreknow is to know earlier in time what is to happen later in time. To predestine is to cause to happen in the future. But it was common doctrine since Augustine and Boethius that none of Aristotle's categories can apply to God except that of substance and perhaps relation, as when we speak of the Divine Fatherhood or Sonship.[60] There is no quality or quantity or condition or situation or place about God, and, equally, no time. 'Now the text of the first question requires us to consider whether God is said to have foreknown or to have predestined properly (*proprie*) or improperly (*abusive*)'.[61] Eriugena's contention is that nothing can be worthily (*digne*) or properly (*proprie*) said of God, but that God provides signs (*signa*) so that the *laboriosa egestas* of human reasoning (incompetent as it has been since the Fall of Adam clouded men's minds with sin) may use them, and in that way somehow 'the rich sublimity of the Creator' (*copiosa conditoris sublimitas*) may be in some way believed and hinted at.[62] As to the actual words of human language, if they are not natural signs (*secundum naturam*) but invented at the whim of men (*ex complacito hominum inventa*), it is not surprising that they are unable to express that nature which alone is truly said to 'be'.[63]

Nothing said of God, then, can be taken quite literally. Everything involves *translatio*. Eriugena thinks that this may take place, broadly speaking, in three ways, or according to three topics. Here he seems to be drawing directly or indirectly on Cicero's *Topics*, or perhaps on Boethius' commentary on Cicero's *Topics*. Cicero described the topics as 'seats of argument' (*sedes argumentorum*). The Roman orator was taught to collect material for his speeches in the form of examples and illustrations on the one hand, and condensed or 'pattern' arguments on the other. The former came to be thought of as 'rhetorical' *topoi* or *loci* and the latter as 'dialectical'. Boethius composed a monograph on the difference (*De Differentiis Topicis*).[64] The orator built up his argument by drawing from these stores the 'seats' or 'starting-points' he wanted. Cicero lists a number of standard patterns for arguments, amongst them arguments from likeness (*a similitudine*), from contrariety (*a contraria*) and from difference (*a differentia*). When Job said, 'Your hands made me' (*Manus tuae fecerunt me*) (Job 10:8), for example, he spoke *a similitudine*. God does not make things with his hands as human craftsmen do.

The topic used in speaking of God's 'foreknowledge' of or 'predestination' to evil is the argument *a contrario*, as in 'the wisdom of this world is foolishness before God' (*sapientia huius mundi stultitia est apud Deum*) (1 Cor. 3:19). There we perceive dimly the greatness of God's wisdom by placing the best of worldly wisdom beside it and seeing that it is folly. Thus, if we recognise that a comparison is being made between temporal things and the Divine, we can see clearly *a contrario* how great is the difference between 'eternity' and 'time'.[65] 'Foreknowledge', 'predestination', 'prevision' and all such terms are 'predicated of God transitively' (*translative de Deo predicari*)[66] and that is how we must understand them when we hear that God 'predestines' or 'has predestined' or 'has prepared' sin and death or any other evil. We must understand what is said entirely *a contrario*, otherwise a heretical wickedness will carry us away.[67]

In this way Eriugena is able to distinguish between statements that God has predestined the elect to salvation (where 'predestine' is a temporal usage *a similitudine*), and statements that he has predestined the wicked to damnation (where 'predestine' is a temporal usage *a contrario*). Then he moves on to arguments *a differentia*, which enable us to distinguish between predestination and foreknowledge – for, says Eriugena, God foreknows everything which he predestines, but he does not predestine everything he foreknows.[68]

In his reply to Eriugena in defence of Godescalc, Prudentius of Troyes discusses the problem of differentiating between one form and another of predestination and foreknowledge. When Godescalc subdivides them, he says, he claims that there are two 'seats of meaning' (*sedes significationum*) used in a transferred way (*translatae*).[69] The scholars of the ninth century lacked the vocabulary to make the technical distinction of the twelfth century between supposition and signification. Lacking this advanced signification-theory, which might have helped them in their differentiations of meanings, our scholars could speak only of *significatio*, and Prudentius claims that in his attempts to distinguish meanings, Eriugena has been led astray. 'In this, while you follow the dialecticians and rhetoricians, you wander far from the truth', he accuses him. 'You wish to understand that God foreknows and predestines only what is good, and that he neither knows nor predestines what is evil; no one before you has been found to have presumed to this perversity.' Thus, in a way which makes it plain that he understood the technicalities perfectly, he refers to Eriugena's distinction between cases where we are to read statements about divine predestination *a similitudine*, by analogy, and cases where we are to read them *a contrario*, as meaning the opposite of what they say.[70]

Godescalc himself speaks of the 'transferred' use of one term for another. 'Foreknowledge' is sometimes used for 'predestination', he says,[71] citing Augustine's *De Dono Perseverantiae*. Hincmar, writing against him, quotes the same work of Augustine. He defines predestination in terms of *praescientia* and *praeparatio*:

Haec est praedestinatio sanctorum, nihil aliud, praescientia scilicet et praeparatio beneficiorum Dei, quibus certissime liberantur quicunque liberantur.[72]

Hincmar was not a technician of the order of Eriugena; nevertheless he displays a grammarian's habits. His concern is to refute Godescalc's contention that predestination is twofold (*gemina*). He tries to make a close study of the word itself, its *rectus sensus* or correct meaning according to the catholic faith, with careful comparisons of apparent pluralities in the Fathers that are intended to be no such thing.[73]

Godescalc had not, it seems, been saying what Hincmar claimed. He defends himself indignantly. To say that predestination is twofold is not to say that there are two predestinations ('perish the thought').[74] It is like saying that charity is twofold and yet one. His body, *exterior homo*, and his soul, *interior homo*, are not two but one. In a similar way, the predestination of God is the mercy by which the elect are freed and saved and the truth by which the wicked are justly judged and condemned is twofold, but still one.[75] Godescalc, too, can quote cases where the Fathers have said that something is *gemina* or indeed *quadripartita* or *quinquepartita*.[76] We are dealing simply with a case of usage, *a genus locutionis usitatissimum*.[77]

If we compare this discussion with its twelfth century equivalents we can see that many of the same assumptions are in force. According to Magister Bandinus, a pupil of Peter Lombard's, such words as *splendor, figura* are said of God *per translationem* in such a way that the 'proper' or literal meaning of these nouns is not expressed, but rather some spiritual sense.[78] Bandinus gives a table of the ways in which language may be used of God by transference. When we speak of God's *splendor*, we compare him to 'brightness' as we know it in this world, and thus we speak of him *per similitudinem*. Such expressions as *splendor, sapientia, virtus, veritas* refer to God as One; others refer to the Persons specifically, but they all refer to God *sempiterne*, always. A further group of transferred usages refers to God *extempore*, in relation to time. We may speak of God as 'Creator', that is, relatively to the temporal created world; or we may speak of one Person only in this way, as *donatus, datus, missus*. Bandinus's classification goes on to place the word *Trinitas* in a category of its own,[79] as the word which refers neither to the essence of God, nor to the Persons individually, but collectively to all three Persons.

3 The four senses

Augustine was not the originator of the fourfold division of the 'senses' of Scripture into literal, allegorical, anagogical and tropological. Clement of Alexandria and Origen have a claim there,[80] but together with Gregory, Augustine was perhaps the principal transmitter to the Middle Ages of the notion that there is more than one 'higher' sense.[81] He says that we learn by analogy that there is no contradiction between the Old Testament and the New. By aetiology we understand for what reason a deed or a saying (*factum vel dictum*) is present in the text. Allegory teaches us that something is not to be taken literally.[82] 'In all the holy books', he explains, in another, fourfold division, one ought to try to see what eternal things are intimated there, what things are related as having been done, what future things are foretold, what we are instructed to do.[83]

As we have seen in chapter 4, Thomas of Chobham's *Summa* of preaching begins by looking at the three ways in which one 'thing' is understood through another (*per unam rem alia intelligitur*). One thing is understood through another in a tropological way when it is made to convey moral instruction (*moralis instructio*) or when by *transumptio* 'night', for example, signifies sin and 'day' signifies virtue. One thing signifies another in another way, allegorically, by changing the subject, as in 'Come, my bride, my beloved'. Christ says this to the Church and thus the subject is changed, for through (*per*) the 'bride' of the flesh is understood the spiritual 'bride'. The word *allegoria* is sometimes taken more generally to cover all three figurative senses, but, says Thomas, this is its strict sense. One thing signifies another in yet another way, when something of heavenly things is understood as concerning God and the angels and the saints in glory; that is the anagogical sense, for *anagoge* means *sursum ductio*, a leading above.[84]

The study of the four senses is not our principal concern here, but something must be said briefly about the distinctive types of 'signification of things' they were believed to involve.

I ALLEGORY

In the multiplication of the figurative senses, the allegorical remained the primary and most important one in certain respects. The term *allegoria* has scriptural authority. St Paul speaks of *allegoroumena* in Gal. 4:21.[85] It had long been standard practice to regard the whole of the New Testament as embodying that which is spoken of allegorically in the Old Testament. The habit of reading the Old Testament on this principle was, for Origen, one of the distinguishing marks of the Christian way of reading Scripture as opposed to that of the Jews. 'If anyone wants to hear and understand these things strictly literally, he ought to address himself to the Jews rather than to the Christians, but if he wants to be a Christian and a disciple of Paul, let him hear him saying "For the Law is spiritual", and when he speaks of "Abraham" and his "wife" and "sons", let him pronounce these to be allegorical.'[86]

The term *allegoria* had currency among secular authors,[87] as well as among Christian authors[88] and, despite Origen's remarks about the literalness characteristic of Jewish exegesis, in the writings of the Jew Philo of Alexandria references to *allegoria* are much in evidence. As its use became the commonplace it long continued to be in Christian exegesis, the link with literary usage was maintained and explored,[89] so that, as we have seen, all the figures a secular poet might use were looked for and many of them identified in the text of Scripture.

II THE ANAGOGICAL SENSE

If the figurative explanation goes beyond words into things, at no point does it proceed so far as in the anagogical sense, where we are at the furthest remove from the ordinary world where human language is adequate. The anagogical sense looks not only upwards to heavenly things, but also onwards to the future, from this world to the world to come. What do we call *anagoge* if not the mystical and upward-directed understanding of things above the heavens?[90] It is the *sensus de superioribus*.[91] Prophecy will often require an anagogical interpretation.

Haymo of Auxerre gives a conventional definition of prophecy.[92] Prophecy is divine inspiration, which demonstrates the outcome of things, through visions or through deeds or through the sayings of certain men, with an unchanging truth:[93] by visions, as in Ezekiel and Revelation; by deeds, such as Abraham's sacrifice of the ram, and Jacob's blessing of Joseph's sons Manasses and Ephraim with his hands crossed; by sayings such as we read in Moses' writings or in the Psalms. Sayings may be inspired by Grace (as in Moses) or by 'permission' as the sibyl and the philosophers of the gentiles, who foretold many things of Christ under divine prompting. Prophecy is characteristic of the Old Testament, not of the New; only the Apocalypse in the New Testament can be called prophetical in the strict sense of the term.[94]

Gregory the Great, introducing his first homily on Ezekiel, suggests that prophecy may refer either backwards or forwards in time, and that its task is to 'unveil' what is hidden; but he concedes that this is a sense of the term 'prophecy' which affronts etymology, and his definition includes what is figurative in the widest sense.[95] Prophecy, properly, is confined to those figurative meanings which point forwards.[96]

This 'prophetic' function of the anagogical interpretation is by no means the highest. There are things which can be learned only by experiencing them, Cassian notes.[97] Pseudo-Dionysius suggests in a comment quoted by Aquinas that they somehow 'happen' to us: *non solum discens sed et patiens divina*.[98] Gregory the Great speaks of the 'sublime and unknown methods of interior speech' which have nothing to do with the tongue's utterances. Such 'speech' is the method of communication used by spiritual beings. When God spoke to the Devil, in the episodes recounted in the Book of Job, he did so by a secret visitation of his mind, and the Devil's answers were not spoken, but simply read by God in his mind, for he was not able to conceal anything from God.[99] Man is not purely a spiritual creature and finds such interior speech difficult. It is easier for him to use his tongue and to speak aloud in words, but he has some power to understand spiritual things, and this is the power which is developed in him by the habit of looking for the spiritual sense of Scripture which lies beyond its words.

In what way can the reference of the anagogical sense be beyond words? Every sign, whether it is a word (*nomen significativum*) or itself a 'thing', signifies a thing. In allegory, the thing signifying – an object or being within the natural world such as a lion – is used to suggest something beyond the natural world in which, it is implied, certain of the lion's properties are to be found, in a higher, super-natural way, but nevertheless, recognisably the same properties. The Lion of Judah in his nobleness and regality and courage is Christ; but he is not Christ in being yellow and four-footed. In an allegory there is thus a point-by-point correspondence between analogy and analogue which extends a certain distance and no further. In the anagogical sense the comparison is not so direct and mechanical. It involves several stages of removal from the original sign, and even then it is not to be arrived at by simply being methodical, although a methodical approach is helpful. When Peter of Celle wrote his mystical and moral exposition of the Tabernacle of Moses, he explained at the outset that: 'The tabernacle which we have planned to expound is not made with hands, that is, it is not of this creation, but it is wonderful, heavenly, spiritual, angelic, everlasting. Let us nevertheless set before our eyes that earthly tabernacle of Moses, built by earthly labour and, transferring our attention from visible to invisible things . . . go up towards the East, singing, "Blessed are those who dwell in thy house, Lord".'[100]

There are many mechanical aids to be had, although they must be used with care. Some of them are likely to lead the reader astray, for as Peter says: 'If you wish to behold the house of Pharaoh, of Nebuchadnezzar, the habitations of the princes of this world, depicted with unspeakable subtlety, collect together trees from the forests of the poets . . . you may construct from reading them the luxurious brothels of the gentiles, not the holy temples of the Christians.'[101]

The sensible exegete will make use of simple comparisons. In human contracts, Peter points out, although there are many different types of contract and just as many different intentions on the part of

the contracting parties, it is always the case that something is pro-
posed to which both parties agree in making the contract. For
example, in buying a horse, the two parties agree on a price for which
it will be handed over by one to the other. Or, if you build a house for
me, it is proper for me to pay you an agreed price. Something is given
and something received on both sides. It would be a rare contract in
which the benefit of only one party is considered. If we turn to the
text where God instructs the children of Israel to make him a
sanctuary, there must surely be a price which God gives for the work.
Indeed, there is, but it is not a fixed price. Scripture says, 'I will dwell
in the midst of them'; but God's habitation among men cannot be
fixed.[102] Peter has led the reader from a consideration of a common
practice with which he is familiar to see in what respects God's acts
transcend and in what respects they fit common experience. There is
method and comparison and even the use of analogy in the anagogic
exposition, but there is something more.

Cassian was one of the first Christian thinkers of the Latin West
to try to describe in one of his talks to his monks the quality of that
contemplatio by which the anagogical or spiritual meaning of Scripture becomes clear to the reader by some process not solely intellectual, but involving an actual experience of it. Man's task is to fix the
eyes of his mind upon God as steadily as he can, bringing his attention back to this 'straightest line of the mind' when it strays.[103] There
are many proper objects of contemplation which will help to keep the
mind there,[104] not only God himself, but all the gifts he gives to man.
We can train our concentration and learn to control and dispel
unruly and unwanted thoughts by frequent reading of Scripture, by
meditating upon Scripture, by frequent singing of Psalms, by vigils
and fasting and prayers.[105] Daily reading will bring us to a progressively greater illumination.[106]

III THE TROPOLOGICAL SENSE
AND THE BENDING OF SIGNIFICATION

In examining the literal or historical sense of Scripture the mediaeval
reader is concerned with decisions about the signification of the
words. In looking for the figurative senses he searches beneath the
surface of the words for the things they signify according to some
adapted usage which gives them a different import from their usual
literal one. In a general way this may be described as *translatio* whatever kind of figurative sense it involves, but the shift or transfer is different in each of the three principal figurative senses. In allegory the

movement is sideways, from one thing in the created world to another. In anagogical interpretation things take an upward turn in their significations, so that, as Thomas of Chobham puts it, they signify 'The Church triumphant, heavenly things such as God and the angels and the saints in glory.'[107] Tropology, on the other hand, involves a substantially different adaptation of normal usage, a deliberate 'bending' to make it instructive about human behaviour. This 'bending' sometimes goes so far that it is difficult to see the application without the interpreter's help. Gregory the Great throws down challenges to his readers, as though he defies them not to see at once the moral application of Job's words. 'What else is this but . . . ?', he asks.

The monastic scholar and younger contemporary of Anselm, Guibert of Nogent, shows clearly what this 'bending' process entails. Guibert wrote a brief treatise on the way to preach[108] as a prologue to his moral exposition of the Book of Genesis. This little manual full of common-sense advice indicates that he saw preaching as an exegetical exercise[109] just as Augustine and Gregory had done before him. Nevertheless, he was conscious that he had entered upon a task which others might see in a different light. In *Proemium* addressed to Bartholomew, bishop of Laon, he refers to the brothers Anselm and Ralph of Laon in order to explain that he takes a humble view of his own powers in comparison.[110] He knows that certain criticisms have already been made of his own work, especially where he seems to disagree with Augustine or to try to replace what he says.[111] It is in order to have legitimate scope for his own reflections that he has chosen to concentrate upon the moral interpretation of Genesis in which it is allowable to explore by reasoning.[112] Guibert is very much aware of the bounds of the various interpretations ('I would have added a number of points about allegorical meanings, if I had not feared to make the work too long.')[113]

The moral sense gave him scope; he was able to make fresh discoveries about the application of Scripture's teachings to man's behaviour. When he speaks of 'taking' an example (*sumamus itaque veracis historiae in exemplum*) he is able to see it as something by which 'while we discover [its] secrets', we reveal 'instruments' (*instrumenta*) for our own use.[114]

Guibert begins by pointing to the opposition within man between the flesh and the spirit, the earthly and the heavenly part. This, he says, makes us perpetually divided against ourselves. The existence of the division ought to come to mind when we read that: 'In the beginning God created heaven and earth.' Guibert explores and develops the text in detail.[115] For example, we might examine the difference it makes if, when interpreting 'And the darkness was upon the face of the abyss', we take it literally or not. Literally it would mean: 'Above the depth of water' which is properly (*proprie*) called the 'abyss'. Taken figuratively (where the 'abyss' stands allegorically for the human mind) *super* would not mean 'above' or 'over' or 'upon', but 'more than', 'greater than' (*plusquam*).[116] Reading further in this spiritual vein, we may say that the 'earth' produces 'grass' (Gen. 1:11) when the heart of the faithful, clean of worldly desires, sends out shoots from the seeds of the Word of God (*verbi Dei semine conversationis initia emittit*).[117]

There is a certain natural order in the progression of the levels of interpretation. Alan of Lille speaks of the 'leaves' of history, the 'flowers' of allegory and the 'fruits' of tropology.[118] It is as though the reader progressively learns to understand not merely what is before his eyes in the historical sense, but what divine truths are spoken of allegorically, and then to apply what he learns to his own behaviour in the tropological sense. 'Holy Writ is set before the eyes of the mind like a kind of mirror', says Gregory on Job, 'so that we may see our inward face in it. For therein we learn about our deformities and our beauties.' It accomplishes this reflection by putting the examples of others before us; we are stirred to follow their example, and helped to resist the vices ourselves by the realisation that they have fought the battles we are now fighting against the vices and have conquered them.[119] Thus history is bent to the purposes of tropology. Gregory envisages this harmonious interconnectedness of the Scriptures as something like a stringed instrument. When one chord is touched, a very different one, which may not be adjacent, begins to vibrate, and when the latter string is touched the first vibrates, without the others being struck at all. It is in this way that Scripture often deals with the various virtues and vices, mentioning one thing only but 'by its silence' irresistibly bringing another before us.[120] 'The Bible speaks to us as to beings brought forth in time. It is appropriate that it should use words which signify time, so that, by coming down to our level, and relating something which belongs to eternity after the manner of time, it may gradually transfer to the eternal world those who are used to time and need help to accustom themselves to think eternally. Thus we are not led to the eternal world at once, but by a progression of cases and words, as though by steps.'[121]

Every art, says Cassian, in a collation on spiritual knowledge, has its own fixed and proper lines along which it proceeds.[122] How much more must this be the case for the *disciplina* and *professio* of our religion? Here there are two aspects to be considered: the theory and the practice.[123] The theoretical side involves us in the study of Holy Scripture in two ways, historical or literal interpretation, and spiritual interpretation, of which there are three kinds, tropological, anagogical and allegorical.[124] History deals with the recognition (*agnitio*) of things visible and things past, allegory with those things which *in veritate gesta sunt*, which have really taken place, but which prefigure the form of some other mysterious thing.[125] The tropological is a moral explanation to help us in living a better life in a practical way.[126] The anagogical sends us on a journey 'from spiritual mysteries to certain more sublime and more holy secrets of the heavens'.[127]

The process of reaching the higher spiritual understanding thus involves a progress through all the other senses, with tropology giving the consummation on the practical side and anagogy on the theoretical side,[128] and so we find the four senses are one.

The unity of the four senses is emphasised by many authors. Richard of St Victor, for example, notes that Scripture says many things to us in one: *Scriptura multa nobis in unum loquitur*.[129] Nowhere is this doctrine more fully worked out in the twelfth century than in Rupert of Deutz's exegetical tour de force, the *De Trinitate et Operibus Eius*. He divided it into three parts. The first, which was concerned with the Old Testament, was a study of the work of the Father; the second, on the New Testament, was a study of the work of the Son. In the third part he comes to the work of the Holy Spirit, drawing freely upon the whole of Scripture. He explains that on the day when man ate from the forbidden fruit he became mortal; the old creature was damaged. On the day when he believes in Christ and is baptised he becomes a new creature at once in his soul, and his body will be renewed on the day of resurrection.[130] God the Father, we are told, 'ceased' from creation on the seventh day (Gen. 2:2–3). It does not follow that the Holy Spirit ceased too. It was the property (*proprium*) or special work of the Father to found the natural world, but it is the *proprium* of the Holy Spirit to bring nature to something better (*meliorare naturam*) and his work of improvement goes on. The Son acts as a *medium*, for the Father created through the Son (*per filium*) and the Spirit re-creates *per Filium iam hominem factum*, through the Son who is 'now made man'.[131] This process of re-creation is intimately connected with the Bible. 'When, therefore, we read the Holy Scripture we deal with the Word of God; we have the Son of God *per speculum et in aenigmate* before our eyes', that is, to be seen dimly and through a mirror. Truly, concludes Rupert, if we attend carefully to the text, we are inflamed by reading or hearing and we make progress towards the love of God, and what is this love of God but the Holy Spirit?[132]

This educative and re-creative work of the Holy Spirit upon man's reading of the Word of God consists precisely in the enlargement of the soul's perception of the depths beyond the literal and surface appearance of the sense. The soul becomes a spiritual paradise, as Christ's soul is a paradise: *paradisus deliciarum Dei [anima] facta est.*[133] A process is going on here which Gerhoch of Reichersberg sums up in a culinary image; it is as though the 'meal' of the Word of God were being cooked in a vessel so as to make bread which is free from all leaven of heresy and vainglory.[134]

The architectural references to be found throughout Scripture were readily interpreted so as to reinforce this picture of the structural unity of the four senses. Noah's Ark, the Tabernacle, the Temple of Solomon, cities, temples, citadels, their windows, walls and doors and roofs, their fortifications, lend themselves to spiritual interpretations. The relation between 'edification' and 'edifice', the building-up of the fabric and the spiritual building-up is explored from Augustine[135] to Bernard of Clairvaux.[136] 'The Temple of God grows through silence' in the human mind, explains Peter Damian, writing on 1 Kings 6:7.[137] 'Unless the foundation of history is laid beneath, upon which the walls of allegory ought to be erected and the roof of tropology (that is, the moral or anagogical understanding), ought to be placed, the whole edifice of the spiritual understanding will collapse', says Peter of Poitiers.[138] Giraldus Cambrensis emphasises the importance of the walls and roof in preserving the foundation. The foundation is frail and useless, soaked with rain and soft with mud and easily broken up, unless the structure of walls and roof strengthens and protects it.[139]

PART III

'DISPUTATIO'

8

QUESTIONS

Out of the work of the glossators of the twelfth century who lectured on the text phrase by phrase arose new and numerous questions about the text of the Bible. Some of them were trivial, or asked in a spirit of contentiousness – questions of the sort of which Hugh of St Victor strongly disapproved. But some, as Abelard's pupil and successor Robert of Melun protests, were constructive and useful. He explains that while questions are sometimes a source of doubt (*causa dubitationis*), they are sometimes a means of instruction (*causa docendi*),[1] a sensible way to learn.

Of such a kind are the *Problemata Heloissae*, a series of questions which his able former pupil Heloise sent to Abelard for his guidance because she herself had not been able to answer them for her nuns. He replied to them for her in a way designed to be straightforwardly helpful to the community. He had sensible advice for her about the usefulness of the study of Greek and Hebrew and he recommended her to look to Jerome as a model (for Jerome believed that holy women best occupied their minds in the study of the Scriptures).[2]

Some of Heloise's 'problems' turn on nothing more than an obscurity in the text ('What is the Lord saying in . . . ?').[3] Some of them involve apparent contradictions. In Matt. 12:40 we read, 'Just as Jonah was in the belly of the whale for three days and three nights, so shall the Son of Man be in the heart of the earth for three days and three nights.' How is that to be reconciled with the fact that the Lord was taken down from the Cross and buried on a Friday, and lay in the sepulchre that night and the following night, and was resurrected on the sabbath before three days and three nights had elapsed? Abelard's answer is that this period falls within the span of three days and three nights, so that if we count a day and a night as a unit the two accounts coincide.[4] A similar difficulty arises out of the discrepancies in the accounts of the resurrection appearances in the Gospels.[5] Again, why did Jesus say when he took the wine at the Last Supper, 'This is my Blood of the New Covenant', and not make a similar reference to the New Covenant when he took the bread in his hands and said, 'This is my Body'?[6] In curing the leper (Matt. 8:2) Jesus touched him; why did he thus break the law?[7] These are acts or sayings in which there appears to be something unfitting or contradictory, and which inescapably raises questions, for it is a first principle of mediaeval exegesis that there can be nothing contradictory in Scripture.[8]

While he was still a pupil of the leading theologian of the first years of the twelfth century, Master Anselm of Laon, Gilbert of Poitiers composed a commentary on the Psalms. When he had completed it he submitted it to his master's judgment so that it could be corrected where necessary (with a humility we do not associate with the mature Gilbert).[9] Peter Abelard also came, briefly, to hear Anselm lecture, but his response to this venerable Master of Theology was different. He describes how he came to hear Anselm at a time when he had decided to move from dialectic and himself became a teacher of theology. He found Anselm like a tree which appears fertile enough from a distance, but which, on closer inspection, proves to carry nothing but bare branches. He challenged the old man, promising to lecture on Ezekiel the very next day, although this book was noted for its difficulty.[10] There was no humble submission to correction. Abelard went his own way.

Nevertheless, he learned something perhaps from Anselm of Laon, and if not from him directly, from those numerous contemporary masters of some standing who had been his pupils.[11] Anselm had been pioneering a new method of exegesis, not perhaps with any intention of innovation, but in an attempt to meet a need which arose when he was lecturing. Questions were raised in the course of the exposition, some of them traditional ones, to which the Fathers had already given an answer of sorts, but others no doubt suggested afresh or for the first time by Anselm's pupils. William of Conches in his *De Philosophia Mundi* is one of many witnesses to the controversies which divided his contemporaries. 'Almost everyone says that . . .'[12] he remarks of one such contentious issue, implying that it was generally discussed.

Anselm of Laon tried to answer the questions which arose by assembling patristic opinions under headings. We do not know how these 'Sentences' were used, whether Anselm broke off his exposition and dealt with the question as it came up, or deferred its consideration until later, as we know was the custom in the later twelfth century;[13] but their survival in a number of collections suggests that advice on certain topics was referred to or looked up conveniently whenever they arose – as a number of questions must have done in more than one place in the exposition of Scripture. Something not dissimilar is to be found in the Abelardian *Sententiae Parisienses*. A term such as *sacramentum* is defined and scriptural and other texts are used to support and illuminate the points made.[14]

The spirit of Anselm of Laon's collections is clear enough. We are told that there are some things in divine Scripture which, although they seem to be contrary to one another as the words sound (*secundum hoc quod verba sonant*), to those who understand them properly it is clear that they are not opposed.[15] These exercises in reconciliation were to be the first of a long line of systematic attempts to settle often very substantial questions arising in the course of the exposition of the Bible.

Their content, in Anselm of Laon's work and that of his immediate circle, is chiefly drawn from the Fathers, but some logical connection, some orderliness of treatment, was required if they were to serve the purpose for which they were compiled, and it is not a long step to questions of the type we find in Peter Abelard's commentary on Romans or his exposition of the Hexameron. In discussing these, Abelard includes a great deal more argument and he tries to arrive at a conclusion, so that his pupils may be brought to a definitive view which they can defend. The *quaestio* becomes at times almost a little treatise. In his discussion of 'a few points' which have arisen concerning circumcision – what it may confer or signify, and why it was instituted in the genital members, and in those of the man not the woman; and why it was ordered to be carried out in infants and on the eighth day[16] – Abelard proceeds in a methodical way as though he were writing a self-contained piece.

Sometimes the *quaestio* looks more like an answer given on the spot to a specific question which has been raised: 'Why, then, you say, was it appropriate for those men to be baptised who were already beforehand just, by the faith or by the love which they had, and who, if they died in that condition would certainly have been saved?'[17]

There is, then, no uniformity in the treatment or in the form of the *quaestio*, but if Abelard's answers and discussions are read in the context of the whole commentary it is clear that he has one consistent purpose in mind. He wants to ensure that the reader misses nothing of importance, is left with no unresolved difficulty. The linear progression through the text is still the vehicle. Abelard does not remove his questions and make a list of them for separate consideration. He regards them as integral to the commentary.

This produces a close-textured treatment by which the reader is carried steadily along. 'It should be noted', says Abelard, 'in this very beginning of Genesis, that the prophet has carefully made explicit (*diligenter expressisse*) the foundation of our faith concerning the unity and Trinity of God.' Abelard explains that in saying *spiritus Domini* Moses distinguishes clearly between the Person of the Holy Spirit and the Person of the Father, and notes that Augustine has said as much. In adding 'God said', Moses points clearly to the Word, who is the Son. Again, where our Latin text has 'God created' the Hebrew has a plural word (*Eloim*) for 'God' to indicate the plurality of the Persons, for *El* means 'God' and *Eloim* is its plural.[18]

Abelard's pupil Robert of Melun had reservations about the incorporation of too much material into the running exposition. In the Preface to his *Sententiae* he says that he finds it pretentious to overlay the text with quotations and explanations beyond what is strictly necessary, and that in any case it has the reverse effect of making what is said not more, but less, profound.[19] His own *Quaestiones de Divina Pagina* have been taken out of the context of running commentary in which they arose; they are full of variety.[20] Someone had asked to whom the Lord spoke, priest or people, when he said: 'If you forgive men their sins, your heavenly Father will forgive you your sins, too.'[21] Someone else had asked whether the wicked can sometimes do good or the good sometimes do evil, for Matt. 7:18, 'A good tree cannot bear evil fruit', and Matt. 7:20, 'By their fruits you shall know them', and other texts, seem to suggest a consistency in these matters which is belied by experience.[22] Other questions ask what is meant by Matt. 24:22 which suggests that 'unless those days were shortened all flesh would perish',[23] or what is meant when it is said that the angels 'carried' Lazarus into the bosom of Abraham, or that angels 'carry' our prayers to God.[24] Some questions (1, 13) are answered in a sentence, others at greater length, but many of them are of this relatively trivial sort; questions – not necessarily merely idle questions – asked out of curiosity perhaps, but distinctly of the kind Robert seems to have had in mind when he complained of excessive elaboration in commentaries where too many such questions were included.

A not dissimilar approach is to be found in Simon of Tournai's *Disputationes* of the second half of the twelfth century. 'In today's disputation three questions arise.' Is servile fear good or evil? What is the use of fear? Is there initial fear in unbelievers?[25] In all these cases the sequence of scriptural exposition is over-ridden and questions arising are grouped together for discussion. Simon's seventy-ninth Disputation, for example, covers four questions arising out of a first: is it true what is said in the Creed, that what the Father is the Son is also? (*Qualis Pater talis Filius.*) *Disputatio* 80 has six questions: Can virtue be lost through venial sin? Is someone corrupt in mind but not in body, still a virgin? Can the loss of virginity be restored through penitence? Will all mankind be resurrected virgin at the Last Judgment? In marrying Joseph did the blessed Virgin break her vow of virginity? *Disputatio* 82 has seven questions on excommunication, and so on.

Robert of Melun's one hundred and twenty-five problems are not arranged in any order, but each question follows a consistent pattern. The questions begin with *queritur*, and there is normally a *solutio*. We have not yet arrived at anything close to Aquinas's fixed order of treatment, beginning with the posing of the question, followed by the case for the opposition, then the correct answer to the question, and ending with replies to the points made by the opposition. Odo of Soissons, like Simon of Tournai, prefers the order: *quaestio, solutio, oppositio*. Odo likes to pose the question, reply to it, explain what the opposition says, reply to the opposition, and then to make a 'determination' of the problem. In Odo's *Quaestio* 58, for example, the question posed is whether a greater sin is followed by a greater penalty. Odo's view is that, on the contrary, a grave penalty follows the least of sins if it is not corrected (*non emendatum*). His opponents, who believe that a greater penalty follows a greater sin, point to a paradox. They argue like this (*sed insistent*): the sin of Adam was followed by a penalty both temporal and eternal; the sin of Judas was not. The sin of Adam was a starting-point for all punishment (*quasi occasio*); the sin of Judas was not. Therefore it seems that the sin of Adam was greater than the sin of Judas, which it was not. In his *determinatio*, Odo distinguishes between the penalty which follows in the person of the sinner and that which follows in a way which is outside this person (*extra personam*) and so he gets round the difficulty.[26]

The *Quaestiones* attributed to Odo of Soissons represent an important stage in the development of techniques of Bible study in the Middle Ages when methods of resolving the problems which arise in the course of the reading were first being systematically explored. They are a product of the schools of mid-twelfth-century

Paris. Composed, it seems, soon after Peter Lombard's *Sententiae* were published, and by one of Lombard's pupils,[27] they stand between Robert of Melun's pioneering collection of brief *Quaestiones* and answers and the more elaborate *Disputationes* of Simon of Tournai.

By the time of Simon of Tournai, who may have been Odo's pupil,[28] we find what may have been an almost daily session for discussing problems (*disputatio*), organised perhaps in the manner which Peter the Chanter describes in his *Verbum Abbreviatum*. A regular hour was set aside in the afternoon and all discussion of *quaestiones* was deferred until then.[29] Odo's *Quaestiones* were composed at a point when the resolving of questions was becoming a serious business, requiring a knowledge of the technical skills of the *artes*. They are innovative and exploratory in their method. In the working out of the answers we have one of the earliest experiments in the exercise which Aquinas was to bring to so high a degree of polish.

A few of the *Quaestiones* of Odo resemble the *Sententiae* of the 'school' of Abelard's master Anselm of Laon in tone,[30] as though they are the work of a master quietly expounding the problem to his class. They have the same reflective air, the same gentle prompting to 'Note', 'Note here' (*ibi est notandum, notandum, nota*). The master is not answering questions raised in any numbers or with any persistence by his pupils, but dealing as it seems with the odd difficulty as it arises. There is little of the *disputatio* about the exercise here. To take an example from the *Sententiae* of one of Anselm of Laon's circle and Abelard's other master, William of Champeaux:

> It is asked (*Queritur*) why, since lust is really in the begetting parents and not in the son who is begotten, perdition does not lie in the lust of the parents who have it, rather than in the son who does not have it. Reply (*Responsio*): through the sacrament of marriage and because of the intention of begetting, the actual lust in the parents is a venial sin, which, since it is the 'efficient cause' of the son who has been begotten, passes on the 'effect' of perdition.[31]

Odo's *Quaestio* 38 (*De Sacramento Eucharistiae*) has a similar tone. It is simply a short exposition of doctrine on the Eucharist. Several questions are asked in the course of the explanation. Some ask, for example, what has happened to the bread, since before the consecration it was, and now it is not. Some say that, like the dove in which the Holy Spirit appeared, it is resolved into elements when its job is done (*expleto officio*). For if the bread were to disappear it would seem that injury had been done to a creature. This seems to Odo a superfluous question, *sed nobis videtur hoc superflue quaeri*, since it is agreed what became of it: it turned into the body of the Lord. That cannot be said to be an injury to any creature, for the body of Christ is that than which nothing is better.[32] *Quaestio* 39, on the coming of Christ, is another such exposition. The main points are set out, then the questions are dealt with. It is asked, concerning those who are to be saved, whether they are to remain in Purgatory until their sin is fully purged; or is perfect remission given them at once, so that they enter heaven immediately? *Dicimus quod*, 'We say', says the master (in the royal plural which is common usage in such cases), that they are to be resurrected with the rest of mankind, given their immortal bodies, and then placed in Purgatory until their sin is fully purged. More questions arise: will the evil which the good have done be as apparent as the good the evil have done? (cf. Ps. 31:1); will cut finger-nails and hair be restored at the resurrection? (Matt. 10:30); what is to be done about the restoration to Adam of his missing rib, which became Eve? (Gen. 2:22).

Despite the proliferation of questions there is still little of the air of *disputatio* about this kind of *Quaestio*. There is no debate: merely the settling of difficulties in the students' minds by a master who expects his words to be authoritative. The difference between *Quaestiones* treated in the manner of Anselm of Laon's *Sententiae* and those which have been subjected to *disputatio* seems to be the answering back by the student, questioning his master further. The appearance of such pointers as 'but they insist' (*sed instant*) marks the presence of a contentiousness in the classroom which we do not find in the *Sententiae* of Anselm of Laon and his fellows.

Although it is probable that the context within which pupils normally raised their questions was the glossed reading of the Bible in class or *lectio*, not every question in Odo's or in the other collections by any means can be traced directly to a passage of Scripture. Perhaps as the master lectured it was usual for him to comment on points of doctrine connected with the text under consideration; the more speculative of our questions may have arisen like this. To take an example from the *Sententiae* of the School of Anselm of Laon, we find: 'Since the body of Christ is inviolable and incorruptible, how can it be gnawed by mice, chewed by teeth, and so on?' Odo certainly has questions which seem to have arisen in this way.

In the course of bringing together passages from Scripture and the Fathers which had a bearing on selected topics, it was inevitable that apparent contradictions should be noticed, and it is here that we begin to see contentiousness arise. Odo has several examples of questions about such apparently opposing texts. *Quaestio* 30 (*De Agno qui tollit peccata mundi*) sets the following passages against one another: John 1:29 tells us that Christ is 'The Lamb who takes away the sins of the world'; Ps. 18:14 tells us that the domination sin has over us is unavoidable. Odo's solution (*determinatio*) involves a distinction of the way in which Christ causes sins not-to-be in the life to come, and the fact that it is impossible for sins to be altogether wiped out in this life. He has an alternative solution, too: Christ takes away sins in such a way that they are utterly discounted for purposes of punishment. *Quaestio* 42 juxtaposes two *contraria capitula*: the law saves no one; the law, kept at the proper time, confers temporal goods and, in addition, eternal life. Again, we must look closely at the meaning here of *lex salvat*. If the law is kept after the flesh (*carnaliter*), it saves no one. If it is kept in due time, and *spiritualiter*, then indeed it confers good things in this world and eternal life in the next. This distinction of the senses of a term has its parallels in the Anselm of Laon sentences,[33] but its full exploitation still lay in the future, even in Odo's day, in the dictionaries of biblical terms.[34] Here, it is not so much the contradiction or apparent contradiction between texts of Scripture which is being noted, but the need to read the Bible with an eye to the special characteristics of its language. There is, as Odo himself points out in *Quaestio* 42, a *lex filiorum* and a *lex servorum*, a law for children and a law for slaves. We cannot read 'law' as if it were all one.

Both the variety and the apparent contradictions in scriptural usage are noted by Odo in the same *Quaestio* 42. In Acts 15:10 Peter says that the law is a burden which neither his contemporaries nor their fathers were able to bear. In Deut. 30:11 Moses says that the *mandatum* of which he is speaking is not beyond man's power to keep. These two statements can perhaps be reconciled if we bear in mind that Moses is speaking of a single precept. It is the whole law which no one can fulfil. But this will not quite meet the difficulty, because Moses also says: 'Cursed is the man who has not done all these things' (Deut. 32:26). The answer lies in the notion that since a man justified by faith is excused condemnation for the sake of his faith, the curse which lies upon him *ex lege* is over-ruled. Again, Odo is directing his reader to make a close scrutiny of the words before him and to look for an interpretation which will smooth out anomalies.

9

CONTRADICTORY AUTHORITIES

No one confronted the problem of contradiction so boldly in the middle years of the twelfth century as Peter Abelard. His thoughts are so striking, and in certain respects in a class of their own, that we must consider them briefly before we look at what was perhaps the most successful solution, technically speaking, to be formulated before the end of the twelfth century.

Abelard the controversialist struck a response from a worthy opponent. William of St Thierry (c. 1085–1148) (aspiring friend of St Bernard whom he came to dominate intellectually and continued to regard with the humblest admiration) had a natural bent for research. After a period as a student, probably at Laon, where he would have been taught by the brothers Ralph and Anselm, he became a Benedictine monk. When he first met Bernard soon afterwards he was powerfully drawn to the Cistercian life. For many years Bernard firmly discouraged him from breaking his former vows, until in 1135 he permitted him to enter the Cistercian monastery at Signy and begin his Cistercian life there. In the meantime William had been abbot of St Thierry and had become a considerable scholar. When he arrived at Signy he had already written several monographs and had a file of notes from his reading.[1] Much of the work he subsequently put together from his notes was not more than compilation, a collection of extracts from Gregory on the Song of Songs[2] and another on the same subject taken from St Ambrose.[3] He had made notes, too, of Bernard's conversations with him on one occasion when they were both ill and spent some time together in the infirmary, reflecting aloud upon the Song of Songs.[4]

William's most systematic research was done for a work which he began at Signy, an exposition of the Epistle to the Romans. He read Abelard in preparation for his own work, and what he found troubled him so profoundly that he wrote to Bernard suggesting that action should be taken to silence Abelard. He gave him details and an account of the difficulty each dangerous opinion raised, and in this way the enterprise which led to Abelard's final condemnation at Sens in 1142 was set in motion.[5]

The same polemical spirit seized William when he read William of Conches, whose *De Philosophia Mundi* had been brought to him by a would-be monk in flight from the world of the schools.[6] In his book *On the Errors of William of Conches* he again tried to stir Bernard to action. 'After the theology of Peter Abelard, William of Conches brings in a new philosophy, confirming and multiplying whatever Abelard has said and, more impudently, adding still more of his own that Abelard has not said.'[7] By his 'philosophy' William proves that the Father is Power, the Son Wisdom, the Spirit Will,[8] 'transferring the words from their common meaning on the basis of some affinity' *vocabula illis a vulgari propter affinitatem quamdam transferentes.*[9] This abuse of the method of analogy which God has provided for human use is at the root of William's errors: 'This physical and philosophical man philosophises physically about God',[10] drawing too much on the natural world for evidence. He claims too much for natural science. He says his body was made not by God but by nature,[11] and he mocks the literal reading of the account of the creation of Eve from Adam's rib.[12]

William's own position is consciously that of the monastic scholar, advocate of the humble reading of the Fathers and of patient *lectio divina*. In an epistle to the brothers of Mont-Dieux written towards the end of his life, he contrasts persuasively the puffed-up wise men of this world with the simplicity and humility of those who are truly wise in God.[13] Thus not contradiction but clarity is to be found in the words of Scripture.[14] William's own commentary on Romans[15] begins with an assurance that it is so faithful a compilation of patristic opinions that it is like a bird clad entirely in borrowed plumes. If each of the Fathers took his own 'feathers' back the little bird would be naked.

Nevertheless, William had an academic training and his academic habits never left him. In the *De Sacramento Altaris* he takes up the double difficulty which prompted so many questions in the reading of the Bible; there are both obscure and apparently contradictory passages in the Bible and the Fathers.[16]

He addresses himself principally to the difficulty as it arises in the case of the Fathers. He makes the point that from the earliest Christian centuries the Fathers treated only controversial issues, 'What was not attacked they did not defend',[17] and there are many controversial statements in their writings which may be misleading when taken out of context by modern scholars who are themselves fond of controversy. There are also passages which have been misunderstood and have thus led to error.[18] The status of Scripture stood so high that there could be no question of real contradiction but the words of the Fathers had always stood high, too, and it was not easy to impute error or inconsistency to them. It was necessary for William to find explanations which involved no accusation.

It has been suggested[19] that either William was deliberately adopting the method of Peter Abelard's *Sic et Non* in his *De Sacramento Altaris* or Abelard owed the idea to him. In his *Sic et Non* Peter Abelard lists the views of the Bible and the Fathers on a number of topics or questions in such a way as to bring out their apparent divergence and even contradictoriness.[20] There are no solutions of the individual examples. Abelard sets out his broad intention in compiling the collection in the Prologue with a number of thoughts on the problems it raises. He groups his one hundred and fifty-eight questions in an order which fits closely with the one Peter Lombard adopts in his *Sententiae* and which was to become the standard order of treatment for the topics of systematic theology. The first four deal with the nature of faith and the mode of knowledge of God which is possible to man, Questions 5–10 cover unity and Trinity, 11–25 the Persons of the Godhead, 26–41 questions concerning divine omnipotence, foreknowledge, ubiquity and such attributes, with their implications for the operation of human free will and the problem of predestination and Grace. With Question 42 we move to a consideration of the created spirits and then, at Question 51, to man. Questions 59–104 cover the Incarnation, the human nature of Christ and a number of difficulties which have been raised about the events described in the Gospels, with a few questions (97–104) on the Apostles. At Question 105 we arrive at the sacraments, the Church, heretics and related matters. Several of these broad themes merge into one another with questions which act as bridges between sections. Between questions on the Persons of the Trinity and the questions on the angels, for example, we have the question whether the Son once appeared to the angels (Question 41). Between 'man' and 'Incarnation' we have (Question 58) 'that Adam was to be saved, and the opposite'. Abelard includes questions which lie at the heart of the faith, questions of the most trivial kind ('that Adam was buried at Calvary and the contrary' (Question 57)), questions which had been raised in the early Christian centuries, and questions of the utmost topicality in his own day.

The citations were not discoveries made in Abelard's own reading. Like Lanfranc, he did not hesitate to make use of the existing collections available in *florilegia*.[21] Indeed the very familiarity of the quotations gave added pointedness to their apparent disagreement with one another. Nor was the notion of making such a collection of opposing authorities new. The method was employed by Berthold of Constance in the late eleventh century in his *De Sacramentis Excommunicatorum*.[22] The use of well-known extracts, the challenge implied in Abelard's making a list of difficulties without answering them, all strongly suggests that he intended the book to be used in the classroom; it is a collection of exercises in reconciliation and clarification.

The only help he gives his readers is in the Prologue. There he sets out general rules. The presumption must be that contradictions and disagreements are apparent only. They merely 'seem' to be *diversa* or *adversa* (*videantur*). It is not difficult to see how difficulties have arisen. 'In such a multitude of words, it is not surprising that some sayings even of the saints seem not only to differ from one another but indeed even to contradict one another.'[23] The reader's first assumption must be that his own understanding has failed: 'Let us believe ourselves to lack the grace of understanding (*gratiam intelligendo deesse*) rather than that they err in writing.'[24]

Abelard suggests that we are impeded in our understanding of these writings of an earlier period by two things above all: the *inusitatus locutionis modus*, the unfamiliar way of speaking, and the habit of using the same words with different significations:

ac plerumque earundem vocum significatio diversa, cum modo in hac, modo in illa significatione vox eadem sit posita.[25]

Augustine himself had been very much aware of the first of these, the question of usage. He often speaks of *usus loquendi* and the special uses of theological language. We have seen how the idea of 'usage' had gained a new technical pointedness in the writings of Anselm of Canterbury and the scholars who followed him.[26] The second again had a long history in early mediaeval exegesis, where there is much talk of the 'signification' of words, but again it was becoming technically a much more advanced question in Abelard's day.[27] He is, in other words, speaking not only of two difficulties which were apparent to common sense, but of two highly technical matters in the vocabulary of the day. The elimination of the apparent contradiction will, then, depend upon the mastery of certain technical principles.

These preliminary considerations help to place Abelard's *Sic et*

Non alongside Bede's *De Schematibus et Tropis* as a more or less systematic attempt to analyse the modes (*modi, tropi*) of speaking and
the significations of words literal and metaphorical (*schemata*) for
the study of the Bible. Bede wrote for readers trained principally in
grammar and in a little rhetoric, Abelard for those perhaps more
familiar with the principles of dialectic. Yet Abelard had an ear for
style and an eye for rhetorical devices. He notes that each writer has
his own way of putting things (*in sensu suo, ita et in verbis suis
unusquisque abundat*). Furthermore, he points out that words are
often used in a deliberately altered way (*verba commutari oportet*),
in order to relieve the tedium for the listener, of which the rhetorician
would approve.[28] The result, he points out, is that it often happens
that the proper signification of the word is unknown to some, or
remains a less common usage (*minus usitata*).[29] Abelard turns to
Augustine for authority for these views.[30] How rash it is, he ends, to
judge another's meaning! Only God reads hearts and thoughts.[31]

That said, Abelard turns to the possibility of there being some
genuine difficulty to be got over in the words, beginning with corruption in the text. Even in the Bible itself there are copyists' errors
(*scriptorum vitio corrupta sunt*). Again Abelard looks for authority,
this time to that 'most faithful scribe and most truthful interpreter
Jerome', and he gives an example.[32]

There is a further possibility: that the author (if it is one of the
Fathers; not of course in Scripture itself) has changed his mind and is
retracting an opinion, not contradicting himself. Augustine is the
obvious example here, and Abelard cites his *Retractationes*.[33] Or
again, perhaps, the author is giving not his own opinion but that of
someone else, perhaps mingling orthodox and heretical views.
Again, the opinion may be not a final determination of the question,
but an interim judgment (later decided one way or the other).[34]

There may be a figurative usage of some sort, which may again
deceive, if it is taken literally. Sometimes, Abelard suggests, the
Fathers may be merely giving an opinion. There is ample precedent
in poetical and philosophical writings for an opinion to be expressed
in a way which makes it seem a statement of the truth (*quasi in
veritate consistant*).[35] It is common usage (*quotidiani sermonis usus
est*) to speak of things as they appear to the bodily senses, even
though we know them to be otherwise in reality.[36] There is no
vacuum in nature, but we still speak of something as vacuous, empty,
when we can see nothing in it. Such usages are found in the Fathers,
too; sometimes the same thing may be spoken of in different ways for

different reasons or purposes (*cum de eodem diversa dicuntur*),[37] as, for example, to exhort or instruct or warn, various different complexions may be put upon the same passage. All these are questions of usage.

He also allows for the possibility that there may be failings in the authors, that not all the oddities and contrarieties can be explained by differences of usage. Even the Prophets have not always been inspired (*quandoque prophetiae gratia caruisse*).[38] It is not a matter of sincerity. Sometimes someone has genuinely believed himself to prophesy truly, and has been mistaken.[39] It is also the case that some truths are revealed to one writer and not to another.[40] Abelard asks, with great daring: would it be surprising if even the Apostles and Prophets were sometimes in error?[41] That is not to call them liars. It is not the same thing to lie as to be in error.[42] Here Abelard is departing from the assumption that the divine inspiration of Scripture extends to the minutest detail of the choice of words, but in his own terms he holds 'the authority of Scripture which God himself gave to be unalterable' (*auctoritatem scripturae quam ipse dedit immobilem teneamus*).[43] This is so, he says elsewhere, 'as though the finger of God had written it, that is, as though it were composed and written at the dictation of the Holy Spirit',[44] by a process which has two parts: first the inward implication and then the writing.[45]

He is careful to distinguish the canonical books from later writings, and he marks degrees of authority even within the canonical books.[46] In conflicts between or within lesser authorities such as reasoning cannot resolve (*ut nulla possit absolvi ratione*) he must compare the authorities and retain as *potissimus* what has the more authoritative testimony.[47]

If in reading Scripture, however, he thinks that something is *absurdum*, the reader does not have the same liberty. He may not say that the author did not grasp the truth, but he must consider whether the copy before him is faulty (*codex mendosus*), the interpreter (that is, the translator) in error, or his own understanding at fault.[48] He may not compare authorities and weigh them against one another here.

There is much that appears inconsistent even if we include Abelard's own provisos and distinctions, and the boldness of some of the views he appears to be putting forward in the Prologue to the *Sic et Non* is by no means fully borne out by his own practice in exegesis. He does not himself consider the possibility of error in Scripture when he has a problem to solve. He tries, like any other contemporary exegete, every possible device to solve problems in such a way that no detail of the text of the Bible is brought into question.

William of St Thierry's modest attempt at imitation – if that is what it is – allows for the possibility that the Fathers sometimes treated their subject-matter 'more obscurely', sometimes 'more openly' (*modo obscurius, modo apertius*). But he is confident that their opinions will be seen to agree in the faith, and that the reader will be delighted with what he sees. At bottom, that is what Abelard believes, too. His more arrogant, guilty and iconoclastic suggestions are usually the result of his being driven to an extreme by following through the logical entailments of a position he has taken up. He seems to have been genuinely surprised and not a little outraged that others thought him unorthodox as a result. The most important thing Abelard has to tell us for our purposes is how closely even his more outré ideas fit into the general scheme of contemporary interpretation in its emphasis on the special usages of scriptural language and the need to examine apparent contradictions in order to resolve them.

10

A NEW APPROACH TO
RESOLVING CONTRADICTIONS

Although many of the questions being raised in the schools took their origin from a problem perceived in the course of the study of the text of the Bible, we have seen that they were not all by any means to do with the Bible's use of language; some were doctrinal, some philosophical. But amongst those arising out of the text of the Bible two kinds of difficulty in particular presented themselves.

We have already looked at one of these difficulties in connection with the problem of signification. Hugh of St Victor confronts it when he examines the peculiar behaviour of biblical language. The literal meaning may be *perfecta*, the text making its statement fully without superfluity or the need to supply anything which has been left out; or it may be *imminuta*, and leave something to be 'understood' (*subaudiendum*); or it may include some extra word or element and repeat itself, and then we may describe it as *superflua*;[1] or, as Hugh says, it may be such that 'unless some alteration is made it means nothing, or it seems incongruous'.[2] The kind of alteration Hugh has in mind here is grammatical, as in a case where the nominative of a noun plus a genitive pronoun replaces the genitive of a noun. He gives examples:

Dominus in coelo sedes eius (Ps. 10:5), id est sedes Domini in coelo.
Filii hominum, dentes eorum arma et sagittae (Ps. 56:5), id est filiorum hominum dentes.

'The Lord in heaven, his throne', for 'the throne of the Lord in heaven'; 'the sons of men, their teeth', for 'the teeth of the sons of men'.[3]

I

On a first reading the student will have questions which will need to be answered. This will be even more the case with passages which have either an obvious meaning, beyond the literal (*sensus*),[4] or a deeper meaning (*sententia*), which is not clear unless it is expounded.[5] Other passages have both a plain meaning in addition

140

to the literal one, and a hidden meaning,[6] and here, too, the Bible's multiple significations will raise questions requiring answers.

The theme of the special usages of biblical language is pursued in Hugh's account of the *sensus*. Here again, some 'unusual way of speaking' may get in the way of our understanding. The *sensus*, if it is *congruus*, will present no problems, but it may be incredible, impossible, absurd or false, as when Job says: 'My soul chooses strangling' (Job 7:15). Sometimes, 'even where the signification of the words is clear, there seems to be no sense, either because of the unusual way of speaking or because of some circumstance which impedes the reader's thinking'.[7] 'You will find many things of this kind in Scripture', Hugh warns, 'and especially in the Old Testament, according to the idioms of the language in which they are said which – although they are clear enough in that language – seem to us to mean nothing.'[8]

Hugh brings us to our second kind of difficulty when he points out that the *sententia*, dealing as it does with the deeper meaning, is not restricted by the limitations from which human language suffers when it is trying to talk about the divine. 'It can never be absurd; it can never be false . . . it admits no contradiction; it is always appropriate, always true',[9] says Hugh. There are in the text of the Bible many statements which appear to be at variance with one another, and, of these, it is those which involve a conflict of the literal sense which present the greatest difficulty to the interpreter; as Hugh of St Victor saw in his discussion of *sententia*, there can be no head-on conflict in figurative interpretations on different levels. Nor, as Philip of Harveng puts it, can there be any conflict between the literal and the figurative. He says that, even in those things which are manifold in their *mysterium*, there is nothing which is contrary to the literal sense.[10] It is as though one interpretation passes over the head of another because they are on different levels.

In any case, there can be no real contradiction, even where two statements, taken literally, appear to be irreconcilable. The Bible is uniformly an expression of divine truth throughout, and it is an axiom of logic that truths cannot be contradictory. Thus any appearance of discord requires comment; something must have been incorrectly understood. Jerome reconciles Isa. 53:8, 'who shall tell his generation', with Matthew's 'telling' of the 'generation' of Christ (Matt. 1:1) by explaining that Isaiah was speaking of divine and Matthew of human generation, so that the word 'generation' has two different meanings.[11] Alcuin's *Quaestiones in Genesim* include a query about Abraham's request for a sign, so that he might be sure that he was to receive what he had been promised by God (Gen. 15:8). Alcuin explains that Abraham did not ask for proof, as though he doubted God's promise, but for information, so that he might know how it was to come about. To ask for a proof would seem inappropriate to Abraham's faith, as Alcuin's questioner points out.[12] If we can remove the anomaly by giving a precise definition of a 'sign', all seems plain. In a later question Alcuin resolves an apparent discrepancy between the number of generations after Abraham when the children of Israel returned from Egypt, which in Genesis are four and in Exodus are recorded as five. Alcuin counts the generations from Levi in one case and from Judah in the other, and finds there to be no conflict.[13] Gregory puzzles over Paul's quotations from the words of one of Job's comforters. God reproves Job's friends for their words (Job 42:7); Paul seems to be giving authority to the same words by citing them (1 Cor. 3:19). The difficulty disappears if we understand that there were things in the sayings of Job's friends which were right, but that by comparison with Job's own words they seem feeble. 'Many things that they say would have been admirable if they were not spoken against the afflicted condition of the holy man.'[14]

If apparent contradiction is a sign that one or both texts have been incorrectly understood, congruity is a test that a correct understanding has been reached. 'And then that chapter will be congruously in harmony' (tunc congrue concordat istud capitulum).[15] How can we fit together the statement of Gen. 2:2 that God rested from his labours on the seventh day, with the statement of St John's Gospel (5:17) which seems to say that God is still working: 'My Father is still working, and I work'? The answer is that God rested from creating but not from the work of governing and directing creation. When we understand that, we see how the two are to be reconciled (quomodo convenit).[16] Similar talk of convenire is to be found everywhere in our commentators.[17] It can even be used as a test to distinguish between the different versions given in two translations in order to determine which is the more satisfactory. Remigius of Auxerre compares dives valde and gravis valde, in order to see which best befits the 'mystery' (bene mysterio convenit).[18] When we get the answer right, the solution seems easy, as Hugh of St Victor remarks.[19] The difficulty disappears and everything has that clarity and smoothness which is the mark of the correct interpretation.

Augustine had attempted a reconciliation of the apparent discrepancies and contradictions between the Gospels in the *De Consensu Evangelistarum*. Cassiodorus had tried to make sense of the *obscuritas* of the Psalms, a mystery he describes as *intexata* and *velata*,[20] in order to show that they contain nothing inconsistent with Christian truth. He explains, for example, how two statements which are in fact not contradictory may appear to stand in opposition to one another if we read both literally; but, if we look at the 'transferred' or figurative sense, they seem to fit perfectly *nimis videntus accommodae*.[21] Gregory the Great discusses the theory of the matter in his *Moralia in Job*. He who reads without trying to understand the sense of the Holy Word in this way, he says, is not so much taking an instruction as confusing himself because he will find the words, taken literally, sometimes contradicting themselves, but they are directing the reader by their very anomalies to a truth he must understand to lie beneath. When we look at the historical or literal sense alone, he says, it is like seeing only someone's face and not knowing what is in his mind.[22]

Bede laid the foundations of the systematic study of the modes of reconciling contradictions in his *De Schematibus et Tropis* by stating squarely that contradictions will always be found to disappear if one or both of the opposing statements is taken in a figurative sense.[23] But this device will not always meet the difficulty. Sometimes the contradiction appears to lie between two literal meanings. It was above all in dealing with such cases that the twelfth century interpreters made their new contribution, although they had an eye to the figurative as they did so, and, as we shall see, they had some success in bringing the figurative within the technical scheme which they devised as a result of studying the literal sense.

II

Zachary, who taught in the school at Besançon from 1131 to 1138, before he became a Premonstratensian canon of St Martin's, Laon, made his own concordance of the Gospels. In this he brought together the views of those who had written since Augustine's time and Augustine's methods of harmonising the discrepancies in the *De Consensu Evangelistarum* with the attempts of other early Christian writers.[24]

Zachary's *Super Unum et Quatuor* met a need and proved a popular work, not only because of his contribution to the task of resolving these contradictions. He includes a general discussion of the excellence of the Gospel; its difference from the law; the individual ways of writing characteristic of each of the evangelists; and an *accessus*[25] to explain what is the subject-matter of the Gospels (the mystery of the Trinity, Christ in his divine and human nature, his sayings and actions and what others did and said to him), the *intentio* and *finis* ('to teach men that they have life through faith in Jesus as the Son of God'). But the central difficulty to which Zachary addresses himself is that of the apparent contradictions and discrepancies between the Gospel accounts. He wants to demonstrate that although there are four Gospels, they are merely four books, not four separate teachings; the doctrine is one.[26] It is with this in mind that Zachary has borrowed his title from Jerome's dictum *quatuor Evangelia esse unum, et unum quatuor*: the four Gospels are one and the one four.[27]

He is sure that the words of the Gospel are not intended to be difficult or confusing. On the contrary, they are 'accessible to everyone'. The Gospel speaks like a familiar friend to the minds of both learned and simple men.[28] Yet it is also designed to exercise men's minds, to teach them not only what is obvious, but something more: the secret[29] hidden beneath the surface.[30] It does so in various ways: by the use of images, comparisons, proverbs, and above all by the transference of signification from its usual reference to the natural world to a special reference to God. When eyes, ears, mouth, lips, head are attributed to God this is not to be taken literally.[31]

So far Zachary has been talking in familiar terms, but he finds in Augustine not only such general explanations as these, but also a detailed and purposeful handling of difficulties at the level of literal reading. One evangelist misses out what another includes. There is no contradiction in that, nor in their adopting a different order for their narratives at times. It is probable that each of the evangelists told the story in the order God suggested it to his recollection, says Zachary. If there appear to be irreconcilable differences in the details, we must conclude that a different incident is being spoken of in the two accounts. Any apparent anomaly may disappear if we remember that the evangelists often recall the reader to a past narrative or incident, as when Matthew mentions Mary Magdalene again in his account of the Passion (Matt. 28:1). Or they mention something which is to happen in the future, as Luke does when he describes Jesus' baptism and refers to the time when Herod was to imprison John the Baptist (Luke 3:20).[32] Sometimes a word is used to express not a fact but an opinion; where Mary finds Jesus in the Temple and says to him 'Your Father and I have sought you sorrowing', 'Father' means 'he who was thought to be the Father of Jesus'.

In Matt. 14:9 we read that Herod was sorry when the head of John the Baptist was presented to him on a dish as he had ordered. 'That is', says Zachary, 'it was thought that he was sorry.'[33] In all these cases the evangelists are following a special rule of scriptural usage. We need not look for a figurative meaning, but simply for an unexpected or surprising literal meaning.

The examination of these and other Gospel usages leads Zachary to draw upon elementary principles of grammar and dialectic. It is here that he begins to point the way to a method of analysis of biblical language which Peter the Chanter was to take substantially further within a few decades.[34]

It is often the case, for example, that a cause is spoken of in the Gospels by the name of its effect. In Mark 9:25, 'Go out, deaf and dumb spirit', the spirit itself is not deaf and dumb but it causes him whom it possesses to be deaf and dumb. *Surde et mute* would read *faciens surdum et mutum* if this were an ordinary piece of writing. Equally, the word for a cause is sometimes given for the effect.[35] St Mark's Gospel says that the Lord cast demons out of Mary but it means literally that he cast out the vices which had been introduced into her by the demons, that is, the effects the demons had had upon her.[36] A further type of apparent anomaly may arise where someone is said to have done something which he did not himself do, but was the responsibility of his ancestors or successors (*de diversis in eadem successione positis*). Zachary refers to the passage where Jesus says that the blood of all the righteous which has been shed upon the earth, 'from Abel's blood to that of Zacharias, whom you slew between the temple and the altar', shall 'be upon' the present generation. The present generation did not slay Zacharias, their fathers were responsible (Matt. 23:35). Similarly, when Jesus says: 'I am with you to the end of the world' (Matt. 28:20) he did not mean only the 'you' of the generation then living, but also those who came after them.[37] There is no figurative use of 'you' but a literal one according to Scripture's own way of speaking.

Often 'the thing signified takes its name from a likeness to the thing signifying' (*significata res ex similitudine rei significantis nomen suscipit*). When Jesus says 'I am the Vine', and in other cases where Christ is said to be a lamb, a lion, an eagle, and so on,[38] he is being described by the name of something which is in some way like him. Again, the thing signifying is understood sometimes by the thing signified. When John the Baptist saw the heavens opened and the Spirit descending like a dove (Matt. 3:16; Mark 1:10; Luke 3:22;

John 1:32) he was seeing the Spirit in reality, but the reader understands what he saw by way of the dove which signifies the Spirit and
which is brought in here for comparison ('like a dove'). When we
read that 'some of those standing here will not taste death until they
see the Son of Man coming in his Kingdom' (Mark 9:1), we understand by the transfiguration the future coming of Christ in glory.[39]

Sometimes, as Tyconius had explained, the whole is understood
by a reference to a part. 'The Word was made flesh': this 'flesh' must
be understood to be 'man' (John 1:14). Sometimes specific numbers
are given, when what is meant is 'all'.[40] The seven demons who were
cast out from Mary stand for the whole collection of vices which
were cast out from her.[41] Sometimes a plural is given for a singular.
In Matthew and Mark two robbers crucified with Christ mock him,
but in Luke only one is mentioned (Mark 15:32; Luke 23:39). Luke
says that two soldiers came and offered the dying Jesus vinegar
(23:36); Matthew and Mark say that only one came (Matt. 27:48;
Mark 15:36).[42]

Zachary does not take us very far with this method, beyond what
may be found in Augustine and elsewhere among Zachary's predecessors and contemporaries, and he himself makes little use of it in
the detailed discussions of the *Super Unum et Quatuor*. When he
comes to the accounts of Jesus' baptism, for example, he does not
give the explanation we have already met where 'the thing signified
takes its name from likeness to the thing signifying', but merely
remarks: 'You will understand that the Evangelists, although they
did not use the same words, conveyed the same meaning.' He
suggests that this difference of wording prevents something being
misunderstood as it might have been if it had been said in only one
way and interpreted incorrectly.[43] This emphasis on the meaning
being the same even though the words are different appears elsewhere,[44] but his provision of a list of types of divergence in scriptural
usage which may be checked against any apparent anomaly is clearly
a step towards the systematic approach of the grammatical and
dialectical theologians of the later twelfth century. Indeed, at times
there is a hint of the schools: 'It is asked why baptism took over from
circumcision.'[45]

III

In his study of the late twelfth century, *Masters, Princes and Merchants*, J.W. Baldwin takes as his central figure Peter the Chanter,
who was precentor of the cathedral of Notre Dame in Paris from

1183. Peter died in retirement as a Cistercian monk at Longpont in the diocese of Soissons in 1197. As a Master of Theology he was held in the greatest respect in Paris in the last decades of the century.[46] His influence spread beyond. William de Montibus, chancellor of Lincoln Cathedral from about 1190 until his death in 1213, is the author of a number of works in imitation of Peter's, where he appears to have tried to produce a version of what he had been taught in Paris suitable for use by less sophisticated readers in England.[47] Peter tried, in his workmanlike, confident way, to resolve some of the problems raised by the Bible's use of language. He had at his disposal the most up-to-date techniques of grammar and dialectic. He is fully aware of the technical implications of the special usages of Scripture as his contemporaries saw them. He is in no doubt that sensible application of familiar rules will make it possible to resolve at least the majority of the difficulties.

Peter is the author of a series of works composed while he was a master at Paris towards the end of the twelfth century. His *Verbum Abbreviatum*[48] divides the study of the Bible into our three parts or stages: *lectio*, the reading of the text itself with glosses, *disputatio*, the discussion of the questions which the text raises, and *predicatio*, preaching based on the Word of God.[49] The *Verbum Abbreviatum* itself is designed for the use of preachers, providing pattern-sermons or selections of texts arranged by topic for easy reference. Peter also put together a series of *quaestiones* in his *Summa de Sacramentis*, to help those in difficulties over a number of points which proved to be open to *disputatio*. His *Summa Abel* is one of the earliest dictionaries of biblical terms.[50] His *De Tropis Loquendi* is a manual of biblical contradictions, together with their resolutions, arranged not as they occur in the Bible but according to a series of divisions by type of contradiction, which reflect the most up-to-date work of his contemporaries.

The *Verbum Abbreviatum*, the *Summa De Sacramentis* and the *De Tropis Loquendi*, like his commentaries on the Bible, were all delivered in the first instance as courses of lectures. In the form in which they survive they are probably based on *reportationes*, notes made by a student at the master's request so that the master could revise and polish the work before copies were made for general circulation.[51] This method of composition lent itself to the making of adaptations and abbreviations, and copyists seem to have felt free to make further modifications, so that a process of growth which was not always under the control of the author can be observed in their development. They should not perhaps be regarded as finished treatises, but as working manuals, constantly being adapted to meet the needs of a fresh generation of students.

This workmanlike, schoolmasterly quality of Peter the Chanter's exegesis is much in evidence in his scriptural commentaries. (He seems to have been the first master at Paris to lecture on all the books of the Old and New Testaments.)[52] He considers the title of the Book of Numbers and the promise God made to Abraham: 'I will multiply your seed like the stars of the sky and like the sands of the sea.' According to the surface of the letter it seems to have been promised that the seed of Abraham was to be multiplied so far that it would become innumerable. It is obvious that this was not fulfilled to the letter, for it is agreed that the people derived from him were often 'numbered'. On the best of evidence (*fortiter*) the name of this book in Latin is said to be the Book of Numbers. Peter the Chanter lists the 'numberings' made in the Book of Numbers: of all men able to bear arms; of the first-born of the Levites; of the dwelling-places (*mansiones*). The word 'numbers' can, Peter explains, be taken as a singular, and then 'book of' is understood (*subintelligitur*), so that 'The Book of Numbers' is meant. Or it can be understood in the plural. On Joshua, Peter writes that *amici* is used ironically, for there is no friendship in the ordinary sense in the passage referred to. There is some discussion of the variations in translations, which are so great, Peter claims, that it is sometimes impossible to find even one letter of the alphabet to correspond between different manuscripts.[53]

Peter is attracted by Gregory the Great's frequently reiterated idea that each book is written both 'inwardly' and 'outwardly'. They all have both an outward purpose (*intentio extrinsecus*) as far as the letter is concerned and an inward one in their spiritual interpretation (*intrinsecam quantum ad spiritualem intelligentiam*). He himself examines both, but with references to the technical aids that grammar and dialectic can provide which bring the 'spiritual' interpretation under the same kind of scrutiny as the literal. Peter finds problems of signification arising in both and he accordingly applies signification-theory to both in his *De Tropis Loquendi*.[54]

In late twelfth and thirteenth century manuscripts Bede's treatise *De Schematibus et Tropis* is sometimes found with the *De Tropis Loquendi* of Peter the Chanter. Peter undoubtedly saw himself as following in Bede's line; he refers to Bede's work in his Prologue.

He draws on other sources, too. He takes as his opening text: 'Now we see through a glass darkly' (1 Cor. 13:12). Here he probably depends directly upon Peter Lombard's exposition of the same passage. Peter Lombard says in his commentary on the Pauline Epistles that the 'glass' through which we see 'darkly' is Scripture's use of tropes and figures. *In aenigmate* means 'through hidden allegory' (*per obscuram allegoriam*). What we actually 'see' is 'certain creatures in which some likeness of God shines, obscurely enough; that is, figures and images'.[55] Peter the Chanter explains conventionally enough that this is a benevolent dispensation of God, because of the limitations of man's understanding and his inability to know God himself directly. 'Because of the dullness of sense' of sinful man we are not always able to understand his meaning even when he speaks to us in figures. Certain passages in Scripture 'seem to be contrary or contradictory' (*videntur esse contraria*) though they are not (*cum non sint*). They are *diversa* but not *adversa*.[56] Until we can see clearly, we must do what we can to help our understanding by reading the Scriptures intelligently in the light of what we know of the technicalities of figurative language. We must read the Bible in the certainty that Scripture's figurative language is 'necessary'; it is a help to us, not a hindrance, and we must above all attempt to understand apparent contradictions so as to see that they are no such thing.

The points made by Zachary of Besançon (which in their turn enlarge a little upon the work of earlier generations, although they involve nothing which is not relatively common doctrine) are amplified and added to considerably, until Peter has arrived at a full and detailed scheme for identifying the special usages which may confuse the reader of Scripture and make him think that the Word of God is contradicting itself. Like Zachary, Peter sets out to teach his pupils how to read with a set of possibilities in mind, which they can apply in the reading of the text as they seem to fit best. The key to the method is the examination of the use of a term or a phrase in a given context.

The contextual approach is characteristic of those logicians of Peter the Chanter's day who are sometimes called 'terminists';[57] it was these scholars who developed the use of the word *suppositio* to denote the actual meaning of a noun in a particular proposition.[58] It might be said that the authors of the dictionaries of biblical terms, too, were concerned with both the signification and the supposition of the terms they list, for they, too, examine the Bible's use of its terms in different contexts.[59] But Peter appears to have been one of the first to attempt to reduce these differences to rule by employing principles of contemporary grammar and dialectic systematically in resolving exegetical difficulties. He takes the contextual approach to its natural conclusion and uses it to examine the apparent contradictions where a word or a term is employed in two passages in ways which appear unreconcilable, so that the passages seem to be saying opposite things. The context of each is scrutinised in order to see whether it is affecting the meaning of the word in question, with the result that the two statements are about different things and not contradictory at all. Peter discovers in every case that this is what has happened, and the apparent contradiction vanishes.

If we take the term 'fallacy' in a broad sense, this is exactly what happens in the resolution of a fallacious argument. The middle term of a fallacious syllogism, for example, may be being used in one sense in the first premise and in another sense in the second, so that in reality no conclusion can follow, although it looks at first as though an absurd conclusion must follow.

Among the simpler methods of clearing up an error based on fallacious reasoning in the *Quaestiones* of Odo of Soissons are questions of this type. On the predestination of Christ, for example, we have in *Quaestio* 6:

Christ is the Son of God from eternity.
Therefore he was not predestined to receive the Sonhood of God in time.

This is false, says Odo. He does not elaborate. He merely draws parallels. It is like saying that Christ 'naturally' (*naturaliter*) had 'power' from eternity (and therefore did not have it in 'time' when he was on earth). We are being invited to look closely at the words of which the propositions are composed in order to see what is implied. We must form the habit of looking for parallels. In this case, we must understand the difference between those things which Christ has from eternity because they are attributes of his nature, and his possession of those attributes in time while he was incarnate on earth; then it will be clearer to us how Christ may be said to have been the Son of God from eternity and to have received his Sonhood in time. It is a method of detecting the weakness in fallacies *a simili*, and it is elementary in the demands it makes on the reader. It is also to be found in Robert of Melun.[60] In a not dissimilar way elsewhere, Odo demonstrates the absurdity of an argument by citing other arguments like it whose absurdity is obvious (*Quaestio* 6).

Even where we are dealing with fallacious syllogisms of some sophistication, Odo's instinct is to encourage the student to examine the propositions and conclusion clearly in order to see what is wrong in this particular case, rather than to try to identify a type of fallacy by its technical name. *Quaestio* 32 is concerned with an apparent contradiction in Scripture. In Exod. 20:7 we are commanded not to covet. Now it is superfluous to commend what cannot be obeyed, but the command 'thou shalt not covet' cannot be obeyed. See how St Paul says in Rom. 7:15 that he does things he does not will to do. Therefore it seems that God has given a superfluous commandment. No, says Odo, we must look more closely at *concupisces*. We cannot help coveting, certainly, but we have it in our power not to consent to our desire. Therefore God has not given a superfluous commandment. A similar fallacy is exposed in *Quaestio* 44; again, not by identifying the technical error, but by looking at the use of words in a particular instance.

The most striking difference between Odo's discussions and resolutions of fallacies and those of Peter the Chanter in the *De Tropis Loquendi* is Odo's use of relatively untechnical language in discussing fallacies. It is true that Odo employs a technical vocabulary (*nomen compositum*; *locutiones adpropriatae*), but it is for the most part the commonplace terminology of grammar and dialectic in general, not the specialist vocabulary developed by writers on fallacies of the second half of the twelfth century. Odo will merely state that a proposition is false, *videtur falsum*; *falsum est*, and show why, in plain language. Peter the Chanter has at his disposal terms to describe fallacies *secundum equivocationem*, *secundum univocationem*, by *diversa pars*, *diversus relatus*, *diversum tempus*, *diversus modus* – the six types of fallacy found in the *logica vetus*[61] – and also words often found in connection with the study of the *Sophistici Elenchi* – *translatio*, *amphibolia*.[62] It is hard to believe that Odo did not know these terms. His understanding of the rules of argument is as extensive as we should expect of any master of his day. His use of relatively little technical language must be a matter of deliberate choice. We can only conclude that Peter the Chanter was able to expect a higher degree of technical expertise from his students, while Odo had found that he must explain himself simply if he was not to confuse the students of his own day, a decade or two earlier.

Quaestio 5 provides an example. Odo discusses the proposition: the less one is obliged to do something, the more does one do it freely, as an act of Grace (*quanto indebita, tanto gratiora*). This gives rise to a paradox. For example, I may take a wife, but for love of God I do not. Therefore I love God more than myself, but I ought to love God more than myself. If what I do beyond what I ought to do is the more pleasing to God, it seems that it is more pleasing to God that I should not take a wife than that I should love God. This is false (*quod falsum est*), for it is a greater good to love God than not to take a wife. Odo explains where the error lies. As a general rule 'it is a greater merit if, for God's sake, I do not do what I can legitimately do than if I avoid what is forbidden'. In our example, a simple positive good (loving God) is being compared with another compound, positive good (renunciation of a legitimate pleasure for love of God) and the element of renunciation is misleadingly being singled out as constituting, in itself, that which makes the second a greater good. The only proper comparison, Odo contends, is between not-doing-what-I-may-do and not-doing-what-I-must-not-do. There is certainly greater merit in the former than in the latter, for by the former I merit a crown, but by the latter I merely avoid just punishment. Instead of comparing *facienda* and *facienda*, or *facienda* and *cavenda*, we must compare *mittenda* and *dimittenda*. That is, instead of comparing positives, or positive and negative, we must compare 'not-doing' and 'renouncing', the two negatives, and then we shall be able to see clearly where the greater merit lies. Odo does not discuss the general rules for recognising and resolving fallacies of this logical type in technical dialectical terms. He allows the principle to make itself clear by discussing a series of similar cases.

The only general principle to be drawn from the *Quaestiones* concerns the need to look closely at the way in which language is being used. This is exactly the policy of Adam of Balsham in his *Ars Disserendi*, written before the advent of the *Sophistici Elenchi*. Among the rules for detecting sophisms, Adam instructs the student to make a systematic enquiry into the usage of words.[63] It is Peter the Chanter's advice, too, throughout the *De Tropis Loquendi*. Odo speaks of the *modus dicendi*,[64] and describes how we are 'accustomed to say' (*consuevimus autem loqui*) what is not strictly accurate, technically speaking.[65] Skill in the detection of fallacies requires a fine eye for the way words are being used. In one of his parallels in *Quaestio 5*, Odo takes the statement: 'Those who speak ill of Christ are worse than those who crucified him.' Here we must understand that the comparison is not between those who do injury in speaking ill of Christ and those who did him injury in crucifying him, but between the damage done to the members of the Body of Christ (*membra Christi*) by speaking evil, and the damage done to Christ himself in the crucifixion. In *Quaestio 3*, Odo considers in what sense the flesh of Christ is said to be corrupted. In the sense that it can be chewed and eaten in the consecrated bread of the Eucharist (*hoc sensu*), it can indeed be corrupted. In any sense which would imply that the flesh of Christ could be corrupt absolutely, in that sense (*hoc modo*) the statement must be false. We must note that this is a composite noun: *caro* and *Christi* can be separated, and then the parts of the *nomen compositum* no longer signify the same.

Odo's *Quaestiones*, then, deal with fallacies and apparent contradictions piecemeal. He considers problems arising out of the study of the Sacred Page where two passages seem to stand in opposition to one another and difficulties of a more speculative kind without discrimination, because he is not concerned with classification of types of fallacy. Each problem is approached in the way which seems most likely to produce a solution. But it would be quite wrong to think of Odo as a master who was not aware of the latest technical developments and willing to make use of the help the study of the *artes* could give him. He understands the technical aspects of the problems before him well enough to point confidently to the weakness in an argument. His own technical competence is beyond question. He wanted, however, to train his students to form the habit of reading the text minutely, and so he encourages them to practise that close scrutiny of the way words are being used which is the first requirement in detecting fallacies. He offers no short cuts. Every problem must be looked at on its own merits. Peter the Chanter, on the other hand, expected his students to come to class well equipped with technical knowledge so that he could classify for them the types of apparent contradiction to be found in Scripture quickly, simply by naming the type of *equivocatio* or *amphibolia* or *consignificatio* involved.

The change which had been brought about in the atmosphere of the schoolroom in these few decades, and which is superbly exemplified in the exploratory *Quaestiones* of Odo of Soissons, had enormous implications. It took the student of the Bible from something not far removed from the *lectio divina* of the monastic schools to the university lecture-room, where there was a syllabus to be covered, an order of treatment, and a certain amount of technical knowledge expected. Odo's pupil could follow his explanations without having studied the *Sophistici Elenchi*. Simon of Tournai's pupil would have found a knowledge of the *Sophistici Elenchi* helpful, but not indispensable. Peter the Chanter's pupil would have made little sense of his lectures *De Tropis Loquendi* without it.

It is instructive to set the *De Tropis Loquendi* beside a more or less contemporary treatise on fallacies which covers much the same ground but draws its examples from secular rather than scriptural sources. Peter draws upon treatises and teaching of this kind in order to give technical exactness to his explanations; he borrows rules from grammar and logic and replaces standard examples with fresh illustrations drawn from Scripture. It is this replacement of the stock examples which is perhaps his most original contribution, for it is in this way that he shows the precise application of contemporary work on fallacies to the study of the Bible.

We must begin with the fallacy treatises themselves. The *Fallacie Londinienses* survives in a single manuscript of the early thirteenth century, British Library MS Royal IX, fos. 127–34. It probably originated in England between 1160 and 1190.[66] If this is indeed the case, the resemblance to Peter the Chanter's teaching requires some explanation, for Peter taught, as far as we know, nowhere outside France. William de Montibus, Peter's pupil, provides one known link, however, and no doubt there were more English scholars who returned home with French treatises. William almost certainly brought a copy of the *De Tropis Loquendi* with him. One group of manuscripts of the *De Tropis Loquendi* preserves a curious version of the text in which the long *reportatio* version begins part of the way through, taking over from an abbreviated version. All these manuscripts were either written in England or are now held in English repositories, and there must be a strong probability that they all derive from the copy brought to England and put into circulation by William. The earliest of them dates from soon after the time of his return. In such circumstances of free movement and exchange of scholarly endeavour there is no difficulty in understanding how an English treatise on fallacies proves to be so close in doctrine to Peter's *De Tropis*. And, in any case, the *Fallacie Londinienses* is close to other contemporary works on fallacy.

The arrival of Aristotle's *Sophistici Elenchi* in the French schools shortly before the middle of the twelfth century[67] stimulated new work on fallacy, but a solid foundation had already been laid by students of Boethius' commentaries on the *De Interpretatione* and the treatise on categorical syllogisms where Boethius outlines the theory of fallacy.[68] In *De Interpretatione* (6.17^4.25–6) Aristotle points out that sometimes a clear view of the opposition between two propositions is impeded by equivocation. The analysis of equivocation is the keynote of the earlier twelfth century study of fallacy, and equivocation continued to be a prominent feature of later treatises. It provides Peter the Chanter with the bulk of his material in the *De Tropis*. Compare, for example, *Ego dico vobis non iurare* (Matt. 5:34) with *Iuravi et statui custodire* (Ps. 118:106). It seems that in the first text the Christian is being told not to swear and in the second encouraged to do so. To swear lightly or falsely is prohibited, Peter explains, but to promise firmly or to take a solemn vow is a virtuous act. 'Swearing' means something different in the two passages, and so they do not contradict one another at all. The equivocal use of words was, even in this relatively simple way, of direct concern to the interpreter of the Bible.

Peter wrote his treatise in the decades at the end of the century when the study of fallacies no longer depended largely on Boethius. The commentaries written in the twelfth century on the *Sophistici Elenchi* distinguish three modes (*modi*) of equivocation. In the first case a noun with several primary impositions or *significationes* has a number of literal or 'proper' senses. This comes about because of that shortage of words in human language upon which Bede as well as Abelard remarks. It is therefore an unavoidable or 'necessary' multiple usage. Abelard suggests that this should be called a *translatio que fit causa necessitatis*.[69] It is also possible for a noun or verb to have only one meaning by primary imposition, but another according to a figurative or metaphorical usage (*translatio*). Abelard calls this *translatio que fit ad ornatus sermonis*.[70] In the third case, the noun in question has only one meaning by itself, but when used in conjunction with other words, it turns out to have other meanings. This threefold division between apparent contradictions arising out of these three types of *equivocatio* provides Peter the Chanter with a system of division for his own treatise. First he deals with a series of equivocations which occur when words are used *proprie*, and then with a series arising when they are used *improprie* or metaphorically, and then with compounds of various sorts.

The parallels between the *Fallacie Londinienses* and the *De Tropis Loquendi* fall, broadly, into three groups: those involving equivocation in the primary or principal signification of the word, that is, its literal meaning; those involving equivocation arising out of a difference in what is consignified by the word in its two contexts; and those arising out of *amphibolia*, or ambiguity. The second group affords the most close and detailed parallels. The author of the *Fallacie Londinienses* divides this category of fallacies into those where what is consignified is, respectively, case, number, genus, time, mood, person. This is much the same list as Peter the Chanter gives under a similar heading.[71]

Under *consignificatio casus*, the consignifying of a case which differs in each premise, the author of the *Fallacie Londinienses* gives the following example:

> quicumque est rationalis, est homo
> sed iste asinus est rationalis

The second proposition may be translated in two ways: 'but that ass is rational', or 'but that is the ass of a rational man', because the nominative case looks the same as the genitive. If we read:

> whoever is rational is man
> but that ass is rational
> therefore it is a man

we have an absurdity. If we read:

> whoever is rational is man
> but that ass belongs to a rational man[72]

no conclusion follows at all. Peter the Chanter's example comes from Acts 1:6: *Domine si in tempore hoc restitues regnum Israel?* Does this mean that the Kingdom is restored to Israel or that the Kingdom *of* Israel is restored? Since *Israel* is indeclinable, we cannot tell what case is intended. The principle is identical with that of the *Fallacie Londinienses*, but Peter has substituted a scriptural example.[73]

For *consignificatio numeri*, the *Fallacie Londinienses* has this example:

> quaecumque sunt alba, sunt plura
> hec mulier est alba
> ergo est plura

> whatever are white are many
> this woman is white
> therefore she is many

The absurdity arises because in the first proposition *alba* is plural (*pluralis numeri*); in the second, although the ending is the same, it is a feminine singular (*singularis numeri*).[74] Peter's example again comes from Acts 4:1: *Principes venerunt et magistratus Templi.* *Magistratus*, Peter claims, again citing Bede, is in the nominative singular, and refers to the Chief Priest,[75] although its ending would allow us to read it as a plural.

Under the heading: *ex diversa consignificatione temporis* the author of the *Fallacie Londinienses* gives this syllogism:

> quidquid legit est legens
> sed Socrates legit
> ergo Socrates est legens

Legit may be either a present tense or a past tense of the verb, so that the syllogism may read either:

> whatever reads is reading
> but Socrates has read
> therefore Socrates is reading

or:

> whatever reads is reading
> but Socrates reads
> therefore Socrates is reading

The former does not yield a valid inference; the second is perfectly satisfactory. Peter the Chanter gives a number of examples to illustrate cases where, for instance, a present participle is made to signify the past; where a verb in the future may refer to the near future or to the distant future; where a past participle may refer to the distant past or to the recent past; where the present refers to the near future; where the past is given for a future which is prophetically certain. Peter's example of the first[76] – again from the Acts of the Apostles (1:1–2) – is of especial interest because he gives a parallel which appears in the *Dialectica Monacensis*; he shows how a present participle may stand for the present or the past, depending on the context. The *Dialectica* borrows from Aristotle, *Sophistici Elenchi* 4.165^b.38ff.:

> whoever was healed is healthy
> the working man was healed
> therefore the working man is healthy

Laborans, the 'working man', may be working at present or he may have been working in the past, and the validity of the conclusion depends upon the tense implied. Peter's example involves the passage: *Precipiens apostolis per Spiritum Sanctum*. This is to be read, he says, as *qui precipiebat*, not as *qui precipit*, just as 'the working man was healed' refers not to him who 'works', but to the man who 'was working': *sicut 'laborans sanabatur', non qui laborat, sed qui laborabat*.

In a similar way, Peter has a scriptural example to offer for cases where a verb in one premise is in one mood and in another in a different mood (although it might on the face of it be either). He also has instances of imperative confused with indicative, indicative for optative, imperative for indicative again; and he matches the points in the dialectical treatise with biblical examples at every point. Some of these involve not cases where confusion arises from the form of the word, but instances where Scripture uses one form in place of another. In *Quod facis, fac citius* (John 13:27), *fac* is used in place of *facies*, says Peter, for the Lord was not giving Judas an order, but recognising that his resolve was already fixed.

Peter does not restrict himself to the use of grammatical and dialectical aids only in dealing with the literal sense. He tries to apply them in, as it were, a 'literal' way to the interpretation of the figurative sense, too. He deals methodically first with 'proper' and then with 'improper' or transferred usages. This is an important aspect of his treatise because it involves him, not in building castles of figurative interpretation in the air, but in subjecting the figurative to the same technical analysis as the literal. It brings the 'higher' senses within the ambit of the skills of the grammarian and dialectician.

'Improper', transferred or figurative usages are divided by Peter into three types: *in demonstratione*; *in relatione*; *in translatione*. Of these only the third always involves a figurative usage. The others may do. Petrus Helias provides a grammarian's definition of the first two in his commentary on Priscian Minor. Under the heading *De Divisione Pronominum et Demonstrativa et Relativa* he points out that some pronouns are demonstrative and others are relative.[77] First and second person pronouns are always demonstrative, says Petrus Helias, but it is not true, conversely, that all third person pronouns are relative. Some of them are demonstrative, like *hic*, one of Peter's favourite examples. A contemporary commentary on Priscian gives a list: 'Some pronouns are demonstrative, some relative, some both demonstrative and relative.' Demonstrative ones are 'I', 'you', 'that' (*iste*), 'this' (*hic*). Relative ones are 'that', 'which', 'the same' (*idem*). Both demonstrative and relative are *ille* and *ipse*.[78] *Relatio* makes a connection with 'the matter with which the preceding word or thought was concerned': *relatio . . . rei de qua precessit sermo vel cogitatio vel recordatio*.[79] The relative pronoun thus recalls to mind the preceding noun. It is inserted in its place, so that there is no need to repeat the noun. We speak of Virgil (*iste*), 'He wrote the *Bucolics*'. 'The same (*idem*) wrote the *Georgics*'. The second assertion makes sense only in relation to the first.[80] A 'demonstrative pronoun makes a new beginning'. It stands in place of a noun different from the preceding one (*ponuntur loco aliorum*), as in 'Socrates reads and I argue'.

The *Fallacie Londinienses* offers helpful definitions of some of the fallacies which arise: *ex diveresa demonstratione* and *ex diversa relatione*. The author distinguishes four kinds of fallacies which occur in connection with equivocation. The first which 'comes from the principal signification of the word' may be further subdivided into six. In one of these subdivisions he touches upon the distinction between *proprietas* and *improprietas* and gives an example which shows that he has in mind the same distinction as Peter the Chanter between the use of a word according to its proper signification and a metaphorical or figurative usage:

> whatever laughs is a man
> but the meadow laughs
> therefore the meadow is a man

(A standard means of identifying man by a characteristic peculiar to him describes him as *risibilis*, capable of laughter, to distinguish him from other animals.)

In the first statement 'laughs' is being used properly, that is, in its literal sense. In the second it is used figuratively. Therefore the conclusion does not follow. The two propositions have nothing in common and so there can be no middle term:

Hec dictio 'ridet' in una propositione tenetur proprie, in alia transumptive. Et ideo non provenit conclusio.

For fallacies *ex diversa demonstratione* the author of the *Fallacie Londinienses* gives the following example:

> this word 'alpha' is a letter of the alphabet
> but this word 'alpha' is a dissyllable
> therefore a dissyllable is a letter of the alphabet

In the first proposition what is 'demonstrated' by the demonstrative pronoun 'this' is that which is signified by the word 'alpha'. In the second type of fallacies *de diversa relatione* what has gone wrong is something like this:

> Socrates is either a rational or an irrational animal
> an ass is an irrational animal
> therefore Socrates is an ass

Irrationality has been incorrectly 'related' to Socrates and thence arises the *deceptio*.

Another dialectical treatise, the *Quaestiones Victorinae*, gives a theological example, which is perhaps a little clearer. It is asked concerning the construction 'God made man in his own image; male and female created he them', whether this relative 'them' refers to the term 'man' or to the terms 'male and female'. The solution offered is that 'them' refers to 'man', which carries a plural sense in this context (that is, it has a plural 'supposition' here).[81]

Peter the Chanter's interest in *equivocatio* is conspicuous in the earliest passages of the *De Tropis Loquendi*. He speaks of *equivocatio* in his headings with a freedom which suggests that he takes the same view of its all-purpose usefulness as a technical term as the author of the dialectical treatise known as the *Fallacie Parvipontane* appears to have done. *Equivocatio* has a narrower meaning (*strictus* as opposed to *largius*) in many contemporary works. Underlying the general consensus that *equivocatio* and *univocatio* are inter-related is a certain amount of confusion – or at least disagreement – about the precise nature of their relationship.[82] The *Fallacie Parvipontane* defines *univocatio* as involving different suppositions of a term which retains the same signification through-out:[83] *univocatio est manente eadem significatione variata nominis suppositio.*[84] In equivocation, taken in its strict sense, one of the terms does not have the same signification as the other, as a result of different *impositiones*.[85] The general use of *equivocatio* for both univocation and equivocation is, however, so widespread that it must have been technically acceptable.

In a case of apparent discrepancy between two biblical passages we may find that in one context a word is being used 'properly', that is, according to its true signification, and in the other in some 'improper' way; or we may find that it is used 'properly' in neither context. But there will sometimes be, in one or the other or both of the passages, an 'improper' usage. The meaning-in-context, which may involve diverse *suppositiones* in the 'improper' usage, will involve some process of transference of signification such as a metaphorical or figurative usage will occasion. Abelard prefers to avoid the term *univocatio* and speaks instead of *translatio* for such 'borrowings'.[86]

Peter distinguishes in the conventional way, as Bede does, between unavoidable transference of usage, or borrowing, where shortage of words makes it necessary to employ the same term for different purposes; and a merely decorative transference, such as occurs in metaphor and other figures of speech.[87] The first always involves equivocation (in the strict sense) because a separate *impositio* is involved, and therefore a separate *significatio*. The second does not.

Abelard takes his subdivisions further, going beyond these two types of *translatio* to make a distinction between 'grammatical' and 'dialectical' *translatio*. In the first, the 'borrowed' term is used as though it were mentioned as exemplifying a grammatical category, as when we say 'man is a word' (*homo est vox*). A man is not a word, but the *word* 'man' is a word. In the second, the borrowed term is used as though it were a logical category, as when we say 'man is a species' (*homo est species*). A man is not a species, but the *species* 'man' is a species. In each case, for lack of a separate term for the-word-man or the-species-man we use *homo* in a transferred sense.[88] He is of course speaking in terms of a language lacking the convenience of some way of explicitly showing diversity of semantic category.

Peter the Chanter, like Abelard, prefers *translatio* for cases where a word is used in a 'transferred way', in a metaphorical or 'borrowed' sense. In theology an 'improper' usage of this kind sometimes has to stretch to refer to something which lies altogether beyond the range of ordinary human language. This, as Peter explains, is 'necessary' because Scripture does not have words for heavenly things (*de rebus caelestibus*).[89] The problems to which he addresses himself are not primarily those which arise as 'grammatical' or 'logical' or 'decorative' *translatio*, but those occasioned by the figurative use of language, and in particular the special difficulties which arise when we talk about God and find ourselves short of words. Although some contemporary treatises on fallacy include theological examples, Peter the Chanter is undoubtedly doing something new and important in attempting a systematic treatment of such *translationes* from this point of view.

Peter the Chanter distinguishes, then, between three kinds of impropriety; that which arises from ambiguity in the use of relative pronouns, that which arises from ambiguity in the use of demonstrative pronouns, and the ambiguities of *translatio*. Certain topics which we have met elsewhere and which had perhaps emerged as those posing classic difficulties appear under all three of these headings: confusions about *accidens* and *subiectum*, about *materia* and *materiatum*, about *persona* and *natura*, about *continens* and *contentum*, about *significans* and *significatum*, about *totum* and *pars*.

Zachary considered confusions of *significans* and *significatum*. Peter, too, is concerned about confusions of the signifier with the thing signified. In the case of *continens* and *contentum* he considers the cases where the container is given instead of the thing contained, or the thing contained instead of the container. In confusions of *materia* and *materiatum*, the matter from which something is made is confused with the thing made from the matter. This principle is stated in a dialectical rule: if the *materiatum* is given, the *materia* is given, too (*posito materiato, ponitur et materia*).[90] For example: 'He possesses a sword; therefore he has iron.' A use of *materia* and *materiale* by dialecticians and grammarians falls into the same category:

Appellant autem antiqui materiale impositum quando nomen imponitur ad agendum de sua materia, *id est de ipsa voce*, ut cum dico: 'homo est nomen' ibi hoc nomen est materiale impositum.[91]

The *antiqui* say that a word is 'imposed materially' when it is imposed so as to refer to its own subject-matter, that is, to the word itself: as when I say *homo est nomen*. There the word 'man' is materially imposed because it refers to itself as a word, not to mankind.[92]

Confusions about parts and wholes are a well-trodden theme; we have seen that Zachary considered them (p. 146). Certain rules are set out by the author of the *Logica 'Ut dicit'*. Given the *pars subiectiva*, the whole is given, too. Given the *totum integrale*, the part is given, too. If the *pars integralis* is destroyed, so is the whole to which it belongs. If a whole quantity is given, so is its part.[93] Peter's concern is with cases where an ambiguity arises because a part is mistaken for a whole, or a whole for a part. We may take, Peter suggests, 'And you are clean, but not all' (John 13:10) to be an instance of the reference to a part as though it were a whole and classify it as a case of *pars in toto* under the general heading of *demonstratio*.[94]

As to confusions of subject and accident: the *Fallacie Londinienses* provides a definition of a *fallacia secundum accidens* which helps to make it clear what Peter has in mind.[95] For *accidens* we must read 'predicate'. The ambiguity arises because the subject and the predicate have had their positions reversed.[96]

With *persona* and *natura* we are in an area which, as we might expect, Peter treats for the most part as theological. Baldwin notes that 'Peter the Chanter contributed only one *quaestio* to the discussion of his contemporaries about the Nature of Christ', but he reckons without the *De Tropis Loquendi*.[97] Peter has a good deal more to say on the matter in his treatise. The contradictions he considers arise out of the difficulty Peter of Poitiers points to in his *Sententiae*: whether the word 'person' follows the rule for those words which are taken *essentialiter*.[98] Peter the Chanter prefers to speak of *natura* instead of *essentia*, but this is the question at the back of his own mind as he looks at the Bible's references to the Persons and Nature of the Trinity.

These parallels show how far grammar and dialectic were penetrating the study of the Bible at its most technically demanding. To the simpler reader they can have had little to offer. To the student of theology in the schools – always a very small minority of the Bible's readers – they were a satisfactory, and surely immensely satisfying, means of understanding the reason why a number of the Bible's statements are puzzling and rendering them clear and straightforward. They are the end of a road on which Abelard set out when he compiled the *Sic et Non* and wrote its challenging Prologue; the ultimate development of the methods of reconciling contradictions which were being developed in the 'sentence' and 'question' literature of the first half of the twelfth century.

CONCLUSION

Gregory the Great prefaced his vast commentary on the Book of Job with a letter in which he explained something of his intention in writing it. 'Whoever speaks about God must take care to search thoroughly for anything which may teach his listeners how to live a better life, and he should be confident that he is arranging his talk along the right lines if, when an opportunity presents itself, he turns aside from the matter in hand to speak about some edifying point'. Gregory sees the exposition of Scripture as a river of discourse. As the river flows along its bed it comes from time to time to open valleys, and it runs into them at once until they are full, and then it pours itself back into its course.[1] This discursiveness of biblical scholarship is the characteristic most likely to strike the modern reader as he comes to Gregory and his mediaeval successors for the first time. The Bible seemed to mediaeval exegetes to be infinitely profuse in its riches, and yet unified in its teaching. Adam the Scot, a Premonstratensian canon of the twelfth century, describes the 'great and wonderful profundity' of Scripture, the veil beneath which it hides its depths; its essentially paradoxical nature, showing God and his works in simple things and at the same time elevating those simple things to a high significance; how it is always one and the same and yet teaches that 'one' in many ways, according to the multiplicity of human needs.[2]

This variety and subtlety of biblical language discouraged more than the broadest attempts at classification for many centuries. The notion that the literal meaning might be only one of several possible meanings for a given passage became current in the first Christian centuries, and we find mediaeval authors from Bede onwards referring familiarly to a 'figurative' sense, allegorical, tropological, anagogical, and sometimes all three in the same passage. Yet the bulk of the work done by mediaeval exegetes up to the twelfth century – and it was an enormous bulk – was chiefly concerned with particular problems within the text rather than with the drawing up of rules.[3] The scale of the operation is clear from every surviving library catalogue of the early mediaeval centuries, where books of the Bible, glossed and unglossed, outnumber every other kind of book, even the liturgical in many cases.[4]

The twelfth century produced new work and new thinking in almost every area of intellectual endeavour. Giraldus Cambrensis, discussing the historian's task, shows how universally the study of the Bible with all its apparatus underlay that work. He defends himself in a letter to Master William de Montibus, chancellor of Lincoln Cathedral, against the contention that he ought to be writing a work of theology not a history. Historians ought to be respected, he says. Jerome and Augustine wrote histories. History is, in Seneca's words, 'the authority of antiquity, the witness of the times, the way of life, the life of memory', and so on. In Giraldus's book on the history of Ireland the reader will find applied, not without stylishness (*non ineleganter*), theological points 'both moral and allegorical'. His defence of history is conducted, in other words, in terms of its theological value as a source of moral instruction, and in terms of its comparability with works of the Fathers. Giraldus is in fact writing a work which has all the value of a 'theological' study with, he insists, the advantage that it is original and not derivative, while the work of contemporary theologians is nothing more than a reshuffling of old material.[5] Whether his assessment is fair or not, it reflects a widespread contemporary feeling for what is new within an old tradition, an interest in schemes and theories which give an overall view of an area of study. The study of the Bible itself was first thought of as an 'academic' discipline in the nascent universities of the twelfth century, and it was within the lifetime of Giraldus (he was born c. 1146) that it came to embrace the speculative study of problems of faith and doctrine in a single subject of study.

There must be both subjective and objective in criticism; both inward perception and response; and some account given in terms intelligible and acceptable to others of the reasons why that response is appropriate. The emphasis of many of the monastic commentators of the twelfth century was upon fostering and cultivating the capacity for response in themselves and others; they try above all to convey the splendour and beauty of the Bible's teaching, to rouse their readers to excitement over it, and to profound devotional feeling. The academics concentrate upon the objective and technical side of biblical criticism – although rarely without, in each case, some consideration of the other side. Even within the comfortable and largely traditional framework of Hugh of St Victor's schoolroom in the 1120s and 1130s, the habit of 'placing' what was studied within a plan or scheme was becoming established. Hugh explains how the novice should approach the study of Scripture. 'You brothers, who have now entered the school of discipline, ought first to seek in holy reading what may instruct you in virtuous behaviour, rather than what will make you sharp-witted, and you should seek rather to be informed by Scripture's precepts than to be impeded by questions.' He goes on to encourage them to seek methodically to learn what Scripture can teach them.[6] The monk is to hold no science or piece of writing cheap; nor is he to be too proud to learn from anyone; nor is he to despise others when he himself becomes expert.[7]

John of Cornwall describes how he had often seen his master, Peter Lombard, with the works of *his* master, Peter Abelard, in his hands, and how there had been frequent discussions by other masters and scholars on certain points.[8] At the end of the twelfth century in Paris a comparatively small number of masters was teaching theology to those relatively few students who remained in the schools after they had equipped themselves in the liberal arts and who had not chosen to enter the ecclesiastical civil service or to go on to take a higher degree in law. They were a close-knit community who had been building for several generations upon the work of previous masters. Their new academic theology was still grounded in the study of the Bible out of which it had grown, and although it had developed into a science with many of the characteristics of the *artes* – with rules and technical aids and a syllabus of topics to be covered – it remained unique in many of its exegetical assumptions and, above all, in its importance.

Twelfth century scholars took a major step forward in their thinking about the nature and functioning of theological language. Their approach took to its technical limits the implications of Augustine's teaching about the special use of language in the Bible. They helped to shift the earlier preoccupation with figurative interpretations to a serious concern with making the literal sense make sense. These developments brought to an end the most notable spurt of new work in exegesis of the Middle Ages. But since there was no questioning of the fundamental assumptions of earlier centuries – the literal inspiration of Scripture word by word and the consequent importance of making sense of it as it stands – it was not possible for them to move far towards modern standards of criticism. A vast amount of intellectual ingenuity was spent in erecting contrivances which now seem absurd. And it cannot be over-emphasised that, alongside all that is new in the areas of *lectio* and *disputatio* we have been examining, the old approach to commentary persisted. Peter the Chanter's technical expertise in the theory of signification gave his treatment of problems raised by biblical language in the *De Tropis Loquendi* a high sophistication, but he had, too, a thoroughly traditional respect for figurative interpretation, as his own scriptural commentaries amply demonstrate, and he was known above all as a moralist. He rarely plunges his hand very deeply into the barrel of his technical knowledge of language theory in his own commentaries.

Nevertheless, stripped of the trappings of the mediaeval tradition, something of importance remains. There is a perennial difficulty for the creature who wishes to talk about his Creator in a language which can be no more than creaturely. The difficulty was described with a new precision and clarity, and some sensible suggestions were made about the ways in which it might be circumvented. If the new look at the Bible's language which began to be taken in these first centuries of the Middle Ages did no more than this, it achieved a very great deal.

II

Protestant theology began with the assertion of the principle of *sola Scriptura*. The Bible had to be its own interpreter (*sui ipsius interpres*).[9] Two centuries after the Reformation the rationalism of the day encouraged the development of a critical method based on the principle that the Bible must be subjected to analysis and investigation like any other ancient document, if it was to be properly understood.[10] Once that was conceded, a variety of approaches became possible, resting on numerous philosophical and critical assumptions. The text has been examined to discover what it meant when it was written, as distinct from what it means for its present-day reader.[11] Or, conversely, it has been read 'in faith' for what it has to teach the Christian reader now.[12] Or an attempt has been made to reconstruct both the historical context and the world of faith within which each book speaks, so as to understand its structural unity.[13]

All these, and a multitude of other approaches, have had in common a desire to find a single method of criticism wholly appropriate to the special status of the Bible and at the same time giving satisfactory answers to minds harbouring the reservations of their day about the validity of different modes of proof and the nature of certainty. Sometimes the endeavour has broken down into a scrutiny of individual fragments, as in 'form criticism'.[14] Sometimes it has been possible to stand back and consider the influence of one book on another, or to look for a human author who can be understood as a person who had his own purpose in mind in writing as he did. All these, *mutatis mutandis*, are equally features of mediaeval exegesis.

It has become possible since the Reformation to ask questions about the Bible which could not be asked in the Middle Ages. But a number of mediaeval critical procedures are still with us. We still compare the views of previous critics; we still compare textually similar usages in different parts of the Bible; we still bring in secular authors of scriptural times for comparison.[15] Some critics still look to typology for illumination.[16] It is still possible to publish a 'religious and theological exposition'[17] which explicitly does not set out to engage with a good many current problems of critical procedure. Above all the commentary is still the natural vehicle of biblical criticism, with its insistence upon word-by-word analysis and the value thus implicitly placed upon every detail of the text. The patristic and mediaeval legacy lingers most strikingly here.

It would be absurd to suggest that little headway has been made since mediaeval times in the understanding of the Bible. The modern critic is vastly better informed than his predecessor on points of history and the transmission of the text. But no consensus has yet been reached on the way in which the Bible should be approached and the questions which should be asked about it. The mediaevals we have been looking at had a consensus. It is no longer a generally tenable one, because it involved a widespread if not universal acceptance of the view that the Holy Spirit dictated the Bible verbatim to its human authors, with all that that implied for mediaeval exegetes. But it was an approach which cast a certain amount of light incidentally on problems of epistemology and theological language, and it deserves perhaps to be more widely known and to take its proper place in the history of exegesis. Here was laid all the groundwork for the technical refinements of the later Middle Ages: the period which preceded the major changes of the Reformation.[18]

NOTES

Preface

1 To take some recent discussions in which questions germane to the work of these mediaeval scholars are raised afresh: R. Bosley, 'Existence and Purported Reference', *Mind*, 77 (1968), 84–95; G. Weiler, 'A Note on Meaning and Use', *Mind*, 76 (1967), 424–7; C.R. Carr, 'Speaker Meaning and Illocutionary Acts', *Philosophical Studies*, 34 (1978), 281–91; V.C. Aldrich, 'Mirrors, Pictures, Words, Perceptions', *Philosophy*, 55 (1980), 39–56; T. Iglesias, 'Russell and Wittgenstein: Two Views of Ordinary Language', *Philosophical Studies NUI*, 28 (1981), 149–63; J.M.E. Moravcsik, 'How Do Words Get Their Meanings?', *Journal of Philosophy*, 78 (1981), 5–24.

Introduction

1 *In Cant.*, p. 3, 9–10.
2 These views are expressed widely in Augustine's writings. See my *Augustine on Evil* (Cambridge, 1983), chapter 3.
3 *In Job*, I.xiii.31; CCSL, 143.42.18.
4 *In Cant.*, p. 3, 14–15.
5 *Ibid.*, p. 3, 18–4.2.
6 Oxford, Bodleian Library, MS Auct. D.3.14, fo. 8^{rc}.
7 *In Cant.*, p. 4, 27–30.
8 *Ibid.*, p. 4, 34–5.
9 See my *Augustine on Evil*, chapter 1. The doctrine that every word of the Bible is there for a purpose is still to be found in Wyclif, for example: *Opus Evangelicum*, I, ed. J. Loserth (London, 1895), pp. 1024–6.
10 *Ibat animus meus per formas corporeas.*
11 DDC, I.xiv.13, p. 13, 2–14, 30.
12 *Ibid.*, I.xii.11, p. 12, 1–5.
13 *Ibid.*, I.xii.12, p. 12, 10–14.
14 *Didasc.*, V.5, PL, 176.793.
15 *In Gen.*, 18.1; PL, 131.89C–D.
16 *De Trin.*, II.xvi.27; CCSL, 50.115–16.
17 *En. Ps.*, 103.iv.1; CCSL, 40.1521.1–19.
18 *Glossa Ordinaria*, PL, 113.747.
19 See B. Smalley, 'Peter Comestor on the Gospels and his Sources', *RTAM*, 46 (1979), 85ff. on the way in which some early exegetes, following Origen, took the figure or metaphor as part of their spiritual interpretation, moving straight to the spiritual sense. They sometimes claimed that a passage had *no* literal sense.

20 *En. Ps.*, 105.18; CCSL, 40.1561.2–3.
21 *Ibid.*, 104.18; CCSL, 40.1546.3–4.
22 *De Civ. Dei*, XX.21; CCSL, 48.738.67–70.
23 *Ibid.*, IX.4; CCSL, 47.251.19, and *En. Ps.*, 108.23; CCSL, 40.1597.14.
24 *In Reg.*, I.2; p. 56, 51–3; cf. Job 1:1; Luke 1:5.
25 *In Reg.*, p. 56, 53–7.
26 *Ibid.*, p. 56, 57–9.
27 *Ibid.*, p. 56, 63–5.
28 *Inst.*, I.xv.i; p. 51, 23–5.
29 *Ibid.*, I.xv.2; p. 42, 8–13.
30 *In Job*, CCSL, 143.7.221–2.
31 See chapter 2.
32 *In Job*, Preface i.2; CCSL, 143.8.21–9, 32.
33 Preface to the Pentateuch, PL, 28.181A–182A.
34 *Q. in Gen.*, PL, 100.677B. See Smalley, 'Peter Comestor', 84–5 on the 'zone of uncertainty' left by the Fathers here.
35 *Ibid.*, PL, 100.678D–679A.
36 *Didasc.*, VI.iii; PL, 176.801: *Illa prima significatio cuiuslibet narrationis quae secundum proprietatem verborum exprimitur.*
37 *Hom. in Eccles.*, Preface; PL, 175.114–15.
38 *Ibid.*
39 See J.W. Baldwin, *Masters, Princes and Merchants* (Princeton, New Jersey, 1969), 2 vols., on Peter the Chanter and his circle.
40 PL, 205.
41 *Ibid.*, 205.25.
42 J.J. Murphy, *Rhetoric in the Middle Ages* (Berkeley, California, 1974), pp. 317–27.
43 B. Smalley, *The Study of the Bible in the Middle Ages* (Oxford, 2nd edn, 1952), p. 27.
44 Murphy, *Rhetoric*, p. 319.
45 Cambridge, Corpus Christi College, MS 455, fo. 1[rb].
46 *Ibid.*, fo. 4[ra].
47 *Ibid.*, fo. 77[rb].
48 *Ibid.*, fo. 77[rb]; cf. fo. 76[ra] on the legal topic.
49 *Ibid.*, fo. 4[ra].
50 Simon of Tournai, *Disp*, p. 39 and *passim* for references to *hodierna disputatio*.

1 The monastic way

1 *Proslogion*, S, I.97.4–9.
2 See my *Old Arts and New Theology* (Oxford, 1980), pp. 57–79 and p. 61 n. 12.
3 *Sup. Matt.*, CCCM, 29.3; 29.4.38–40.
4 *In Hiez.*, CCCM, 23.1643.5–8.
5 *Ibid.*, CCCM, 23.1643.35–1644.43; Jerome, *In Hiez.*, Prol., 25–30; CCSL, 75.75.3ff.
6 *In Hiez.*, CCCM, 23.1644.47–50.
7 Evans, *Old Arts*, pp. 59–79.
8 *In Ex.*, CCCM, 22.802.2199–2204.

9 *Trin.*, XXXV–VI; XL; CCCM, 24. This is an Augustinian distinction. See, for example, *De Trin.*, XII.
10 *De Conversione Sua*, p. 74, 9.
11 *In Ex.*, CCCM, 22.584.137.
12 *In Deut.*, CCCM, 22.1065.117.
13 *In Ex.*, CCCM, 22.583.111–584.
14 *Trin.*, Epistola ad Cunonem; CCCM, 21.119.18–21.
15 *Ibid.*, Prologue; CCCM, 21.125.22.
16 *In Deut.*, CCCM, 22.1062.16–19.
17 *Trin.*, Prologue; CCCM, 21.126.46–57.
18 *In Ex.*, CCCM, 22.801.2147–84.
19 *Sup. Matt.*, CCCM, 29.19, especially lines 546–7.
20 *In Deut.*, CCCM, 22.1016.84.
21 *Cur Deus Homo*, I.i; S, 2.48.8–9.
22 For Anselm, see especially the final chapters of the *Proslogion* on the pleasures of heaven, S, I.9ff., chapters 25 and 26.
23 *In Hiez.*, CCCM, 23.1644–5.
24 *Sup. Matt.*, CCCM, 29.397.25–6.
25 *In Gen.*, CCCM, 21.129.
26 *Ibid.*, CCCM, 21.148.723–149.760.
27 S, I.98.4.
28 *Excitatio mentis ad contemplandum deum, ibid.*, I.97.3.
29 On Anselm's life, see R.W. Southern, *St Anselm and his Biographer* (Cambridge, 1963). His thorough reading of the Fathers, especially Augustine, had, however, clearly done a great deal to form his ideas.
30 On the history of these explanations, see H. de Lubac, *Exégèse médiévale* (Paris, 1959), 2 vols.
31 S, I.173.2–3.
32 For a study of Anselm's use of these devices, see D.P. Henry, *The Logic of St Anselm* (Oxford, 1967).
33 S, I.173.2–3.
34 *Ibid. (feci diversis temporibus).*
35 *Ibid.*, I.7.3–4.
36 Ordericus Vitalis, *Hist. Eccl.* II.246. II.296 mentions the *rustici* who seem philosophers at Bec.
37 S, I.93.9–10.
38 *Monologion*, 18; S, I.33.11–22; *De Veritate*, S, I.176.4–40.
39 *Letters*, 64; S, III.180.5–6; *Letters*, 19–20; S, III.127.7–9.
40 S, I.177.10–12.
41 *Ibid.*, I.177.19.
42 *Ibid.*, I.178.1–4.
43 *Ibid.*, I.178.25–6.
44 *Ibid.*, I.179.1–15.
45 *Ibid.*, I.179.15–19.
46 *Ibid.*, I.179.19–21.
47 *Ibid.*, II.60–4.
48 *Ibid.*, II.61.8–10.
49 *Ibid.*, II.62.5–27.
50 *Ibid.*, II.62.13–16.
51 *Ibid.*, II.62.17–63.18.
52 *Ibid.*, II.63.17–64.11.

53 For a bibliography of Gilbert Crispin, see *The Works of Gilbert Crispin*, ed. G.R. Evans and A. Abulafia (London, forthcoming).

54 *Disputatio* (ed. B. Blumenkranz (Antwerp, 1956), p. 31.31.

55 *Ibid.*, p. 29.11.

56 *Ibid.*, p. 31.20–2.

57 *Ibid.*, p. 31.22–6.

58 *Ibid.*, p. 51.1–2.

59 *Ibid.*, p. 34.29–30.

2 Bible study in the schools

1 On Hugh's career and the beginning of the Victorine Order, see J. Ehlers, *Hugo von St Viktor* (Weisbaden, 1973).

2 See Smalley, *The Study of the Bible*, pp. 87–8 on Hugh's system.

3 See *Epistola anonymi ad Hugonem amicum*, ed. E. Martène and A. Durand, 'Thesaurus Novus Anecdotorum', I.487–8.

4 On the *accessus*, see R.B.C. Huygens, *Accessus ad Auctores* (Leiden, 1970).

5 Oxford, Bodleian Library, MS Rawl.G.17, fo. 1ra. See Smalley, 'Peter Comestor on the Gospels', 110–11 on Abelard's claim to be the first to use the *accessus* in this way.

6 Oxford, Bodleian Library, MS e.Mus.3, fo. 1ra.

7 *In Hexaemeron*, PL, 178.731A–B.

8 *Ibid.*, 178.731–3.

9 *In Isaiam*, PL, 194.997C.

10 *Ibid.*, 194.1001.

11 'Epitome Dindimi in Philosophiam', *Opera Propaedeutica*, pp. 187–207.

12 *Ibid.*, pp. 192–3.

13 Some of these tables are reproduced in my *Old Arts*, pp. 15–16.

14 Oxford, Bodleian Library, MS Add. C.269, fo. 2ra.

15 *Q. in Ep. Paul.*, PL, 191.1327.

16 *Didasc.*, VI.12; PL, 176.809.

17 PL, 64.875–92.

18 *Didasc.*, VI.12; PL, 176.908.

19 *Adnotationes Mysticae in Psalmos*, 28; PL, 196.299C.

20 *Ibid.*, 196.300.

21 *Ibid.*, 196.295.

22 *Ibid.*, 196.306.

23 For a recent study, see H. Kirkby, 'The Scholar and his Public', in *Boethius, His Life, Thought and Influence*, ed. M.T. Gibson (Oxford, 1981), pp. 44–69.

24 Cassiodorus, *Inst.*, Pref., I.

25 *Four Labyrinths*, III.viii, p, 257, and IV.i, p. 270. On *proponere, assumere, concludere*, see Henry, *Logic*, p. 241.

26 V. Law, *Insular Latin Grammarians* (Studies in Celtic History, III (London, 1982)), p. 11.

27 *Ibid.*, p. 2.

28 *In Job*, Epist. Miss., V; CCSL, 143.7.220–2.

29 *Ibid.*

30 See *The Commentaries on Boethius by Gilbert of Poitiers*, ed. N.M. Häring (Toronto, 1966), pp. 189–90.

31 Paul Alvarus of Cordoba, *Epistula*, I.ii; PL, 121.413C.

32 See p. 100.
33 *Ecrits de l'école d'Abélard*, ed. A. Landgraf, SSL, 14 (1934), pp. 5–7.
34 Hugh of Amiens, *Hexameron*, I.i, 140.
35 Lubac, *Exégèse*, II'.113–28 considers the *bovinus intellectus*.
36 Sapientia 11:21.
37 Lubac, *Exégèse*, II'.13ff. examines number symbolism.
38 *Commentaries on Boethius by Thierry of Chartres and his School*, ed. N.M. Häring (Toronto, 1971), includes an edition.
39 *Hom. in Eccles.*, PL, 175.116B.
40 On the existence of these barriers, see my *Alan of Lille* (Cambridge, 1983), pp. 33–53. On the wish for precision in men trained in the arts course, see Smalley, 'Peter Comestor on the Gospels', 88.

3 A standard commentary: the 'Glossa Ordinaria'

1 *Hist. Calam.*, pp. 68–70. On Abelard's use of an *Expositor*, see B. Smalley, 'Some Gospel Commentaries of the Early Twelfth Century', *RTAM*, 45 (1978), 153, and *Hist. Calam.*, p. 69: *Assumpto itaque expositore statim in crastino eas ad lectionem invitavi*. See Smalley, 'Some Gospel Commentaries', 149 on the attitude of secular masters.
2 *Hom. in Eccles.*, PL, 175.114.
3 *In Psalmos*, PL, 195.154B, on Ps. 66.
4 B. Smalley, 'La *Glossa Ordinaria*, quelques prédécesseurs d'Anselme de Laon', *RTAM*, 9 (1937), 365–400. In what follows I have depended largely upon Miss Smalley's pioneering work. For more recent published material, see B. Smalley, 'An Early Twelfth Century Commentary on the Literal Sense of Leviticus', *RTAM*, 36 (1969), 78–99, and her 'Peter Comestor on the Gospels', 84–129; J. McEvoy, 'The Son as *res* and *signum*: Grosseteste's Commentary on *Ecclesiasticus*, ch. 43, vv. 1–5', *RTAM*, 41 (1974), 38–9; Smalley, 'Some Gospel Commentaries', 147–80, pp. 147–8 on the importance of the Psalter and Paul; E. Bertola, 'La *Glossa Ordinaria* biblica ed i suoi problemi', *RTAM*, 45 (1978), 34–78, and Bertola's earlier articles listed there on p. 44, nn. 12, 13.
5 Oxford, Bodleian Library, MS Lyell 1, from Augustine's Canterbury manuscript. On this manuscript, see A. de la Mare, *Catalogue of the Lyell Manuscripts in the Bodleian Library, Oxford* (Oxford, 1971).
6 Smalley, *The Study of the Bible*, p. 63, and B. Smalley, 'Les Commentaires bibliques de l'époque romane: glose ordinaire et gloses périmées', *Cahiers de Civilisation Médiévale*, 4 (1961), 23–46; R. Wasselynck, 'L'Influence de l'exégèse de S. Grégoire le Grand sur les commentaires bibliques médiévaux', *RTAM*, 32 (1965), 157–204.
7 Smalley, 'Some Gospel Commentaries', 140.
8 E.g. Oxford, Bodleian Library, MS Lyell 1, fo. 100.
9 B. Smalley, 'Gilbertus Universalis, Bishop of London (1128–34) and the Problem of the *Glossa Ordinaria*', *RTAM*, 7 (1935), 242.
10 Smalley, *The Study of the Bible*, p. 47.
11 *Ibid.*, p. 48.
12 J.M. de Smet, 'L'Exégète Lambert, écolâtre d'Utrecht', *Revue d'Histoire Ecclesiastique*, 42 (1947), 103–10.
13 Smalley, *The Study of the Bible*, pp. 52–5.
14 M.T. Gibson, *Lanfranc of Bec* (Oxford, 1978), pp. 39–40.

15 Smalley, *The Study of the Bible*, pp. 52–5.
16 Gibson, *Lanfranc*, pp. 51–2.
17 *Ibid.*, p. 53; cf. Smalley, 'La *Glossa Ordinaria*', 375.
18 Gibson, *Lanfranc*, p. 54, and see the same author's 'Lanfranc's Commentary on the Pauline Epistles', *JTS*, 22 (1971), 86–112.
19 Gibson, *Lanfranc*, p. 55.
20 *Ibid.*, p. 53 and Smalley, 'La *Glossa Ordinaria*', 376.
21 Gibson, *Lanfranc*, p. 53.
22 *Ibid.*, pp. 57–8.
23 *Ibid.*, pp. 56–7 has examples.
24 Lanfranc wrote to Domnald, bishop of Hibernia to say that he had given up dialectic since he became archbishop. See Lanfranc's *Letters*, Letter 49, p. 161.
25 Pl, 150.102B–C; and see Gibson, 'Commentary on the Pauline Epistles'.
26 *Ibid.*, 150.103A.
27 Gibson, *Lanfranc*, p. 65.
28 Smalley, 'La *Glossa Ordinaria*', 372–99, especially pp. 391–4, and Smalley, *The Study of the Bible*, p. 47.
29 Smalley, 'La *Glossa Ordinaria*', 392; MS Berne 334, fo. 100^v.
30 On the possibility that this is Bernard of Tours' friend Drogo, see Smalley, 'La *Glossa Ordinaria*', 380–1.
31 Smalley, *The Study of the Bible*, p. 396, from MS Berne 334, fo. 120^v and MS Vat. Lat. 143, fo. 92^r on Gal. 2:16. On hypothetical syllogisms, see Boethius, *De Syllogismis Categoricis*, PL, 64.831–76 and Abbo of Fleury.
32 Gibson, *Lanfranc*, pp. 36–7, 139–40, 143, 150.
33 See Smalley, 'La *Glossa Ordinaria*', 390–1 for examples.
34 On Bruno, see A. Stoelen, 'Les Commentaires scripturaires attribués à Bruno le Chartreux', *RTAM*, 25 (1958), 177–247.
35 *In Psalmos*, PL, 152.652C, on Ps. 5. See, too, *Les 'tituli Psalmorum' des manuscrits latins*, ed. P. Salmon (Rome, 1959), pp. 149–86, 'Série de Cassiodore, résumée par Bède'.
36 *In Psalmos*, PL, 152.647, on Ps. 3.
37 Noted by Stoelen, 'Les Commentaires scripturaires', 192; *In Psalmos*, PL, 152.684C; 808D; 874A–B; 981D.
38 Smalley, 'La *Glossa Ordinaria*', 373–4.
39 G. Morin, 'Le Pseudo-Bède sur les Psaumes et "L'opus super Psalterium" de maître Manégold de Lautenbach', *RBén*, 28 (1911), 331–40.
40 Smalley, *The Study of the Bible*, pp. 49, 60–2 (on Ralph of Laon).
41 *Hist. Calam.*, pp. 68–70.
42 Oxford, Balliol College, MS 36, fo. 145^v, ed. R.A.B. Mynors, *Catalogue of the Manuscripts of Balliol College, Oxford* (Oxford, 1963), p. 26.
43 O. Lottin, *Psychologie et morale aux xiie et xiiie siècles*, 6 vols. (Gembloux, 1957–60), V, p. 9; and F. Bliemetzrieder, 'L'Œuvre d'Anselme de Laon et la littérature contemporaine, II: Hughes de Rouen', *RTAM*, 6 (1934), 261–83 and 7 (1935), 28–52. See, too, T. Waldman, 'Hugh "of Amiens" archbishop of Rouen 1130–64', Oxford D.Phil. thesis, 1970.
44 Smalley, 'La *Glossa Ordinaria*', 400; Paris, MS Nat. Lat., 12011, fo. 173^b.
45 Lottin, *Psychologie*, V draws together a series of articles.
46 Lottin, *ibid.*, V, 11; Troyes Bib. Mun., MS 425, fo. 95ra.
47 See chapter 8 on *quaestiones*.
48 A. Wilmart, 'Un Commentaire des Psaumes restitué à Anselme de Laon', *RTAM*, 8 (1936), 325–44; cf. Lottin, *Psychologie*, V, 170–5.

49 Smalley, 'La *Glossa Ordinaria*', 365.
50 Smalley, 'Peter Comestor on the Gospels', 84; and see Lottin, *Psychologie*, V, 153 and 169 on the commentary on Matthew, PL, 162.1227–500. The latter now seems unlikely to be Anselm's. See Smalley, 'Peter Comestor on the Gospels', 95ff.
51 Smalley, *The Study of the Bible*, pp. 50–1.
52 Lottin, *Psychologie*, V, 83, no. 98.
53 *Ibid.*, 84, no. 100.
54 *Ibid.*, 97–18–9, no. 1120.
55 Smalley, *The Study of the Bible*, pp. 364–5; 'Gilbertus Universalis', 235–62 and 'Gilbertus Universalis, Bishop of London (1128–34) and the Problem of the *Glossa Ordinaria*: 2', *RTAM* 8 (1936), 24–64.
56 Smalley, Gilbertus Universalis', 237.
57 *Ibid.*, 238.
58 *Ibid.*, 243.
59 *Ibid.*, 247–8.
60 *Ibid.*, 235.
61 Hugh's pupil Andrew of St Victor did, however, use the *Glossa Ordinaria* in the 1140s.
62 Oxford, Bodleian Library, Laud. Misc. 2/391, fo. 3C.
63 *Ibid.*, fo. 9^d. On Petrus Manducator, see A. Landgraf, 'Recherches sur les écrits de Pierre le Mangeur', *RTAM*, 3 (1931), 366–72.
64 Without title or author. Presented by the Dean and Canons of Windsor in 1612.
65 J. de Ghellinck, *Le Mouvement théologique du xiie siècle* (Bruges, 1948), col. 98. Herbert of Bosham suggested later in the century that when he revised the work he did not intend it for use as a class-book, but for independent reading.
66 *Q. in Ep. Paul.*, PL, 191.1302.
67 *Ibid.*, 191.55.
68 *Ibid.*, 191.57.
69 *Ibid.*, 191.58B.
70 *Ibid.*, 191.58A–B.
71 See Smalley, *The Study of the Bible*, pp. 46ff.; and for the borrowing process in the formation of the commentary on Matthew attributed to Anselm of Laon in Migne (n. 50), see Smalley, 'Peter Comestor on the Gospels', 95ff.
72 See J. Blic, 'L'Œuvre exégétique de Walafrid Strabon et la *Glossa Ordinaria*', *RTAM*, 16 (1949), 5–28; and e.g. PL, 114.795A–B for a reference to Strabo.
73 PL, 64.306.
74 Oxford, Bodleian Library, MS Lyell 1, fo. 4. See Smalley, *The Study of the Bible*, p. vii on the importance of this manuscript.
75 Martianus Capella, *De Nuptiis Philologiae et Mercurii*, ed. A. Dick (Leipzig, 1925), p. 186, 9–12; cf. John's own *Annotationes in Marcianum*, ed. C.E. Lutz (Cambridge, Mass., 1939), p. 100, 14–16.
76 Cf. John Scotus Eriugena, *Commentaire sur l'Evangile de Jean*, ed. E. Jeauneau, SC (Paris, 1972), p. 100 (I.xxi).
77 John Scotus, *Homélie sur le Prologue de Jean*, ed. E. Jeauneau, SC (Paris, 1969), pp. 226.1–228.3 and p. 227 n. 2 on the sources of John's remarks in the Greek Fathers.
78 *Glossa Ordinaria*, PL, 113.77D.
79 *Ibid.*, 113.91C.

80 *Ibid.*, 113.97B–C.
81 *Ibid.*, 113.288B.
82 *Ibid.*, 113.290A.
83 *Ibid.*, 113.289D (Augustine Q. 154).
84 *Ibid.*, 113.104D.
85 *Ibid.*, 113.196B.
86 *Ibid.*, 113.199C.
87 *Ibid.*, 113.114C.
88 *Ibid.*, 113.115.
89 *Ibid.*, 113.93D.
90 *Ibid.*, 113.93B.
91 *Ibid.*, 113.126A.
92 *Ibid.*, 113.129A.
93 *Ibid.*, 113.144B; 150B; 205A.
94 *Ibid.*, 113.178A.
95 *Ibid.*, 113.261C.
96 *Ibid.*, 113.275B.
97 *Ibid.*, 113.295C–296A.

4 Words and things and numbers

 1 Peter Lombard, *Sent.* I.i.1.
 2 *Ibid.*, I.xxi.1ff.
 3 Augustine, *DDC*, IV.i.1; CCSL, 32.
 4 *DDC*, I.ii.2; CCSL, 32.
 5 *The Rules of Tyconius*, p. xi.
 6 *Ibid.*, p. xiii.
 7 *Ibid.*, p. xiii.
 8 *Ibid.*, pp. 11, 22–5.
 9 *Ibid.*, Rules I, VII.
10 *Ibid.*, p. xiv.
11 *DDC*, II.i.2; CCSL, 32.
12 Augustine read the *Categoriae* as a young man and was much influenced by the work, but his knowledge of Aristotle was never extensive.
13 *DDC*, II.i.2; CCSL, 32.
14 Gregory the Great, *In Cant.*, p. 5, 49–54.
15 Hugh of St Victor, *Didasc.*, V.iii; PL, 176.790; cf. *De Sacr.*, Prologue, V; PL, 176.185B–C.
16 *De SS*, xiv; PL, 176.20–1.
17 Peter Abelard, *Dialectica*, p. 111, 13.
18 *Ut vox leo animal ipsum significet, animal vero diabolum designet*; *Didasc.*, V.iii; PL, 176.791.
19 Gregory, *In Job*, V.xxi.41; CCSL, 143.246–7.
20 On the Latin *Physiologus*, see F.M. McCulloch, *Mediaeval Latin and French Bestiaries* (University of North Carolina Studies in the Romance Languages and Literature 33, 1962) and the edition of F.J. Carmody, *Physiologus Latinus* (Paris, 1939).
21 London, British Library, MS Royal 12C XIX.204, fo. 6ᵛ.
22 *DDC*, I.i.2; CCSL, 32.
23 *De Trin.*, XV.ix.15; CCSL, 50.
24 *In Job*, II.ii.2; CCSL, 143.

25 PL, 116.195B.
26 *In Ps.*, PL, 191.55–62.
27 Oxford, Bodleian Library, MS Add. C 169, Flanders, late twelfth century.
28 *LM* I^i.180ff.; and see Boethius on primary signification, PL, 64.159B–C.
29 Hugh of St Victor, *De Sacr.*, Prologue, IV; PL, 176.184–5.
30 Cf. Magister Bandinus, *Sententiae*, PL, 192.1031B.
31 Cf. *Glossa Ordinaria* on Babel, Gen. 11:8–9; PL, 113.115.
32 Gregory, *In Reg.*, I; CCSL, 144.
33 *Didasc.*, VI.2–3; PL, 176.799B–C.
34 PL, 70.30B.
35 S, II.51–2; Gerhoch, *In Psalmos*, PL, 194.147–8, on Ps. 66. .
36 G. Ropa, ed., *L'Enarratio Genesis di Donizone di Canossa* (Bologna, 1977), p. 71.
37 Cambridge, Corpus Christi College, MS 455, fos. 1^{ra}ff.
38 See PL, 64.297A for the Latin text of Boethius' lemma.
39 See H. Lange, 'Traités du xiie siècle sur la symbolique des nombres: Odo de Morimond', *Cahiers*, 40 (1981), xxviii–xxxiii, for a preliminary discussion of these and other sources. See, too, the sources identified in this text, and the same editor's 'Traités . . . Geoffroy d'Auxerre et Thibault de Langres', *Cahiers*, 29 (1978).
40 Lange, 'Traités du xiie siècle', xxviii–xxxii.
41 On the relationship of these treatises, see Lange, 'Traités . . . Geoffroy d'Auxerre', ix–xi.
42 See Augustine, *DDC*, I.ii.2 and II.i.2.
43 *Quaestiones*, Prologue, pp. 3, 6–8.
44 *Ibid.*, p. 3, 13–16.
45 *Ibid.*, p. 4, 1–2.
46 *Ibid.*, p. 4, 22–5.
47 *Ibid.*, p. 3,10–11; and cf. p. 15, 1–2.
48 *Ibid.*, p. 15, 1–2 and p. 4, 11.
49 *Ibid.*, pp. 4–5.
50 *Ibid.*, p. 6, 5–6.
51 *Ibid.*, p. 17, 1–13.
52 *Ibid.*, p. 18, 15–19.
53 *Ibid.*, p. 3, 10–11.
54 *Ibid.*, p. 7, 42–8, 3.
55 *Ibid.*, p. 6, 4.
56 *Ibid.*, p. 6, 9–16.
57 *Ibid.*, pp. 19–20; cf. p. 21, 10ff. for a summary of the ways in which words signify things.
58 *Ibid.*, pp. 25–7.
59 *Ibid.*, p. 28, 5–15.
60 *Ibid.*, p. 70, 3–5, opening of Part III.
61 *Ibid.*, p. 8, 2–6.
62 *Ibid.*, p. 18, 8–19, 3.
63 J. Pinborg, introduction to J. Pinborg, O. Lewry, K.M. Fredborg, N.J. Green-Pedersen, Lauge Nielsen (eds.), 'The Commentary on "Priscianus Maior" Attributed to Robert Kilwardby', *Cahiers*, 15 (1975), 9$^+$–10$^+$.
64 See *Quaestiones*, p. 32 for a list.
65 H. Lange, 'Les Données mathématiques des traités du xiie siècle sur la symbolique des nombres', *Cahiers*, 32 (1979), covers the material in all the

twelfth century treatises. See p. 14 for a list of nine *modi significationum* culled from these authors.

66 *Ibid.*, 13 for terminology.
67 *Ibid.*, 34.
68 See my article, '*Duc oculum*: Aids to Understanding in Some Mediaeval Treatises on the Abacus', *Centaurus*, 19 (1976), 252–63.
69 Lange, 'Les Données', 35.
70 *Ibid.*, 34.
71 *Ibid.*, 35.
72 *Ibid.*, 32; Gregory, *In Job*, XVIII.xlii.67; CCSL, 143^A.
73 See Henry, *Logic* for a study of Anselm's use of the concepts of direct and oblique signification in the *De Grammatico*.
74 Abelard, *Dialectica*, p. 118, 14–16.
75 *LM*, III^{ii}.371.21–2; PL, 64.305.
76 For a summary of these *modi*, see Lange, 'Les Données', 42.
77 Bede on Genesis, *In Gen.*, II.viii.14; p. 126, 1906–7.
78 *Ibid.*, p. 126, 1922–5.
79 *Ibid.*, II.vi.14; p. 103, 1067–9.
80 *Ibid.*, II.vi.15; p. 106, 1179.
81 *Ibid.*, p. 106, 1198–1201.
82 *Ibid.*, p. 114, 1473.
83 Hugh of St Victor, *De Inst. Nov.*, PL, 176.629–33.
84 See Pinborg *et al*, 'The Commentary on "Priscianus Maior" ', 66.
85 Bede, *De Temp.*, PL, 90.187–277.
86 Theobald, in Lange, 'Traités . . . Geoffroy d'Auxerre', 64.
87 See my '*Duc oculum*: Aids to Understanding'.
88 Theobald gives tables, see Lange, 'Traités . . . Geoffroy d'Auxerre', II.
89 *Ibid.*, 53–4.
90 *Ibid.*, 61.
91 *Ibid.*, 53ff.
92 *Ibid.*, 68.
93 *Ibid.*, 70.
94 The opening chapters of Boethius' *De Institutione Arithmetica* are concerned with this principle.
95 Theobald, in Lange, 'Traités . . . Geoffroy d'Auxerre', 42.
96 Lange, 'Les Données', 42.
97 Theobald, in Lange, 'Traités . . . Geoffroy d'Auxerre', 106–7.

5 The historical sense and history

1 Alcuin, *Q. in Gen.*, Preface; PL, 100.517A.
2 Hugh of St Victor, *Didasc.*, VI.iv; PL, 176.802C–D.
3 See Lubac, *Exégèse*, I^{ii}.481 on architectural images.
4 *Didasc.*; PL, 176.804.
5 *De SS*, PL, 175.12A.
6 E.g. PL, 92.957C.
7 *In Psalmos*, PL, 194.175C.
8 *Ibid.*, 194.174B, verse 9.
9 *Ibid.*, 194.175C–D.
10 On Hugh on history, see R.W. Southern, 'Aspects of the European Tradition of Historical Writing: 2. Hugh of St Victor and the Idea of Historical

Development', *Transactions of the Royal Historical Society*, 21 (1971), 159–79.

11 Hugh of St Victor, *Didasc.*, VI.ii; PL, 176.800C.

12 *Ibid.*, VI.ii–iii.

13 W.M. Green, 'Hugh of St Victor: *De Tribus Maximis Circumstantiis Gestorum*', *Speculum*, 18 (1943), 484–93.

14 PL, 175.75–8.

15 *Ibid.*, 175.87A.

16 *Ibid.*, 175.32–3.

17 *Ibid.*, 175.32–3: *Quia per istam historicam narrationem ad altiorum rerum intelligentiam provehimur.* On *veritas rei*, cf. Jerome, *In Matth.*, 15 and Henry, *Logic*, p. 234.

18 Cf. Cicero, *Orator*, II.9 on history as the mistress of life; Lubac, *Exégèse*, I^{ii}.467; and Gregory, *In Job*, XXIII.xix.34.

19 Abelard, *Comm. in Rom.*, p. 44, 112–19.

20 *Ibid.*, p. 45, 143–4.

21 *Ibid.*, p. 87, 362.

22 *Ibid.*, p. 53, 194–211.

6 Exegesis and the theory of signification

1 See pp. 51–3 and *DDC*, I–II. This area is conveniently covered in *The Cambridge History of Later Mediaeval Philosophy* (Cambridge, 1982), especially for the thirteenth century.

2 Boethius, *De Interp.*, p. 32, 10–12; cf. Abelard, *Dialectica*, p. 582, 29–30, from an unidentified source: *interpretatio* is a *definitio per quam ignotum alterius linguae vocabulum exponitur.*

3 And also the phrase or saying: Boethius, *De Interp.*, p. 32, 22–5.

4 Boethius, *De Interp.*, p. 37, *passim* on signification; see too, *LM*, II^i.177–80.

5 Boethius, *De Interp.*, p. 37, 25.

6 Alcuin, *Q. in Gen.*, PL, 100.523.

7 Remigius of Auxerre, *In Gen.*, II.1; PL, 131.81B; cf. PL, 131.115 quoting Alcuin.

8 On the *accessus*, see R.B.C. Huygens, *Accessus ad Auctores* (Leiden, 1970).

9 For examples of diagrams showing the *schemata* of the sciences, see my *Old Arts*, pp. 16–19.

10 On the arrival of the *Posterior Analytics*, see L. Minio-Paluello, *Posterior Analytics (Post. An.)*, ed. E.S. Forster (London, 1976), I.ix.76^a, 17–19.

11 This is the subject of *Post. An.*, I.

12 *Commentaries on Boethius by Gilbert of Poitiers*, pp. 189–90.

13 Pinborg *et al.*, 'The Commentary on "Priscianus Maior" ', 30–1. The thirteenth century developments go technically beyond the level of the twelfth century exegetical use of signification.

14 See O. Lewry's discussion, in *ibid.*, 12$^+$–17$^+$.

15 *Post. An.*, 61^{b15}.

16 'Kilwardby', Pinborg *et al.*, 'The Commentary on "Priscianus Maior" ', 9.

17 *Ibid.*, and cf. *Post. An.*, 87^{a38-9} and 95^{a1-6}.

18 'Kilwardby', Pinborg *et al.*, 'The Commentary on "Priscianus Maior" ', 10.

19 See Pinborg, in *ibid.*, 6$^+$–7$^+$.

20 'Kilwardby', *ibid.*, 49.

21 *Ibid.*, 12 and 50.

22 *Ibid.*, 50.
23 *Ibid.*
24 *Ibid.*
25 *Ibid.*, 50–1.
26 *De Interp.*, 16$^{a4–9}$.
27 'Kilwardby', Pinborg *et al.*, 'The Commentary on "Priscianus Maior" ', 51.
28 *Ibid.*
29 *Ibid.*, 52. 'Kilwardby' acknowledges his debt to Petrus Helias; Paris, Arsenal, MS 711, fo. 21vb.
30 'Kilwardby', Pinborg *et al.*, 'The Commentary on "Priscianus Maior" ', 56–7.
31 *Ibid.*, 64.
32 *Ibid.*
33 Hugh of St Victor, *Adnot. in Pent.*, PL, 175.29; on this gloss, see *LM*, II^i.255–63, and R.W. Hunt, 'Studies on Priscian in the Twelfth Century', *MARS*, 2 (1950), 1–55.
34 Garlandus, *Dial.*, p. 65, 26–7.
35 Abelard, *Theol. Chr.*, III.162; CCCM, 12,255; Aristotle, *De Interp.*, I.16^a.
36 *Commentaries on Boethius*, p. 285, 51 (*intellectus enim constituunt vocabula*).
37 *Ibid.*, p. 172, 114; cf. p. 277, 83–4.
38 *Ibid.*, p. 278, 88–90.
39 PL, 194.1080B.
40 *LM*, II^i.206.
41 S, I.157.1–8 and Henry, *Logic*, pp. 18–26.
42 Abelard, *Dialectica*, p. 87, 38–88.1; cf. p. 82, 32 and p. 151, 35–152.1. Abelard cites Priscian, *Inst. Gram.*, I.175; II.213; and cf. *Log. Ingr.*, p. 218, 17–99.
43 *Sup. Matt.*, 1.2; CCCM, 29.9.177.
44 Remigius of Auxerre, *In Gen.*, PL, 131.83.
45 PL, 116.718A, Haymo on Isaiah; and cf. Lanfranc, *In Rom.*, PL, 150.115C.
46 'Kilwardby', Pinborg *et al.*, 'The Commentary on "Priscianus Maior" ', 64–5.
47 *Ibid.*, 65–6.
48 *Ibid.*, 66.
49 *Ibid.*; cf. Priscian, *Inst. Gram.*, II.iii.14, p. 53.
50 'Kilwardby', Pinborg *et al.*, 'The Commentary on "Priscianus Maior' ", 71.
51 *Ibid.*, 67.
52 See Henry, *Logic*, p. 207 (on *De Magistro*).
53 *De Interp.*, I, 17^a,28–30.
54 Cf. Anselm, *De Veritate*, I; S, I.178–9.
55 Cf. Anselm, *Proslogion*, I; S, I.100.
56 'Kilwardby', Pinborg *et al.*, 'The Commentary on "Priscianus Maior" ', 73–5.
57 *Ibid.*, 79.
58 *Ibid.*, 17–18.
59 *Ibid.*, 6–7.
60 *Ibid.*, 23.
61 R.H. Rouse and M. Rouse, 'Biblical Distinctions in the Thirteenth Century', *AHDLMA*, 41 (1974), 29; and in *Renaissance and Renewal in the Twelfth Century*, ed. R.L. Benson and G. Constable with C.D. Lanham (Cambridge, Mass. and Oxford, 1982), pp. 201–25.

62 *Ibid.*, 27–8. Cambridge, Pembroke College, MS 8 is an example of a fine large concordance, the chapters of the Bible numbered in Roman figures with subdivisions labelled by letters of the alphabet (four or seven, depending on the length of the chapter). The words are arranged alphabetically, each with a brief context. Related words are grouped together, as: *signare, non signare, signans, signator, signum, signaculum, significare, non significare, significans, significatio*, and subtle distinctions are possible.

63 Gregory, *In Job*, IV.xiii.25.

64 *In Gen.*, PL, 131.83.

65 PL, 210.161D.

66 *Q. in Gen.*, PL, 175.35.

67 *Ibid.*, 175.36.

68 *In Psalmos*, PL, 194.214B–D.

69 *In Psalmos*, PL, 189.1569–72, Homily I.

70 *Ibid.*, 189.1583–4, Homily V.

71 *Prob. Hel.*, PL, 178.757D.

72 *Ibid.*, 178.735.

73 Peter of Poitiers, *Sent.*, pp. 1–2.

74 Richard of St Victor, *Adnotationes Mysticae in Psalmos*, PL, 196.268.

75 *Ibid.*, 196.270D.

76 On this gloss, see *LM*, II^i, pp. 255–63, and Hunt, 'Studies on Priscian', 1–56.

77 *In Rom.*, PL, 150.161.

78 Oxford, Bodleian Library, MS e. Mus. 3, fo. 1ra.

79 On *suppositio*, see *LM*, II^i.205.

80 *Prob. Hel.*, PL, 178.741C, and see *Dialectica*, p. 151, 30–6.

81 Alcuin, *Q. in Gen.*, PL, 100.526.

82 *Ibid.*, 100.546.

83 *Ibid.*, 100.527B.

84 *Ibid.*, 100.1094D. Alcuin himself gives a definition of a sign as a 'seal' (*sigillum*) and says that 'to sign' is therefore 'to seal'.

85 Rabanus Maurus, *Hom.*, IV; PL, 110.141A.

86 *Ibid.*, XLI; PL, 110.221A.

87 *Ibid.*, XLIV; PL, 110.249A.

88 *Ibid.*, XLIV; PL, 110.250C.

89 *LM*, II^i.195–205.

90 Ralph of Beauvais, *Glose Super Donatum*, pp. xxiv, 147.29–148.3.

91 *Ibid.*, p. xix.

92 *Ibid.*, p. xviii.

93 *Ibid.*, p. 10, 9–18. Ralph has a notable chapter on *regimen*, pp. 11–12.

94 *Ibid.*, p. 37, 25–7.

95 *Ibid.*, p. 36, 16–17.

96 *Ibid.*, p. 37, 10–13.

97 *Ibid.*, p. 53, 25.

98 *Ibid.*, p. 147.29–148.3.

99 *LM*, II^{ii}.371.21–2.

100 *Ibid.*, II^i.227.

101 Boethius, *De Interp.* I, p. 46, 1–2.

102 *Ibid.*, p. 48, 18; cf. D.P. Henry, *Commentary on 'De Grammatico'* (Dordrecht, 1974), p. 259.

103 *Vim temporis in significationibus trahit.*

104 Thierry of Chartres, *Commentaries on Boethius*, p. 524, 10.

105 PL, 210.640A, Rule 40.

106 PL, 64.305, for example.
107 *LM*, II^i.227.
108 Garlandus, *Dial*, pp. lvi and 115; cf. Abelard, *Dialectica*, p. 166, 27–9.
109 Abelard, *Dialectica*, p. 118.
110 *Theol. Chr.* I.7; CCCM, 12.74.89–90.
111 D. Luscombe, *The School of Peter Abelard* (Cambridge, 1969), pp. 103–42.
112 H.C. van Elswijk, *Gilbert Porreta*, SSL, 33 (1966), pp. 77–128.
113 *In Psalmos*, PL, 194.1078D.
114 *Ibid.*, 194.1079A–B.
115 *Ibid.*, 194.1089B.
116 On Boethius, see H. Chadwick, *Boethius* (Oxford, 1981), pp. 203–11, especially p. 208.
117 PL, 194.1089B.
118 *Ibid.*, 194.1090A.
119 *Ibid.*, 194.1093A–B.
120 PL, 210.628B–C.
121 *Ibid.*, 210.629A–B.
122 *Ibid.*, 210.630B–C.
123 I am indebted to F. Giusberti for much of what follows. See his article 'A Treatise on Implicit Propositions from Around the Turn of the Twelfth Century', *Cahiers*, 21 (1978), 45–115.
124 *De Interp.*, p. 219.
125 *LM*, II^i.354.
126 *Ibid.*, II^i.268.
127 Giusberti, 'A Treatise on Implicit Propositions', 55.
128 *Ibid.*, 58.
129 J.E. Tolson, 'The Summa of Petrus Helias on Priscianus Minor', with an introduction by M.T. Gibson, *Cahiers* (1978), 27–8, and see R.W. Hunt, 'Studies on Priscian in the Eleventh and Twelfth Centuries, I, Petrus Helias and his Predecessors', *Mediaeval and Renaissance Studies*, 1 (1943), 194–231.
130 Paris, Arsenal, MS 711, fos. 16, col. 2–16^v, col. 1. See Henry, *Commentary on 'De Grammatico'*, pp. 262–3. I am indebted to Dr Henry for his helpful comments on an early draft of what follows.
131 Boethius, *De Interp.* I, p. 4, 5; p. 4, 26; p. 5, 12.
132 Abelard, *Dialectica*, p. 118, 4–5: *Oportet enim ut etiam per se dictae coniunctiones vel prepositiones aliquam significationem habeant.*
133 *Ibid.*, p. 118, 12–13.
134 *Ibid.*, p. 118, 14–15: *Suspensum tenent animum auditoris, ut aliud expectet cui illa coniungantur.* The conjunction is behaving as a *functor*. See D.P. Henry, 'Mediaeval Critics of Traditional Grammar', *Historiographia Linguistica*, VII, 1/2 (1980), 85–107.
135 Abelard, *Dialectica*, p. 118, 26–9: *pro appositione diversarum.*
136 *Ibid.*, pp. 118, 29–119, 2.
137 *Ibid.*, p. 119, 16.
138 *Ibid.*, p. 119, 20–2.
139 *De Syllogismis Categoricis*, PL, 64.796D.
140 Abelard, *Dialectica*, p. 119, 29.
141 *Ibid.*, p. 120, 4–5.
142 *Ibid.*, p. 120, 5–13.
143 *LM*, II^{ii}.150.7; cf. Boethius, *De Syllogismis Categoricis*, PL, 64.796D, and see Henry, *Commentary on 'De Grammatico'*, p. 262.

144 Paris, Arsenal, MS 711, fo. 16ᵛ.
145 *Ibid.*, fo. 120.
146 *Ibid.*, fos. 111ff.
147 See *LM*, IIⁱ.89–91 on this manuscript, and *ibid.* p. 240 for the passage in question (fo. 23ᵛᵇ); cf. *ibid.* pp. 226ff. and p. 254.
148 J. Pinborg, 'Ein frühes *Compendium Modorum Significandi*', *Cahiers*, 1 (1969), 13–14.
149 PL, 100.1033. On the authenticity of Alcuin's work on Hebrews, see F. Stegmüller, *Repertorium Biblicum Medii Aevi* (Madrid, 1940–), II, 1099.
150 Alan of Lille, *Regulae Theologicae*, PL, 210.634–46, Rules 27–53.
151 Thierry of Chartres, *Commentaries on Boethius*, p. 487, 42–5; cf. Alan of Lille, *Regulae Theologicae*, IV; PL, 210.625.
152 *Regulae Theologicae*, PL, 210.640.
153 *Ibid.*, Rule 41.
154 *Ibid.*, Rule 43.
155 *Ibid.*, Rule 44.
156 *Ibid.*, Rule 45.
157 *Ibid.*, Rules 46 and 47.
158 *Ibid.*, PL, 210.703.
159 *Ibid.*, 210.750.
160 *Ibid.*, 210.756.
161 *Ibid.*, 210.910.
162 The most recent study of Peter the Chanter is Baldwin's *Masters, Princes and Merchants*.
163 The edition of the Prologue by the late F. Giusberti is shortly to be published. See, too, my article, 'Peter the Chanter's *De Tropis Loquendi*: The Problem of the Text', *The New Scholasticism*, 55 (1981), 95–103.
164 B. Smalley, 'The School of Andrew of St Victor', *RTAM*, 11 (1939), 145–67 and 'Andrew of St Victor, Abbot of Wigmore: A Twelfth Century Hebraist', *ibid.*, 10 (1938), 358–74.
165 See my article, 'A Work of "Terminist Theology"?', *Vivarium*, 20 (1982), 40–58.
166 See my 'Peter the Chanter's *De Tropis Loquendi*' for a list of manuscripts. See pp. 150ff. on this section of the work.
167 *LM*, IIⁱ.491–512.
168 Oxford, Bodleian Library, MS Rawl. C 161, fo. 170ᵛᵃ.
169 Troyes, Bib. Mun., MS 398, fos. 89ʳᵃ–115ʳᵇ.
170 *LM*, IIⁱⁱ.320.24ff.
171 *Ibid.*, IIⁱⁱ.340.24–30.
172 Luke 13:4.
173 *Regulae Theologicae*, PL, 210.687–8.
174 E.g. *ibid.*, 210.943.

7 Transference of meaning

1 PL, 202.1051D.
2 *Q. in Gen.*, PL, 100.520C.
3 Cf. Rupert of Deutz, *Trin.*, CCCM, 24.433–40.
4 Aristotle, *Categoriae*, I.1a.
5 PL, 64.164A and see Henry, *Logic*, p. 47.
6 *In Psalmos*, PL, 189.1527D–1573A; on this division of the uses of *similitudo*, cf. Bede, *De Sch. et Tr.*, PL, 90.175A; p. 607; and pp. 101–5.
7 PL, 194.1109.

8 See my article, 'St Anselm's Images of the Trinity', *JTS*, 27 (1976), 46–57; and Anselm, *De Processione Spiritus Sancti*, II.199–201.

9 *Memorials of St Anselm*, ed. R.W. Southern and F.S. Schmitt (London, 1969), pp. 296–7 and 302–3.

10 Anselm, *De Incarnatione Verbi*, XIII; S, II.31–2.

11 *De Processione Sancti*, S, II.201–5.

12 Abelard, *Theol. Chr.*, IV.83; CCCM, 12.304.

13 *Ibid.*, V.135; CCCM, 12.333–4.

14 *Ibid.*, IV.86; CCCM, 12.306.

15 *Ibid.*, IV.87; CCCM, 12.307 and cf. *ibid.*, p. 287.

16 *Ibid.*, IV.5; CCCM, 12.287.

17 See my article, 'A Work of Terminist Theology?', 55–6.

18 *Q. in Gen.*, PL, 175.42D.

19 *Ibid.*, 175.43C.

20 *Dies, inquam, ironice, vere autem nox*, *Trin.*, CCCM, 24.1866.173.

21 DDC, III.xxix.41.

22 DDC, III.xxix.40.

23 *In Ps.*, Preface, xv; CCSL, 97.19.50–4; Cassiodorus cites Augustine, *DDC*, III.xxix.40: *Haec multis modis genera suae locutionis exercet, definitionibus succincta, schematibus decora, verborum proprietate signata, syllogismorum complexionibus expedita, disciplinis irrutilans.*

24 *Etym.*, I.xxxvii.1.

25 *Q. in Vet. Test.*, PL, 83.207B.

26 *Ibid.*, 83.208B.

27 *In Cant.*, p. 7, 105–7.

28 *De Sch. et Tr.*, PL, 90.175A; p. 607.

29 *Ibid.*, 90.175B; p. 607.

30 *Ibid.*

31 *Ibid.*, 90.176C; p. 608.

32 *Ibid.*, 90.176D–177A; p. 608.

33 *Ibid.*, 90.179C–180C; p. 611.

34 *Ibid.*, 90.180D; p. 612.

35 *Ibid.*, 90.181B; pp. 612–13.

36 *Ibid.*, 90.181C–D; p. 613.

37 *Ibid.*

38 *Ibid.*, 90.182A; p. 613.

39 *Ibid.*, 90.182B; p. 513.

40 *Ibid.*, 90.182B–C; p. 614.

41 *Ibid.*, 90.182C; p. 614.

42 *Ibid.*, 90.183D; p. 615.

43 *Ibid.*, 90.184A–B; p. 615.

44 *Ibid.*, 90.184A; pp. 615–16.

45 *Ibid.*, 90.184B; p. 616.

46 *Ibid.*, 90.184C; p. 616.

47 *Ibid.*, 90.184D; p. 616.

48 *Ibid.*

49 *In Eccles.*, PL, 100.672D.

50 PL, 116.720A–B.

51 *Ibid.*, 116.720C.

52 *Q. in Gen.*, PL, 175.57.

53 *De Sch. et Tr.*, PL, 90.175.

54 C. Iulius Victor in C. Halm, *Rhetores Latini Minores* (Leipzig, 1863), p. 431, 30–4; cf. Fortunatianus, *ibid.*, p. 121, 17.

55 Albinus, *Rhetorica*, p. 544, 35–7; cf. Petrus Helias's *Commentary on Priscian*, Paris, Arsenal, MS 711, fo. 21ᵛᵇ.

56 Albinus, *Rhetoric*, p. 545, 4–5.

57 Robert of Melun, *Sententiae*, pp. 164–5; 206 (cf. 170).

58 On the work of some of the outstanding scholars of the day, see J.M. Clark, *The Abbey of St Gall as the Centre of Literature and Art* (Cambridge, 1936); L.M. de Rijk, 'On the Curriculum of the Arts of the Trivium at St Gall from c. 850–c. 1000', *Vivarium*, 1 (1963), 35–86; J.J. Contreni, *The Cathedral School of Laon from 850–930: Its Manuscripts and its Masters* (Munich, 1978).

59 Aquinas examines the problem of analogy in *Summa Theologica*, Iᵃq.13, a.5; *Summa Contra Gentiles*, I, chapter 34; *De Veritate*, q.2, a.11c.

60 Boethius gives the main points in his discussion in *De Trinitate*, IV; pp. 17–25.

61 Eriugena, *De Praed.*, pp. 55, 5–8.

62 *Ibid.*, p. 56, 20.

63 *Ibid.*, p. 56, 22–3.

64 Cicero, *Topics*, ii.7–8. G. Madec finds Eriugena using Cicero's *Topics* in chapters 3 and 9 of the *De Praed.* and Boethius on the *Topics* in chapter 3, PL, 64.1039–1174.

65 Cicero's *Topics* has these forms; it seems unlikely that Isidore, commonly used in the ninth century as a source of the elements of logic, can have been Eriugena's source here (*Etym.*, II.xxx.7–8).

66 *De Praed.*, p. 58, 70ff.

67 *Ibid.*, p. 63, 30–3.

68 *Ibid.*, 10, pp. 62–6.

69 PL, 115.1124.

70 *Ibid.*, 115.1124–5.

71 *Œuvres théologiques et grammaticales de Godescalc d'Orbais*, ed. C. Lambot, SSL, 20 (1945), p. 471, 5–7.

72 *De Praedestinatione*, PL, 125.110.

73 *Ibid.*, PL, 125.170–81.

74 Lambot, *Œuvres théologiques*, p. 339, 8–9.

75 *Ibid.*, p. 342, 15.

76 *Ibid.*, p. 67.

77 *Ibid.*, p. 66, 22.

78 PL, 192.1013A–B.

79 *Ibid.*, 182.999.

80 Lubac, *Exégèse*, Iⁱ, chapter 3.

81 Lubac discusses the extent to which Origen was read in the Middle Ages, see Index to Iⁱⁱ, p. 703.

82 *De Ut. Cred.*, III.5–6; cf. *De Gen. ad Litt.*, I.ii.5; iii.6.

83 *De Gen. ad Litt.*, I.i.1.

84 Cambridge, Corpus Christi College, MS 455, fo.1ᵛᵇ

85 Lubac, *Exégèse*, IIⁱ, p. 550.

86 Cf. Origen, *Homily in Genesim*, 6.1ff.; Augustine, *De Ut. Cred.* III.8, on 1 Cor. 10:1–11.

87 Lubac, *Exégèse*, Iⁱⁱ, p. 373 gives Pseudo-Heraclitus of Pontus; Longinus, *On the Sublime*, 9; Strabo, *Geographia*, I.ii.7; and other examples.

88 See Lubac, *Exégèse*, Iⁱⁱ, p. 377 on Clement of Alexandria and Philo, with numerous citations.
89 See M.D. Chenu, 'Les Deux Ages de l'allégorisme scripturaire au moyen âge', *RTAM*, 18 (1951), 19–28; and 'L'Usage de la notion d'*integumentum* à travers les gloses de Guillaume de Conches', *AHDLMA*, 24 (1957), 35–100.
90 PL, 196.200.
91 PL, 195.205.
92 PL, 116.195B.
93 *Ibid.*
94 *Q. in Gen.*, PL, 100.1088.
95 Gregory, *Hom. in Ez.*, p. 5, 25–32.
96 On prophecy, see J.P. Torrell, *Théorie de la prophétie*, SSL, 40 (1977). Introduction to Hugh of St Cher.
97 Cassian, *Collat.*, XIV.xviii; p. 421, 26–7.
98 Pseudo-Dionysius, *De Divinis Nominibus*, II; Aquinas, *Summa Theologiae*, I.q.1, a.7.
99 Gregory, *In Job*, II.vii.9–ix.12.
100 Peter of Celle on Moses' Tabernacle, Ps. 83:5; PL, 202.1047. Thomas of Chobham, one of the circle of pupils and fellow-scholars influenced by Peter the Chanter, makes a list of the words which can be used to describe the 'ways of signifying' employed by the Bible: *mystice, typice, parabolice, enigmatice* (Cambridge, Corpus Christi College, MS 455, fo. 2vb). The first refers to the secrecy under which the thing signified is hidden, the second to the use of figures (or 'types'), and these two together form a genus whose species are the familiar tropological, allegorical and anagogical senses. Parables and enigmas are used in secular and theological writings alike, and it is possible to distinguish four types of these similitudes: icons, paradigms, parable and enigma. Reflecting on the enigma, Thomas points to the text '*Videmus nunc per speculum in aenigmate*'. Augustine says that the enigma is an obscure similitude (*obscura similitudo*) and gives an example which no one would understand unless he had some grasp of the *modis significandi* of Scripture (*ibid.*, fos. 2vb–3ra). Thomas thus places the *similitudo* squarely in the area of the theory of signification.
101 *Ibid.*, 202.1047C.
102 *Ibid.*, 202.1050C.
103 Cassian, *Collat.*, I.xiii.1–2.
104 *Ibid.*, I.xvii.2.
105 *Ibid.*, I.xv.1; p. 25, 3–29.
106 *Ibid.*, III.xv.
107 Cambridge, Corpus Christi College, MS 455, fo. 1ra.
108 *Liber Quo Ordine Sermo Fieri Debeat*, PL, 156.21–32.
109 Smalley, *The Study of the Bible*, p. 27 (on preaching as an exegetical exercise).
110 PL, 156.19–22.
111 *Ibid.*, 156.19D.
112 *Ibid.*, 156.20D.
113 *Ibid.*, 156.21A.
114 *Ibid.*, 156.32C.
115 *Ibid.*, 156.31D–33D.
116 *Ibid.*, 156.36C.
117 *Ibid.*, 156.45A.

118 *Elucidatio in Canticum Canticorum*, PL, 210.102C–D; cf. Lubac, *Exégèse*, II^i, p. 558, who cites this example.
119 Gregory, *In Job*, II.i.1; p. 59.
120 *Ibid.*, I.viii.11; pp. 30, 34.
121 *Ibid.*, II.xx.35; p. 81.
122 *Collat.*, XIV.i.3.
123 *Ibid.*, XIV.i.3; XIV.ii.1.
124 *Ibid.*, XIV.viii.1.
125 *Ibid.*, XIV.viii.2.
126 *Ibid.*, XIV.viii.3.
127 *Ibid.*
128 *Ibid.*
129 PL, 196.151C.
130 *Trin.*, CCCM, 24.1823.9–19.
131 *Ibid.*, 24.1824.47–62.
132 *Ibid.*, 24.1827.181ff.
133 *Ibid.*, 24.1842.735–41.
134 PL, 194.1075.
135 *En Ps.*, 95.2; CCSL, 39.1343.
136 Bernard, *De Spirituali Aedificio*.
137 PL, 144.444B.
138 Peter of Poitiers, *Allegoriae Super Tabernaculum*, 2.
139 Giraldus Cambrensis, *Opera*, I, Letter 24.

8 Questions

1 Robert of Melun, *Quaestiones de Epistolis Pauli*, p. 3, 18–19.
2 Abelard, *Prob. Hel.*, PL, 178.325B. On 'Heloise's Problems', see Luscombe, *The School of Peter Abelard*, p. 18, Problem 3, on Matthew 26:25.
3 E.g. Problem 1 on John 16:8–11; Problem 2 on James 2:10–11; *Prob. Hel.*, PL, 178.678–9.
4 Problem 4; *ibid.*, 178.682.
5 Problem 5; *ibid.*, 178.683–4.
6 Problem 6; *ibid.*, 178.685–6.
7 Problem 7; *ibid.*, 178.687–8.
8 Problem 8; *ibid.*, 178.690–1.
9 Oxford, Balliol College, MS 36, fo. 145vb.
10 *Hist. Calam.*, PL, 178.124A–125B; pp. 68–70.
11 See V. Flint, 'The School of Laon: A Reconsideration', *RTAM*, 43 (1976), 89–111.
12 PL, 172.53B; *Dicunt omnes fere . . .*
13 Simon of Tournai, *Disputationes*, p. 39.
14 *Sent. Par.*, p. 5.
15 Lottin, *Psychologie*, V, p. 141, no. 224.
16 *Comm. in Rom.*, II (iv.11); pp. 129–42.
17 *Comm. in Rom.*, II (iii.27); pp. 119–295.
18 *Prob. Hel.*, PL, 178.739B.
19 Robert of Melun, *Sententiae*, pp. 3–25.
20 Robert of Melun, *Quaestiones de Divina Pagina*, I.ii.
21 *Ibid.*, p. 4.
22 *Ibid.*, p. 8; Question 11.
23 *Ibid.*, p. 21; Question 354.

24 *Ibid.*, Questions 43, 44.
25 Simon of Tournai, *Disputationes*, p. 39.
26 Odo, *Quaestiones, Quaestio* 58.
27 B. Haureau, *Notices et extraits de quelques manuscrits latins de la Bibliothèque Nationale*, 24, 2 (Paris, 1876), pp. 204–35.
28 Simon of Tournai, *Disputationes*, p. xiii.
29 Baldwin, *Masters, Princes and Merchants*, I, p. 97; II, pp. 66–7, nn. 43, 52; Simon of Tournai, *Disputationes*, p. 237.
30 Lottin edits the surviving sentences of Anselm of Laon and his School in *Psychologie*, V.
31 *Ibid.*, no. 255.
32 Odo, *Quaestiones, Quaestio* 58.
33 *Ibid.*, nos. 27, 37.
34 *Ibid.*, no. 19.

9 Contradictory authorities

1 *William of St Thierry on the Song of Songs*, tr. C. Hart, introduction by M. Dechanet (Shannon, 1976), p. vii.
2 PL, 180.441–74.
3 PL, 15.1497–2060.
4 *Vita Prima*, I.xii.59; PL, 185.258–9.
5 *In Errores Abaelardi*, PL, 180.547–694.
6 *De Sacramento Altaris*, PL, 180.333A.
7 *Ibid.*
8 *Ibid.*, 180.333B.
9 *Ibid.*, 180.333C.
10 *Ibid.*, 180.339A.
11 *Ibid.*, 180.339D.
12 *Ibid.*, 180.340A.
13 *Epistola ad Fratres Monte Dei*, PL, 184.309D; I.i.2.
14 *Ibid.*, 184.310B; I.i.3.
15 *In Errores Abaelardi*, PL, 180.547B.
16 *De Sacramento Altaris*, PL, 180.359B–C, xi.
17 *Ibid.*, 180.359C.
18 *Ibid.*, 180.359D.
19 J.M. Dechanet, *William of St Thierry*, tr. R. Strachan, *Cistercian Studies*, 10 (Spencer, Mass., 1972), pp. 146–7.
20 *Sic et Non*, PL, 178.1329–1611.
21 J.R. McCallum, *Abelard's Christian Theology* (Oxford, 1948), p. 98.
22 PL, 178.1344D; McCallum, *ibid.*, p. 98; and cf. the Preface to Ivo of Chartres' *Decretum* and *Panormia*, PL, 160, for discussions of contradictory authors in canon law.
23 Pl, 178.1339A.
24 *Ibid.*
25 PL, 178.1339B.
26 See pp. 17–27.
27 See pp. 72ff.
28 PL, 178.1339C.
29 *Ibid.*
30 *Ibid.*, 178.1339–41.
31 *Ibid.*, PL, 178.1340D.

32 *Ibid.*, 178.1341A.
33 *Ibid.*, 178.1341.
34 *Ibid.*, 178.1342A.
35 *Ibid.*, 178.1343D. Abelard quotes Ovid, *Ars Amatoria*.
36 PL, 178.1344A–B.
37 *Ibid.*, 178.1344.
38 *Ibid.*, 178.1345A.
39 *Ibid.*
40 *Ibid.*, 178.1345B.
41 *Ibid.*, 178.1345C.
42 *Ibid.*, 178.1346D.
43 *Comm. in Rom.*, II.iv.11; CCCM, 11, p. 132. On Abelard's view of divine authority see R.E. Weingart, *The Logic of Divine Love* (Oxford, 1970), pp. 8–11.
44 *Comm. in Rom.*, III.vii.15; CCCM, 11, p. 205, 598–9.
45 PL, 178.514, Sermo XIX.
46 Weingart, *Divine Love*, p. 9.
47 PL, 178.1347C.
48 *Ibid.*, 178.1347D.

10 A new approach to resolving contradictions

1 *Didasc.*, VI.ix.
2 *Ibid.*
3 *Ibid.*
4 *Ibid.*, VI.viii; cf. J. Marenbon, *From the Circle of Alcuin to the School of Auxerre* (Cambridge, 1981), p. 199: *unus sonus syllabarum, sed divisus sensus et intellectus.*
5 *Didasc.*, VI.viii.
6 *Ibid.*
7 *Ibid.*, VI.x.
8 *Ibid.*
9 *Ibid.*; cf. Anselm's use of *sententia* in the *De Grammatico* (Henry, *Commentary on 'De Grammatico'*, pp. 53 and 112–13); the terminology Hugh uses here is not yet quite precise technically speaking. In Alcuin, *sententia* had been used more broadly for 'opinion'. He speaks of the *sententia* of the Psalmist, who thinks that 'every man living is vanity', and the *generalis sententia* or *communis sententia*, the common opinion of ethics, a usage still current in the twelfth century. Alcuin thinks of the *sensus* of a passage as something arrived at by paraphrasing and thus putting it into familiar language. He endorses the sentiment of Eccles. 1:8: 'All things are difficult; man cannot explain them in words.' Hugh himself uses *sententia* and *sensus* in his little treatise on grammar to refer to the marks used in the text to indicate omissions, superfluities, dubious passages, and punctuation marks respectively. Alcuin, *In Eccles.*, PL, 100.671; *ibid.*, 100.672 and cf. 675A; *ibid.*, 100.673A; Hugh of St Victor, *Opera Propaedeutica*, pp. 123–7.
10 Philip of Harveng, *Epistolae*, PL, 203.12C–D; Lubac, *Exégèse*, I^{ii}, p. 465.
11 Jerome, *In Matt.*, p. 72.
12 *Q. in Gen.*, PL, 100.536; Question 166: *Numquid convenit fidei Abrahae.*
13 Gen. 15:16; Exod. 13:18; *Q. in Gen.*, PL, 100.538.
14 Gregory, *In Job*, V.xi.27; CCSL, 143.236.250–1.
15 Hugh of St Victor, *Q. in Gen.*, PL, 175.69.

16 Alcuin, *Q. in Gen.*, PL, 100.517B; Question 1.
17 *Ibid.*, 100.522C; Question 58.
18 Remigius of Auxerre, *In Gen.*, 13.1; PL, 131.83B.
19 Hugh of St Victor, *Q. in Gen.*, PL, 175.38.
20 PL, 70.9.
21 PL, 70.16, chapter 10.
22 Gregory, *In Job*, IV.i.1; CCSL, 143.163.
23 *De Sch. et Tr.*, PL, 90.175.
24 On Zachary, see A. Landgraf, *Introducción a la historia de la literatura teológica de la escolástica incipiente* (Barcelona, 1956), pp. 113–14; Luscombe, *The School of Peter Abelard*, p. 224; Zachary's *Super Unum et Quatuor* in PL, 186.11–620; Augustine's *De Cons. Ev.*
25 Huygens, *Accessus ad Auctores*.
26 *Super Unum et Quatuor*, PL, 186.11A.
27 *Ibid.*, 186.14A.
28 *Ibid.*, 186.14C.
29 *Ibid.*, 186.16C, from Augustine to Volusian.
30 *Ibid.*, 186.18A.
31 *Ibid.*, 186.18–19D; Augustine, *De Cons. Ev.*, II.xix.69, and pp. 172–3.
32 *Super Unum et Quatuor*, PL, 186.20A–B; cf. *De Cons. Ev.*, II.xvii.36, pp. 136–7, where Augustine makes a related point, and II.xiv.93, p. 199, 23–5.
33 *Super Unum et Quatuor*, PL, 186.20B.
34 On Peter's *De Tropis Loquendi*, see my articles, 'Peter the Chanter's *De Tropis Loquendi*', 95–104, and 'A Work of Terminist Theology?', 40–58.
35 *Super Unum et Quatuor*, PL, 186.20B.
36 *Ibid.*, 186.20C–D.
37 *Ibid.*, 186.20D.
38 *Ibid.*, 186.21A.
39 *Ibid.*, 186.21A–B.
40 *Ibid.*, 186.21C. On wholes and parts, cf. Burkitt, *The Rules of Tyconius*, p. 55, 1–5: *Temporis quantitas in Scripturis frequenter mystica est tropo synechdoche . . . synechdoche vero est aut a parte totum, aut a toto pars.*
41 *Super Unum et Quatuor*, PL, 186.21C. See, too, Tyconius, *The Rules of Tyconius*, p. 55, 1–5, on numbers.
42 *Super Unum et Quatuor*, PL, 186.21D.
43 *Ibid.*, 186.100B.
44 *Ibid.*, 186.82C.
45 *Ibid.*, 186.101B–C.
46 Baldwin, *Masters, Princes and Merchants*, includes a full bibliography and a detailed study of Peter the Chanter.
47 On William de Montibus, see R.W. Hunt, 'English Learning in the Late Twelfth Century', *Transactions of the Royal Historical Society*, 4th Series, 19 (1936), 19–42, reprinted in *Essays in Medieval History*, ed. R.W. Southern (London, 1968), pp. 119–30; and Hugh McKinnon, 'William de Montibus', in *Studies in Medieval History Presented to Bertie Wilkinson*, ed. T.A. Sandquist and M.R. Powicke (Toronto, 1969), pp. 32–45. D.E. Greenway gives evidence suggesting a date slightly earlier than 1190 (Le Neve, *Fasti*, III (1977), pp. 16–17).
48 Bernard of Clairvaux uses the expression in his Sermon for the Nativity, I; *Opera Omnia*, ed. J. Leclercq, C. Talbot and H. Rochais (Rome, 1957–80), 8 vols., III.
49 PL, 205.

50 MSS listed in Baldwin, *Masters, Princes and Merchants*, II, Appendix II.
51 Smalley, *The Study of the Bible*, pp. 200–6; *Verbum Abbreviatum*, PL, 205.1–1554.
52 Smalley, *The Study of the Bible*, chapter V; cf. Oxford, Balliol College, MS 23, fo. 2ra.
53 Oxford, Balliol College, MS 23, fo. 2rb; fo. 113rb; fo. 128rb.
54 *Ibid.*, fo. 128rb.
55 *Q. in Ep. Paul.*, PL, 191.1662.
56 Peter's Prologue, PL, 205.105.
57 *LM*, II^i, p. 95ff.
58 Boethius uses *supponere* only for *subicere*, PL, 64.768. Abelard normally speaks of *res subiecta* where a later thinker would use *suppositum*. See *LM*, II^{ii}, p. 205.
59 See chapter 6.
60 *Quaestiones de Divina Pagina*, 3.
61 *LM*, I, p. 56.
62 *Ibid.*, pp. 96–7.
63 Adam of Balsham, *Ars Disserendi*, p. 59, 11–13.
64 *Quaestio* 2, p. 2.
65 *Quaestio* 5.
66 *LM*, II^{ii}, pp. 21–2 discusses this manuscript and see pp. 504–8 of the treatise, which is printed in *LM*, II^{ii}, pp. 639–78.
67 See S. Ebbesen, 'Anonymi Aurelianensis, I, Commentarium in *Sophisticos Elenchos*', *Cahiers*, 34 (1979), p. vii on the work of James of Venice, and a list of Latin works on fallacies in the twelfth century. See too, I. Iwakuma, '*Instantiae*', *Cahiers*, 38 (1981), for a study of the various types of counter-arguments marshalled by contemporaries.
68 *LM*, I.24.
69 Peter Abelard, *Log. Ingr.*, p. 121, 3–7.
70 *Ibid.*, p. 121, 7ff.
71 Cambridge University Library, MS Gg.4.17, fo. 22^v.
72 *LM*, II^{ii}, p. 650, 32–5.
73 Cambridge University Library, MS Gg.4.17, fo. 22^v; *LM*, II^{ii}, p. 651, 6–9.
74 Cambridge University Library, MS Gg.4.17, fo. 23.
75 *LM*, II^{ii}, p. 651, 18–20.
76 Cambridge University Library, MS Gg.4.17, fo. 23.
77 Petrus Helias's *Commentary on Priscian*, p. 82, 49–50; p. 83, 92–4. See, too, Paris, Arsenal, MS 711, fos. 96^v–7.
78 Petrus Helias's *Commentary on Priscian*, p. 83, 92–4.
79 *LM*, II^i, p. 250.
80 Paris, Arsenal, MS 711, fo. 96^v.
81 *LM*, II^i.
82 *LM*, I.51; cf. Abelard, *Dialectica*, p. 564, 25.
83 On the rules for recognition, see *LM*, I.40 and *Dialectica*, p. 563, 11ff.
84 *LM*, I; *Dialectica*, p. 562, 11–12.
85 *LM*, II^i.495; *LM*, I.50; *LM*, I.67–70.
86 Abelard, *Log. Ingr.*, p. 399, 26–7.
87 The distinction is in Boethius, PL, 64.166–7.
88 *LM*, I.51ff. De Rijk suggests we call the first *translatio equivocationis* and the second *translatio poetica*.
89 Cambridge University Library, MS Gg.4.17, fo. 8^v.
90 *Ibid.*

91 *LM*, II^{ii}.405.
92 Petrus Helias's *Commentary on Priscian*, I, p. 54, 34–8, on Priscian XVII.33–5; cf. *LM*, II^{i}.260–1, and *ibid.*, II, p. 125, 93.
93 On *antiqui* and *moderni*, see *LM*, I.16–17.
94 *LM*, II^{ii}.402–3; cf. *LM*, II^{i}.135–6 on *totum, pars*.
95 *LM*, II^{ii}.669.
96 *LM*, I.146, and *Dialectica*, p. 593, 17–18.
97 *Summa de Sacramentis*, III.353, p. 26, 471–9; and see Baldwin, *Masters, Princes and Merchants*, I, p. 49; and II, p. 38, n. 16.
98 Peter of Poitiers, *Sent.*, I.3; cf. *LM*, I.167.

Conclusion

1 Gregory, *In Job*, Pref. Ep. II, to Leander.
2 Adam the Scot, *De Tripartito Tabernaculo*, PL, 198.629.
3 See Tyconius, *The Rules of Tyconius*, for one influential set of rules, and especially pp. xxff. for the use made of Tyconius in the Middle Ages.
4 See, for example, the *Catalogue générale de manuscrits des bibliothèques publiques de France*, X (Paris, 1889), for a list of the Bibles and commentaries owned by the monastery of Mont-Saint-Michel.
5 Giraldus Cambrensis, *Speculum Duorum*, Letter 3, p. 170.
6 *De Inst. Nov.*, PL, 176.933D–4A.
7 *Ibid.*, 176.877A–D.
8 E. Rathbone, 'John of Cornwall: A Brief Biography', *RTAM*, 17 (1950), 49–55.
9 See G. Ebeling, 'The Meaning of "Biblical Theology" ', in *Word and Faith* (London, 1963), pp. 81–6.
10 E.g. J.E. Benson, 'The History of the Historical–Critical Method in the Church', *Dialogue*, 12 (1973), 94–103.
11 See for example Johann Philipp Gabler's inaugural lecture of March 1787, at the University of Altdorf (*Gableri Opuscula Academica*, II (1831), pp. 183ff.).
12 E.g. R. de Vaux, 'Peut-on écrire une théologie de l'Ancien Testament?', in *Bible et Orient* (Paris, 1967), pp. 59–71.
13 E. Eichrodt, *Theology of the Old Testament*, I (Philadelphia, Penn., 1961), p. 31.
14 J. Rohde, *Rediscovering the Teaching of the Evangelists* (Philadelphia, Penn., 1968), pp. 1–8, 31–46.
15 All these things are done in the opening pages of, for example, I. Howard Marshall, *The Gospel of Luke* (The New International Greek Testament Commentary (Exeter, 1978)).
16 L. Goppelt, *Typos: The Typological Interpretation of the Old Testament in the New* (Grand Rapids, Mich., 1982).
17 R.H. Lightfoot, *St John's Gospel: A Commentary* (repr. Oxford, 1983).
18 On these developments and problems, see Stephen Neill, *The Interpretation of the New Testament, 1861–1961* (Oxford, 1964).

SELECT BIBLIOGRAPHY

Baldwin, J.W. *Princes and Merchants*, Princeton, New Jersey, 1969, 2 vols.

Bertola, E. 'La *Glossa Ordinaria* biblica ed i suoi problemi', *RTAM*, 45, 1978, 34–78.

Chatillon, J. 'Sermons et prédicateurs victorins de la seconde moitié du xii⁰ siècle', *AHDLMA*, 32, 1965, 7–60.

Chenu, M.D. *La Théologie au douzième siècle*, Paris, 1957.
  '*Involucrum*: Le mythe selon les théologiens médiévaux', *AHDLMA*, 22, 1955, 75–9.

Contreni, J.J. 'The Biblical Glosses of Haimo of Auxerre and John Scotus Eriugena', *Speculum*, 51, 1976, 411–34.

Evans, G.R. *Old Arts and New Theology*, Oxford, 1980.
  Augustine on Evil, Cambridge, 1983.

Ghellinck, J. de *Le Mouvement théologique du xii⁰ siècle*, Bruges, 1948.

Gibson, M.T. *Lanfranc of Bec*, Oxford, 1978.

Green, W.M. 'Mediaeval Recensions of St Augustine', *Speculum*, 29, 1954, 531–4.

Häring, N.M. 'Berengar's Definitions of *Sacramentum* and Their Influence on Mediaeval Sacramentology', *Mediaeval Studies*, 10, 1948, 109–46.

Henry, D.P. *The Logic of St Anselm*, Oxford, 1967.

Hunt, R.W. 'Studies on Priscian in the Twelfth Century', *MARS*, 1, 1941–3, 194–231, and 2, 1950, 1–55.

Huygens, R.B.C. *Accessus ad Auctores*, Leiden, 1970.

Jeauneau, E. 'L'Usage de la notion d'*integumentum* à travers les gloses de Guillaume de Conches', *AHDLMA*, 24, 1957, 35–100.

Kenny, A., Kretzmann, N. and Pinborg, J. (eds.), *The Cambridge History of Later Mediaeval Philosophy*, Cambridge, 1982.

Landgraf, A. *Introduction à l'histoire de la littérature théologique de la scolastique naissante*, Montreal and Paris, 1973.

Lange, H. 'Traités du xii⁰ siècle sur la symbolique des nombres: Odo de Morimond', *Cahiers*, 40, 1981.

Leclercq, J. 'The Exposition and Exegesis of Scripture from Gregory the Great to St Bernard', *Cambridge History of the Bible: The West from the Fathers to the Reformation*, Cambridge, 1969, 183–97.

Lecomte, F. 'Un Commentaire scripturaire du xii⁰ siècle', *AHDLMA*, 25, 1958, 227–94.

Lottin, O. *Psychologie et morale aux xii⁰ et xiii⁰ siècles*, vol. V, Gembloux, 1959.

Lubac, H. de *Exégèse médiévale*, Paris, 1959, 2 vols.

Luscombe, D.E. *The School of Peter Abelard*, Cambridge, 1969.

193

McCulloch, F.T. *Mediaeval Latin and French Bestiaries* (Studies in the Romance Languages and Literature, 33), Durham, North Carolina, 1962.

McEvoy, J. 'The Son as *Res* and *Signum*: Grosseteste's Commentary on Ecclesiasticus 43.1–5', *RTAM*, 41, 1974, 38–9.

O'Donnell, J.J. *Cassiodorus*, Berkeley, California, and London, 1979.

Ohly, F. *Hohelied Studien*, Wiesbaden, 1958.

Randolph, D.E. 'The Double Procession of the Holy Spirit in Joachim of Fiore's Understanding of History', *Speculum*, 55, 1980, 479–83.

Riché, P. 'Le Psautier, livre de lecture élémentaire', *Etudes Mérovingiennes*, 3, 1953, 3–33.

Rijk, L.M. de *Logica Modernorum*, Assen, 1967, 2 vols.

Smalley, B. (with G. Lacombe) 'Studies on the Commentaries of Stephen Langton', *AHDLMA*, 5, 1930, 1–220.

Smalley, B. 'Stephen Langton and the Four Senses of Scripture', *Speculum*, 6, 1931, 60–76.

'Gilbertus Universalis, Bishop of London (1128–34) and the Problem of the *Glossa Ordinaria*: 1 and 2', *RTAM*, 7, 1935, 235–62; and 8, 1936, 24–64.

'La *Glossa Ordinaria*, quelques prédécesseurs d'Anselme de Laon', *RTAM*, 9, 1937, 365–400.

'Andrew of St Victor, Abbot of Wigmore: A Twelfth Century Hebraist', *RTAM*, 10, 1938, 358–74.

'The School of Andrew of St Victor', *RTAM*, 11, 1939, 145–67.

The Study of the Bible in the Middle Ages, Oxford, 1941, 2nd edn, 1952.

'Some Thirteenth Century Commentaries on the Sapiential Books', *Dominican Studies*, 2, 1949, 318–55; 3, 1950, 41–77 and 236–74.

'Some Latin Commentaries on the Sapiential Books in the Late Thirteenth and Early Fourteenth Centuries', *AHDLMA*, 18, 1950–1, 103–28.

'A Commentary on the Hexameron by Henry of Ghent', *RTAM*, 20, 1953, 60–101.

'Les Commentaires bibliques de l'époque romane: glose ordinaire et gloses périmées', *Cahiers de Civilisation Médiévale*, 4, 1961, 23–46.

'L'Exégèse biblique dans la littérature latine', *La Biblia nell'Alto Medioevo*, Spoleto, 1963, 631–55.

'An Early Twelfth Century Commentary on the Literal Sense of Leviticus', *RTAM*, 36, 1969, 78–99.

'Some Gospel Commentaries of the Early Twelfth Century', *RTAM*, 45, 1978, 147–80.

'Peter Comestor on the Gospels and his Sources', *RTAM*, 46, 1979, 84–129; reprinted in *The Becket Conflict and the Schools*, Oxford, 1973.

'The Gospels in the Paris Schools in the Late Twelfth and Early Thirteenth Centuries: Peter the Chanter, Hugh of St Cher, Alexander of Hales, John of La Rochelle: I and II', *Franciscan Studies*, 39 (1979), 230–55; and 40 (1980), 298–369.

'An Early Paris Lecture-Course on St Luke', *Sapientiae Doctrinae: Mélanges . . . offerts à Dom Hildebrand Bascour*, *RTAM*, no. spécial 1, 1980, 299–311.

'L'uso della Scrittura nei "Sermones" di Sant'Antonio', *Rivista Antoniana di Storia Dottrina Arte*, 21, 1981, 3–16.

Smet, J.M. de 'L'Exégète Lambert, écolâtre d'Utrecht', *Revue d'Histoire Ecclésiastique*, 42, 1947, 103–10.

Southern, R.W. *St Anselm and his Biographer*, Cambridge, 1963.

Spicq, C. *Esquisse d'une histoire de l'exégèse latine du moyen âge*, Paris, 1944.
Stegmüller, F. *Repertorium Biblicum Medii Aevi*, Madrid 1940–, vols. I–.
Thompson, A. Hamilton (ed.), *Bede: His Life, Times and Writings*, Oxford, 1935.
Van de Vyver, A. 'Les Etapes du développement philosophique de haut moyen-âge', *Revue Belge de Philologie et d'Histoire*, 8, 1929, 425–52.
Wasselynck, R. 'L'Influence de l'exégèse de S. Gregoire le Grand sur les commentaires bibliques médiévaux', *RTAM*, 32, 1965, 183–92.
Wells, D.A. 'Imperial Sanctity and Political Reality: Bible, Liturgy and the Ambivalence of Symbol in Walther von der Vogelweide's Songs under Otto IV', *Speculum*, 55, 1980, 469–83.

INDEX

Abraham 4
Adam 1
Adam of Balsham 152
Adam the Scot 164
Alan of Lille xvi, 80, 88, 92, 96, 97, 100, 120
Alcuin xvi, 7, 67, 72, 73, 95, 101, 141, 142, 143
Alexandria 32
allegory 58, 109, 114, 115–22, 164
Ambrose 39, 42, 133
anagogy 58, 116–18, 164
analogy 106
Andrew of St Victor 97
Anselm of Bec and Canterbury xvi, 13, 15, 17–26, 27, 33, 56, 70, 78, 84, 104, 119
Anselm of Havelberg xvi, 29
Anselm of Laon xvi, 28, 38, 41, 42, 43, 126, 127, 130, 131
antiphrasis 109
antonomasia 108
Aquinas 74, 111, 116, 129
argument 57
Aristotle 53, 72, 73, 74, 79, 88, 101, 153
Arnald of Bonneval, *see* Ernald
artes 31–6, 57
asteismus 109
Augustine of Hippo xvi, 1, 3, 4, 5, 25, 29, 37, 38, 39, 42, 46, 51, 52, 53, 55, 72, 79, 95, 96, 106, 107, 111, 113, 114, 119, 122, 136, 142, 144, 146

Bandinus 114
Bede xvi, 38, 42, 59, 64–5, 107, 108, 137, 143, 148, 156, 160

Berengar of Tours xvi, 38, 40
Bernard of Clairvaux xvii, 27, 29, 82, 122, 133
bestiaries 54
Boethius xvii, 45, 59, 72, 87, 88, 90, 92, 93, 111, 112, 155
Bruno the Carthusian 38, 40

Calcidius 59
Carolingian 4, 28, 101, 107
Cassian 118, 121
Cassiodorus 6, 33, 56, 59, 143
charientismus 109
Chartres 28
Church 33, 58, 63, 115
Cicero 7, 10, 112
Clement of Alexandria 114
Cur Deus Homo 22–4

dialectic, *see* logic
dictionaries 80–5
disputatio 8, 125–63
Donatus 6, 34, 35, 74, 86, 100
Donizone of Canossa 57
Drogo 40

enigma 109
Ernald of Bonneval xvii, 82, 102, 103
Eriugena xvii, 45, 111, 112
ethics 32
Eusebius 70
Ezekiel 13

fable 57
fallacies 153–7
Fathers 18, 39, 42, 59, 131, 137

figurative senses 14, 53, 105–14,
  115–22, 164
figures of speech 105–14

Garlandus 78, 88
Geoffrey of Auxerre 59
Gerhoch of Reichersberg 31, 37,
  56, 68, 76, 82, 89, 90, 91
Gilbert Crispin xvii, 25
Gilbert of Poitiers xvii, 29, 41, 73,
  76, 89, 95, 126
Gilbert the Universal xvii, 38, 43
Giraldus Cambrensis 122, 165
Glossa Ordinaria 37–47
Godescalc of Orbais xvii, 110,
  111, 112, 113
grammar xvii, 14, 57, 72, 100
Greek 75, 86, 125
Gregorian Reform 28
Gregory the Great xvii, 1, 2, 6,
  7, 13, 34, 35, 37, 42, 53, 56, 59,
  63, 81, 83, 87, 107, 116, 119,
  120, 133, 143, 148, 164
Gregory of Tours 70
Guibert of Nogent 27, 119, 120

Haymo of Auxerre 70, 109, 116
Hebrew 39, 40, 75, 125
Heloise 125
Herbert of Bosham 39
Hermannus 14
Hilary of Poitiers 91
Hincmar 113
history, historical sense 57, 67–71,
  118, 120
Hugh of Amiens, 35, 41
Hugh of St Victor xvii, 3, 8, 29, 30,
  31, 32, 33, 37, 42, 43, 53, 54, 55,
  56, 67, 68, 69, 71, 81, 101, 105,
  125, 140, 141, 142, 165

imposition 76–80
irony 109
Isidore xvii, 42
Ivo of Chartres 42

Jerome xvii, 5, 13, 38, 42, 68, 70,
  141
Jerusalem 58

Jewish exegesis 14
John of Cornwall 166

katachresis 108

Lambert of Utrecht 38, 41
Lanfranc xviii, 17, 27, 38, 39, 81,
  84, 136
language, biblical viii, 20, 31, 35,
  46, 72 and *passim*
Laon 28
Latin vii, 6, 7, 75, 86
law 107
lectio 8
literal sense 8, 67–71
logic 14, 57, 72–100 and *passim*

Macrobius 59
Manegold of Lautenbach xviii, 38,
  40
Martianus Capella 45, 59
mechanica 32
metaphor 57, 108
metonymy 108
modi loquendi 5 and *passim*
Moses 4, 15, 69

Nestorians 77
Noah's Ark 122
numbers, number-symbolism
  59–66

Odo of Morimond xviii, 59, 60
Odo of Soissons 129, 130, 131,
  132, 150, 151, 153
Old Latin translation 34
Origen xviii, 32, 56, 114, 115

paradox 22
paroemia 109
Peter Abelard xviii, 27, 35, 38, 41,
  43, 53, 70, 71, 83, 89, 92, 93, 95,
  104, 105, 125, 126, 127, 128,
  130, 133, 134, 135, 136, 137,
  138, 160, 161, 163, 166
Peter of Celle 117
Peter the Chanter xviii, 8, 10, 41,
  80, 96, 97, 98, 99, 105, 145,
  146, 147, 148, 149, 151, 152,

155, 156, 157, 158, 159, 160, 161, 162, 167
Peter Comestor xviii
Peter Lombard xviii, 43–5, 51, 130, 135, 149, 166
Peter of Poitiers 80, 122
Petrus Helias 84, 92, 94, 95, 114, 158
Philo of Alexandria 115
Physiologus 54
Plato 36
predicatio 8
Prepositinus 80
Priscian 34, 73, 74, 86, 88, 92
prophecy, Prophets 116–18, 138
Prudentius of Troyes 112–13
Psalms 43–4
Pseudo-Dionysius 116

quadrivium 14, 35–6

Rabanus Maurus xviii, 85
Ralph of Beauvais 86, 87
Ralph of Laon 28, 38, 41, 42
Reformation 2, 168
Reims 28
Remigius of Auxerre 4, 73, 81, 142
Richard of St Victor xviii, 33, 83, 84, 121
Robert Kilwardby 73, 74, 75, 78, 79, 85
Robert of Melun xviii, 110, 125, 128, 129, 150
Rome vii, 107
Rupert of Deutz xix, 13–17, 32, 78, 106, 121, 122

St Victor 28, 29
sarcasmos 106, 109

schemata 106–10
science vii
senses of Scripture, the four 114 and *passim*
signification 21–2, 57, 60, 72–100 and *passim*
Simon of Tournai 128, 129, 130, 153
Song of Songs 32
synechdoche 109

Theobald of Langres 59, 62, 66
theorica 32
Thierry of Chartres xix, 28, 36, 76, 88, 95, 96
things 51–9
Thomas of Chobham xix, 9, 10, 57, 114, 119
translatio, transumptio 57, 101–22
tropi 106, 110
tropology 58, 118–22, 164
Tyconius 52, 146

Vulgate 34, 38

Walter of St Victor xix, 34
William de Montibus 147, 154, 165
William of Auberive 59
William of Champeaux xix, 29, 41, 42, 130
William of Conches xix, 77, 84, 86, 87, 88, 126, 134
William of St Thierry xix, 133, 134, 135, 139

Zachary of Besançon 143, 144, 146, 149, 161, 162

Printed in the United States
54697LVS00001B/256-267